LOVE AND HATE
IN THE
ANALYTIC SETTING

LOVE AND HATE
IN THE
ANALYTIC SETTING

by
Glen O. Gabbard, M.D.

JASON ARONSON INC.
Northvale, New Jersey
London

Production Editor: Judith D. Cohen

This book was set in 11 pt. Melior by Alabama Book Composition of Deatsville, Alabama and printed and bound by Book-mart Press of North Bergen, New Jersey.

Library of Congress Cataloging-in-Publication Data

Gabbard, Glen O.
    Love and hate in the analytic setting / by Glen O. Gabbard.
       p. cm.—(The Library of object relations)
    Includes bibliographical references and index.
    ISBN 1-56821-671-8 (alk. paper)
    1. Transference (Psychology) 2. Countertransference (Psychology)
3. Psychoanalysis. 4. Psychotherapist and patient. 5. Love.
6. Hate.   I. Title. II. Series
    [DNLM: 1. Psychoanalytic Therapy. 2. Transference (Psychology)
3. Love. 4. Hate. 5. Professional-Patient Relations. WM 460.6
G112L 1996]
RC489.T73G33   1996
616.89′17—dc20
DNLM/DLC
for Library of Congress   96-7484

Manufactured in the United States of America. Jason Aronson Inc. offers books and cassettes. For information and catalog write to Jason Aronson Inc., 230 Livingston Street, Northvale, New Jersey 07647.

THE LIBRARY OF OBJECT RELATIONS

A SERIES OF BOOKS EDITED BY
DAVID E. SCHARFF AND JILL SAVEGE SCHARFF

Object relations theories of human interaction and development provide an expanding, increasingly useful body of theory for the understanding of individual development and pathology, for generating theories of human interaction, and for offering new avenues of treatment. They apply across the realms of human experience from the internal world of the individual to the human community, and from the clinical situation to everyday life. They inform clinical technique in every format from individual psychoanalysis and psychotherapy, through group therapy, to couple and family therapy.

The Library of Object Relations aims to introduce works that approach psychodynamic theory and therapy from an object relations point of view. It includes works from established and new writers who employ diverse aspects of British, American, and international object relations theory in helping individuals, families, couples, and groups. It features books that stress integration of psychoanalytic approaches with marital, family, and group therapy, as well as those centered on individual psychotherapy and psychoanalysis.

Refinding the Object and
Reclaiming the Self
David E. Scharff

Object Relations Family Therapy
*David E. Scharff and
Jill Savege Scharff*

Scharff Notes: A Primer of
Object Relations Therapy
*Jill Savege Scharff and
David E. Scharff*

Projective and Introjective
Identification and the Use
of the Therapist's Self
Jill Savege Scharff

Object Relations Couple Therapy
*David E. Scharff and
Jill Savege Scharff*

Foundations of Object
Relations Family Therapy
Jill Savege Scharff, Editor

From Inner Sources: New Directions
in Object Relations Psychotherapy
N. Gregory Hamilton, Editor

The Practice of Psychoanalytic
Therapy
Karl König

CONTENTS

INTRODUCTION

In the last decade or two, a sea change has occurred in the way that we conceptualize the analytic relationship. The analyst is no longer viewed as a dispassionate interpreter of the patient's intrapsychic conflict. We now recognize that analysts are likely to experience feelings similar to those that stir the patient and often with the same degree of passion. Moreover, these intensely felt affects are now viewed as having the potential to discombobulate the analyst and lead to enactments that reflect the analyst's involvement. Fortunately, the psychoanalytic profession has reached the point where feelings of love, hate, sexual arousal, envy, contempt, boredom, and assorted other affects can be openly discussed and understood as useful contributors to the analytic work.

In 1991 I chaired a panel at the annual meeting of the American Psychoanalytic Association in New Orleans entitled "Hate in the Analytic Setting." With considerable candor, the panelists, including the late Donald Kaplan, Milton Horowitz, Alan Skolnikoff, and Stanley Coen, spoke openly about their experiences of hating and being hated in the consulting room. The following year, Henry Smith and I proposed another panel entitled "Love in the Analytic Setting." This proposal was accepted by the Program Committee, and at the December meeting of the American Psychoanalytic Association in 1992, Dr. Smith chaired the panel and I presented some case material illustrating a particularly challenging clinical situation I had encountered. Other presenters included Otto Kernberg, Estelle Shane, and Theodore Jacobs.

These panels helped crystalize my thinking about the manner in which love and hate sweep over both participants in the analytic enterprise and generated several more papers in addition to those I had already contributed to the literature. As my colleagues and I struggled to articulate our experiences, I recognized that those aspects of the analytic work we would most like to keep secret and not expose to the scrutiny of our colleagues may be just those areas in which we most need such input. Fortunately, the profession has developed a greater acceptance of countertransference as a useful tool in the analytic process, and colleagues are increasingly willing to help one another without resorting to censure or exhortation.

My vantage point on these issues is undoubtedly colored by the fact that I have spent much of my professional career involved in the evaluation and treatment of analysts and other mental health professionals who have become sexually involved with their patients. My observations of these involvements have been reported elsewhere (Gabbard and Lester 1995), but those observations have certainly informed the way I think about the optimal analytic approaches to heated passions kindled by both parties in the analytic dyad. In this volume I confine myself to love and hate as they occur within the boundaries of the analytic frame, however stretched those boundaries may be at times by the challenge of containing such passions.

Some of the case material in this book, especially the patients described in Chapters 7 and 8, reflect the nature of our work at The Menninger Clinic, where I have spent my professional life, and where there is a tradition of analyzing patients who might be regarded elsewhere as a bit too disturbed for analytic work. However, some of these patients have been tried in numerous other treatments and seem reachable only by the unique characteristics of the psychoanalytic approach.

The Menninger Clinic and its sister institution, the Topeka Institute for Psychoanalysis, have always fostered an openness to diversity in terms of theoretical perspective. This tolerance of pluralism has served me well in my development as an analyst. Early in my career it became apparent to me that no one theory had all the answers to the challenges we confront in clinical practice. On the other hand, it seemed that most theories had something to offer that was worthwhile. Empirical validation of one theory as superior to another is so complicated in our field that we must use clinical usefulness as the major test.

My own character is inclined to be synthetic and integrative rather than divisive and polarizing. I have always been wary of those under the influence of charismatic leaders who advocate a quasi-religious adherence to a particular theory. Although I am sometimes characterized by others as a proponent of object relations theory, I have been influenced by a number of divergent trends in psychoanalytic thought. The ego psychological tradition nurtured at Menninger by David Rapaport and others was the basis of much of the teaching I received as a candidate. The South American and British Kleinians have also been influential in my development, and though I am not a Kleinian I find certain concepts, such as projective identification, the emphasis on the role of aggression in human interaction, and the depressive and paranoid-schizoid modes of experience, extremely useful. The work of Winnicott, Fairbairn, and Sutherland, all "Middle Groupers" from the British School of object relations, has been important to me as my thinking has evolved, as have the writings of their American counterpart, Thomas Ogden. In recent years constructivists and relational theorists have also played key roles in defining my own approach to analytic material. In the pages that follow, the reader will note that threads of all these influences are woven together in the fabric of my work.

Pulver (1993) has persuasively argued that the era of the monolithic analytic school is over and that most analysts, whether they are officially adherents of a specific theoretical school or not, use a blend of the features from different schools. Sandler (1983) has made a similar point. In particular, he has suggested that what analysts actually do in private may differ from their public theoretical positions. Most analysts, in his view, borrow whatever is useful from a variety of theories when they are in the privacy of their consulting room. The notion that multiple theoretical points of view are commonly used by most analysts is echoed by Jacobson (1994), who has argued that by studying the experiential core of signal affects, the analyst can use such affects to facilitate switching points where the theories intersect. He also has stressed that the available psychoanalytic approaches each may have particular relevance to specific aspects of psychological functioning, a view shared by Pine (1990).

Much of the current controversy in psychoanalytic discourse involves exaggerated polarizations of one-person versus two-person, intrapsychic versus interpersonal, drive versus relational, and so forth. I find some arguments on both sides of the controversies to be compelling, and I share Sandler's (1983) view that in private each analyst probably evolves a unique integration of the most useful aspects of the theoretical positions. Like Benjamin (1995), I do not experience a sharp opposition between these perceived polarities, and I feel it is imperative to sustain a dialectical tension in practice that allows for the paradoxical coexistence of the intrapsychic and the interpersonal as well as the drive and relational points of view. As Coen (1992) has observed: "The analyst thus must maintain both an interpersonal and an intrapsychic focus for himself and especially for his analysand. It is not an either/or choice; both are necessary" (p. 11). The intrapsychic and the intersubjective, like the domain of drives and the domain of internalized object relations, are distinct from one another but cannot be completely separated in the crucible of the analytic process.

As I reflect on my experience as an analyst in a typical week, I find myself shifting my frame of reference with the ebb and flow of the analytic process. At times I am predominantly a relatively objective observer of the patient's intrapsychic world, tracking defenses and resistances. At other moments, I'm swept up in two-person transference–countertransference enactments, and I'm struggling to think clearly about what is transpiring around me and within me. While there are oscillations between one-person and two-person emphases, both are ever-present and must be taken into account.

I owe a debt of gratitude to my many colleagues across the country and overseas who have consulted with me on difficult clinical situations and have kept me on track when I felt overwhelmed by the affects generated in the consulting room. I also appreciate the helpful suggestions of colleagues who read and commented on portions of this manuscript, including Drs. Irwin Rosen, Sallye Wilkinson, Thomas Ogden, Jane Kite, Arnold Richards, Henry Smith, Stanley Coen, Lawrence Friedman, Owen Renik, Steven Mitchell, Lee Grossman, and Joyce McDougall. Mrs. Sandy Knipp assisted in typing some of the chapters and is also deserving of my thanks. I am grateful to Mrs.

Faye Schoenfeld for her role in typing, editing, and shaping the final version of the manuscript.

I reserve my final thanks for my wife, Dr. Joyce David-son Gabbard. As I have noted in many of my writings over the years, analysts must work diligently to create a loving environment in their personal lives so that they are not forced to seek gratification of their emotional needs from their patients. I have been fortunate in this regard to have a consistently loving companion to come home to after being subjected to a roller coaster of feelings throughout the day at work. I dedicate this book to Joyce and wish to thank her for the best years of my life.

PROLOGUE:
BAPTISM BY FIRE

Love doesn't make the world go 'round. It simply
makes the affected parties dizzy.
                                        —George Bernard Shaw

One sparkling fall day when I was a young psychiatry
resident, I walked into my cramped cubicle, euphemisti-
cally referred to as an office, and I sat down across from
my patient. Ms. S, a shy young woman about my age,
stared intently at me and blurted out, "I think I'm in love
with you."

With masterful poise I responded, "What do you mean?"

Ms. S looked at me incredulously, "What do I mean?!
Just what I said! I think I'm in love with you. Look, don't
make this any harder than it already is. My sister's in
therapy, and she said I should tell you."

The already confining dimensions of my consulting
room suddenly seemed even smaller. My throat was dry
and the pounding of my heart was palpable in my ears. I
contemplated my options carefully. I could, of course, run
out of the office screaming (a course of action that seemed
most in keeping with my affective state). I could be silent
and mysterious in the same way my analyst was with me.
I could explain to her that her feelings were a form of
resistance to the therapy and tell her to stop having such

feelings. I could fake a nosebleed and tell her I'd be right back after tending to it (that would at least buy some time to think).

I leaned back in my chair (trying to get a bit of distance from the patient's intensity), and I tried to look as thoughtful and accepting as I could. In a reassuring way I said to the patient, "Well, this sort of thing happens quite frequently in psychotherapy."

Ms. S glared back at me: "How is that supposed to help me?"

"Well, uh, it may make you feel a little less embarrassed about it if you know you're not alone with these kind of feelings."

"Oh, so you mean *all* the girls you treat fall in love with you? That's supposed to make me feel better? To be one of your harem girls?"

"No, no, you misunderstand me," I explained. "I meant psychotherapy patients *in general* often experience loving feelings for their therapist. I wasn't talking about my own patients in particular."

"That may be true," Ms. S responded, "but I'm not just any patient. I am *really* in love with you. This isn't the kind of love a patient has for a therapist. This is *real* love. You're exactly the kind of man I've been looking for."

At this point in the session, I had an ominous feeling that Ms. S wasn't going to be easy to reason with on this matter and that I wasn't going to be able to extricate myself from the situation with my dignity intact. I assumed a bit of a didactic posture and explained, "I hear what you're saying, but I don't think the feelings are as real as you think they are."

"Not real?! Don't tell me these feelings aren't real. I've been in love before. I *know* what love is. Besides, how would you know whether my feelings are real anyway?"

Undaunted, I continued: "What I mean is that the feelings stem from old relationships in your past. Maybe they're closely related to feelings you had for your father."

The patient guffawed at that suggestion: "My father? That's a good one, Sigmund. My dad was a jerk. I never felt this way towards him." At this point, my thoughts were racing. I was interpreting the erotic transference as a manifestation of oedipal longings for her father, just like I was taught, but it just wasn't working.

Ms. S continued to rail at me: "What am I supposed to *do* with these feelings? You're the therapist! I know we can't go out together, but I'm still stuck with these feelings."

Like many patients in therapy with supervised trainees, Ms. S was not to receive an answer to the question until a week later, after I'd had the opportunity to speak with my supervisor. I met with him two days later and recounted what had happened. He irritated me no end by repeatedly chuckling to himself as I read from my notes and described my struggles. At one point he noted, "It sounds like she tickled your balls a little?"

"Come again?" I replied.

"I think she's exciting you," he clarified.

"You mean sexually," I queried.

"That's the general idea," he responded.

I reflected a moment and said, "I think I was too flustered to feel any sexual excitement." I paused. My supervisor said nothing. "She *is* very attractive," I acknowledged. He said, "I think that's the starting point for this discussion."

My supervisor, in his crude but well-meaning way, was trying to help me see that much of my struggle with Ms.

S was related to my own feelings about her and uncertainty about the way to handle them, even though my presentation to him had focused on how I should manage *her* feelings.

Although humorous in retrospect, this baptism by fire is a meaningful part of the initiation rites of the neophyte therapist. As I reflect back on this incident many years ago, I now recognize that many of the concerns of this book had their origins in my ordeal with Ms. S. Several of the questions raised in my own mind when I treated Ms. S are larger questions with which I still struggle as a mature psychoanalyst. Is the love experienced by patient and/or analyst "real"? How does the analyst respond to a patient who professes love? How much of the love is "really" for the analyst, and how much is displaced from other figures in the patient's past? How does one "help" the patient who is in the throes of transference love? What does it mean to conceptualize love as "resistance" to the analytic work? To what extent does the analyst's "love" for the patient play a role?

My encounter with Ms. S reawakened more fundamental questions. The word *love,* though used as a lyric in virtually every verse of every song on the radio, was not clearly defined in my view. I consulted Karl Menninger's thoughts on the idea and found the following definition: "Love is experienced as a pleasure in proximity, a desire for fuller knowledge of one another, a yearning for mutual identification and personality fusion" (1942, p. 272). The humorist James Thurber was less ambitious in his attempt to define love. He was alleged to have quipped that love is what you've been through with someone.

The questions raised by my encounter with Ms. S did not confine themselves to the affect of love. One of the most disconcerting aspects about the session described was my sense that Ms. S was growing increasingly angry and hostile toward me the more I tried to clarify and help her deal with her feelings. Indeed, I had the impression that her love was about to be transformed into hate at any moment if I continued to pursue the course I had started. I also can reconstruct the session well enough now, some twenty years later, to know that my supervisor was only partly right. I *did* find the patient sexually attractive, but that was only half the picture. I also found myself hating her and wanting to escape because of what she was doing to me.

Another reason that I felt myself hating Ms. S was that she was destroying my capacity to think. As the session went on, the feelings stirred within me overrode my professional role and my capacity to be reflective and thoughtful. It now reminds me of the anecdote about Wilfred Bion's reaction to a particularly chaotic group relations conference. At a moment of maximal turbulence, a colleague turned to Bion and asked him what he thought was going on. Bion responded that he did not find the situation conducive to thought (Symington 1990).

The fact that love and hate coexist in the analytic situation should come as no surprise. One might even say that the two conflicting feelings are inherent in the treatment. Winnicott (1954) made an apt observation in this regard: "At a stated time . . . the analyst would be reliably there, on time, alive, breathing. . . . For the limited period of time prearranaged (about an hour) the analyst would keep awake and become preoccupied with the patient. . . . The analyst expressed love by the positive interest taken, and hate in the strict start and finish and in the matter of fees and so forth" (p. 285).

Even experienced analysts find that feelings of love and hate disturb their sense of poise and their ability to maintain evenly suspended attention. Now as a supervisor of and consultant to other analysts, I find myself continuing to ponder some of the same questions that had their seeds on that autumn day long ago in the company of Ms. S. The ensuing chapters are devoted to contemplating, if not answering, some of those questions.

1   LOVE IN ANALYTIC AND NONANALYTIC SETTINGS

> In their choice of lovers, both the male and the female reveal their essential nature. The type of human being which we prefer reveals the contours of our heart.
>
> —José Ortega y Gasset

"Essentially, one might say, the cure is effected by love." This statement, made *en passant* by Freud in a December 6, 1906, letter to Jung (McGuire 1974, p. 10), unequivocally placed love at the heart of Freud's thinking about the therapeutic action of psychoanalysis. To imagine such words flowing from Freud's pen is perhaps a bit jarring. Is this the same Freud we have come to know as the detached archaeological investigator, steeped in Helmholtzian tradition, listening to his patients' associations with the objectivity of a surgeon?

The founder of psychoanalysis was not, of course, implying that it was the force of the analyst's love that cured the patient. What he clearly meant was that transference love was the vehicle of cure. In the same letter, he confided to Jung, "You are probably aware that our cures are brought about through the fixation of the libido prevailing in the unconscious (transference), and that this transference is most readily obtained in hysteria. Transference provides the impulse necessary for understanding and translating the language of the ucs.; where it is lacking, the patient does not make the effort or does not listen when we submit our translation to him" (McGuire 1974, p. 10). Influenced by his forays into hypnotic suggestion, Freud was convinced that erotic attraction was the active ingredient in the treatment. Suggestion itself was always suffused with erotic undercurrents, as far as Freud was concerned. In fact, as late as 1921, he defined suggestion as ". . . a conviction which is not based upon perception and reasoning but upon an erotic tie" (p. 128).

Yet Freud also discerned a dark side to transference love that could pose formidable obstacles to the treatment. A decade earlier he had noted that the patient might be "seized by a dread of becoming too much accustomed to the physician personally, of losing her independence in relation to him, and even of perhaps becoming sexually dependent on him" (Breuer and Freud 1895, p. 302). Freud went on to link this particular obstacle to "the special solicitude inherent in the treatment" (p. 302). By solicitude Freud apparently meant that the analytic setting itself is conducive to this sort of problem. In other words, the analyst who listens with care and concern to the patient's inner thoughts and seeks to understand her (it was almost always a female patient in the 1890's) ends up soliciting a kind of sexual dependency in the patient. Friedman (1994) has gone so far as to view this as an attenuated form of seduction. As he noted, "By seduction I mean an arrangement whereby the patient is led to expect love while the analyst, in Freud's words, plans to provide a substitute for love. Admittedly, the love substitute is something very special with secrets we have yet to fathom, but it is not the love the patient is imagining" (p. 10).

What was less anticipated by Freud—in an era in which the term *countertransference* had scarcely been defined—was that the patient might have a similarly seductive effect on the analyst. Disclosure of one's most personal thoughts in an intimate setting has its indubitable charms. The analyst may be moved that someone would place such trust in a figure who is relatively less self-disclosing. Freud soon became familiar with the two-way nature of the seductiveness of the analytic situation when one disciple after another succumbed to the siren song of transference love (Gabbard 1995a, Gabbard and Lester 1995).

Hence, from the veritable birth of the field of psychoanalysis, Freud was vexed by the powerful forces of love activated between patient and analyst. Was it resistance or vehicle of cure? Was it real, as Ms. S had insisted, or unreal, as I had tried to convince her? And perhaps most of all, was it similar to or different from love outside the analytic setting. In this chapter I shall trace Freud's struggles with whether love in the analytical setting was the same as love in the nonanalytic setting, from his early works to more contemporary perspectives on the same issue.

PSYCHOANALYTIC PERSPECTIVES ON LOVE

In the same year that Freud wrote to Jung about the role of love in psychoanalytic cure, he received a novella from Jung entitled *Gradiva* by Wilhelm Jensen. Freud was so taken by it that he wrote a lengthy psychoanalytic essay about the story (1907). A young archaeologist, Norbert Hanold, is the protagonist of the story. While visiting Rome, he becomes enamored of a sculpture of a Grecian girl and arranges to have a plaster cast of the bas-relief hung in his study so he could admire it. He cannot understand his obsession with Gradiva, but after a nightmare he becomes delusionally preoccupied with her and goes to Pompeii to search for her. Although his obsession with Gradiva is actually a displacement from a childhood playmate from his past, Hanold is unable to make the connection, and the real life Gradiva, Zoe Bertgang, attempts a cure that Freud found to be remarkably similar to the psychoanalytic process.

Hanold's inability to experience love and sexual excitement in the present is linked to his fixation on the buried past (i.e., the archaeological world which he inhabits), so Zoe must bring him to his senses and liberate his repressed love. Freud, noting that, "Every disorder analogous to Hanold's delusion, what in scientific terms we are in the habit of calling 'psychoneurosis,' has as its precondition the repression of a portion of instinctual life, or, as we can safely say, of the sexual instinct" (p. 89), drew an analogy between the process that transpires between Zoe and Hanold and the psychoanalytic situation. Specifically, he noted:

> The process of cure is accomplished in a relapse into love, if we combine all the many components of the sexual instinct under the term 'love'; and such a relapse is indispensable, for the symptoms on account of which the treatment has been undertaken are nothing other than precipitants of earlier struggles connected with repression or the return of the repressed, and they can only be resolved and washed away by a fresh high tide of the same passions. Every psycho-analytic treatment is an attempt at liberating repressed love which has found a meagre outlet in the compromise of a symptom. Indeed, the agreement between such treatments and the process of cure described by the author of *Gradiva* reaches its climax in the further fact that in analytic psychotherapy too the re-awakened passion, whether it is love or hate, invariably chooses as its object the figure of the doctor. [p. 90]

Freud, however, stopped short of sanctioning a reciprocal kind of love in the process of the psychoanalytic cure. In fact, he commented that one distinction between the novella and the work of a psychoanalyst is that Gradiva was able to reciprocate the love, while the psychoanalyst could not. He again referred to "substitutes" that the doctor must use to "help him to approximate with more or less success to the model of a cure by love" (p. 90), but he did not define exactly what that substitute is, just as he failed to do in his 1895 paper on hysteria. Although we know from other letters to Jung that Freud certainly was aware that the analyst might experience powerful attraction to the patient, he made it clear throughout his writing that one must abstain from reciprocating in action as one would outside the analytic setting.

A few years later, when Freud's papers on technique appeared, he seemed to have shifted a bit in his view of erotic attraction as the vehicle of cure. Only the *conscious* transference, the unobjectionable positive transference, was the ally of the treatment. Erotic transference was relegated to one of two types of unconscious transferences that serve as resistances to the process (1912). The other unconscious transference that could prove problematic was, of course, the negative transference.

In his paper, "Observations on Transference-Love" (1915b), Freud tried to make a more-or-less definitive statement on the subject. Indeed, the paper still stands today as a valuable guide to the analytic management of erotic transference despite its sexist language (the analyst was always male and the patient female) and its confusion about whether transference love was a help or a hindrance. As Friedman (1991) commented, Freud appeared to be saying that the analysand's love for the analyst could be used by the analyst to ultimately give up those same transference longings. This paradoxical state of affairs reflects a trend throughout Freud's technique papers to redefine resistance. Rather than regarding it as simply a stoppage of associations, there was a recapitulation of old conflicts and desires brought forth in the transference by the analytic setting.

Freud (1915b) was ambiguous in his position about the difference between transference love and extra-analytic love (Bergmann 1994, Brenner 1982, Coen 1994, Friedman 1991, Gabbard 1993a, 1994e, Hill 1994, Hoffer 1993, Schafer 1977, 1993). This ambiguity is perhaps best conveyed in the following quotation:

> It is true that the love consists of new editions of old traits and that it repeats infantile reactions. But this is the essential character of every state of being in love. . . . Transference-love has perhaps a degree less of freedom than the love which appears in ordinary life and is called normal; it displays its dependence on the infantile pattern more clearly and is less adaptable and capable of modification; but that is all, and not what is essential. [p. 168]

On the same page of that classic paper, Freud asks:

> Can we truly say that the state of being in love which becomes manifest in analytic treatment is not a real one? . . . We have no right to dispute that the state of being in love which makes its appearance in the course of analytic treatment has the character of "genuine" love. If it seems so lacking in normality, this is sufficiently explained by the fact that being in love in ordinary life, outside analysis, is also more similar to abnormal than normal mental phenomena. [1915b, p. 168]

In these quotations, we can glimpse Freud's struggle. There are certainly the residuals of old object relations brought into the transference, but the same can be said of any other kind of love. It may be a little more infantile because of the analyst's abstinence and the setting itself, but that difference is probably a trivial one. Having identified only insignificant differences between transference love and "real" love, Freud nevertheless advised the analyst to proceed as though the love is unreal: "He must keep firm hold of the transference-love, but treat it as something unreal, as a situation which has to be gone through in the treatment and traced back to its unconscious origins . . ." (1915b, p. 166). This somewhat confusing advice may well have grown out of Freud's concern that his colleagues were falling in love with their patients and behaving as though transference love should be acted upon in the same way as love outside the analytic setting. Coen (1994) has suggested that Freud stressed that both analyst and patient must regard the feelings as unreal to encourage both parties to analyze rather than act on the feelings.

Subsequent writers have made other comparisons about the similarities and differences. Kernberg (1994b) emphasized that the lack of reciprocity in transference love sharply differentiates it from extra-analytic love. In addition, transference love allows the patient to fully explore unconscious determinants of the oedipal situation, a possibility that is not generally available in other forms of love. Brenner (1982), on the other hand, argued that transference love does not differ in any essential way from romantic love in other situations. In his view, the unique feature of analysis is that the analyst analyzes the love. Bergmann (1985–1986) averred that transference love is more primitive and more dependent than romantic love outside of analysis.

Schafer (1977) felt that transference love must be viewed as having a dual nature. On one hand, it is a new edition of an old and regressive object relationship, while on the other it is an aspect of a new and real relationship adapted to the treatment setting, "a transitional state of a provisional character that is a means to a rational end and as genuine as normal love" (p. 340). In his view, the chief problem facing the analyst is how to integrate the two aspects of transference love in an effective, interpretive approach.

One fundamental difference between love in analysis and other love relationships has been pointed out by Modell (1991). Both members of the analytic dyad know they will ultimately separate, no matter how compatible or mutually loving they may be. This dimension of the analytic relationship reflects a fundamental paradox in the analytic situation; while the affective responses of both patient and analyst are real, they occur in the context of a relationship that is unreal in terms of ordinary social intercourse.

Hoffer (1993) has stressed that regarding love in the analytic relationship as anything but real is highly misleading to both patient and analyst. The love itself is virtually identical to love felt outside of treatment. He argued that one must look elsewhere for the distinctive features:

> The difference is not to be found in its reality but in its unique one-sidedness. On the analyst's part, the loving relationship is one-sided because of its purpose—namely, that the *raison d'être* of the relationship is that it exists for the patient's benefit. That, after all, is why the patient is in analysis. Moreover, the analytic setting, context, and frame are naturally defined and subordinate to its purpose. Therefore, although the analyst and patient may "really" love each other, the relationship is not equal and thus not mutual in the ordinary sense. [p. 349]

Most psychoanalytic writing about transference love appears to operate on the assumption that we understand what love is *outside* of the clinical setting. Before going any further in this exploration of similarities and differences, a consideration of the fundamental character of romantic love in everyday life is likely to be of heuristic value in our continued exploration of the nature of transference love.

ROMANTIC SPACE

Discussions about the differences between love in analytic and nonanalytic settings often read as though love is a monolithic entity. Love, of course, is actually protean, and there are infinite variations of states that we refer to as love. The Greeks recognized this multiplicity by applying different names to different kinds of love (e.g., *agape* or brotherly love, *eros* or sexual love, and *philein* or love of truth, knowledge).

It takes only a moment's reflection to recognize that even within an individual, love has strikingly different connotations in different relationships. Love directed toward one's spouse or lover is likely to be substantially different from the love felt for one's grandfather, daughter, friend, boss, student, mentor, dog, or country. Similarly, love within one relationship obviously changes over the course of time. Consider the difference between "love at first sight" and love between the same two individuals after fifty years of marriage.

Most writings about transference love, however, focus on romantic love. Hence, a useful starting point is to try to understand the complexities of romantic love with full recognition that this is only one type of love occurring in analysis or in extraanalytic situations. Wilkinson and I

(1995) have defined the experience as the achievement of "romantic space." More specifically, we defined romantic space as "both an intrapsychic and an interpersonal experience that sustains a feeling of being in love" (p. 210).

Although psychoanalytic writers have tried to define romantic love, they have generally focused more on the vicissitudes of falling in love than how it is sustained (Altman 1977, Balint 1948, Bergmann 1980). Freud (1905b) considered falling in love to be a process of restoration in which "the finding of an object is in fact the refinding of it" (p. 222). He suggested that the choice of romantic partners stemmed from the opportunity to reexperience the happiness and excitement embodied in the prohibited oedipal wish. Later, his theory of love moved beyond a topographical focus on the dormant oedipal wish to encompass the structural influence of the ego ideal and the economic forces inherent in narcissistic libido. As a result, Freud (1914) argued that not only the parent but also the self, through the projection of the ego ideal, can be taken as a model for the love object.

More contemporary psychoanalytic thinkers share Freud's view that love is fueled by an experience of refinding. However, in contrast to Freud, current views emphasize a forward-looking force in love that enriches the self (Bergmann 1987, Kernberg 1974, 1995b, Person 1988). These writers underscore how romantic love consists of a hope that the beloved will heal the wound inflicted by the less-than-good-enough early object. They invite us to consider how that wound is dressed and mended through internalization of the partner's loving concern.

Integration of intrapsychic elements and capacities has long been thought of as a cornerstone in the lover's ability to sustain romantic love. For example, Freud (1905a) spoke about the convergence in puberty of the sensuous component instincts predominating in early childhood with the tender currents ascending during latency. Waelder (1936) addressed the importance of integration from the structural point of view. He considered love to be evidence of the ego's capacity to choose a partner who could be sexually gratifying, unconsciously reminiscent of past love objects, sufficiently admired to garner approval of the ego ideal, and appropriate in meeting the demands of reality.

Others such as Bergmann (1980) have stressed the importance of integrating the longings arising during the separation-individuation phase. Similarly, Kernberg (1974, 1977, 1995b) detailed how the establishment of ego identity and whole-object relatedness, together with overcoming of oedipal conflicts and related prohibitions against a full sexual relation, are necessary to achieve mature love. These divergent theoretical perspectives have one fundamental assumption in common: what has been internalized from earlier relationships and integrated into the very fabric of the individual self-experience becomes a template for seeking out future romantic partners. Freud's assumption that *refinding* guides the course of love continues to be a basic premise.

Presumably, the integration of intrapsychic elements and capacities prepares the lover for being able to adapt to the beloved's needs. Adaptation, as an evolving mode of relatedness, calls on lovers to reconcile interpersonal demands with their own intrapsychic resources. Balint (1948) focused on the adaptation required in romance by discussing how genital love was the fusion of disagreeing elements: genital satisfaction and pregenital tenderness. He considered genital love to be a state in which mature identifications between lovers provide an anchor point for their regression to pregenital expectations of receiving perpetual kindness, regard, and consideration. Reading between the lines of Balint's thought, a lover must balance his or her own separation anxieties and concomitant wishes to command the other's abiding care with an intuitive appreciation for the other's personal needs.

Through his explorations of the dual origin of love, Balint was among the first to address the relevance of the evolving relationship for staying in love. Yet he did so only from the perspective of one of the partners. In discussing the need for the lover to conquer personal desires while attending closely to the needs of the beloved, he brought us to the threshold of exploring what transpires between the two. But he did not pass on into the intermediate area of their experience.

To enter the area in which the lover's restraint and desire overlap those of the beloved, one must allow for the paradoxical coexistence of union and individuality that accompany romantic attachment. No longer confined to the lover's personal experience, this kind of perspective begins to weave the intrapsychic stirrings of each partner with the interpersonal impact they have on each other. Such exchange of deeply personal wishes and reactions may be reminiscent of primitive object relatedness. Relatively stable couples often work out primitive object relationships in their attachment to each other (Dicks 1963, Gabbard 1994c, Kernberg 1995b). More specifically, through a process of projective identification, the beloved may be the recipient of traits, weaknesses, or faults rejected by the self and may be subsequently persecuted for manifesting those qualities. Or the beloved may be fervently sought out, often in vain fantasy, for access to those parts of the self that are missing. From this point of view, the lover is *refinding* elements of self-experience in the beloved that were put there via the intrapsychic–interpersonal process of projective identification (Ogden 1982).

By projectively casting, then acting coercively to engage the other in an internally derived role, lovers may behave in highly stereotyped and constricted ways. Dicks (1963) observed that even for partners with considerable ego strength, couples tended to deteriorate regressively into polarized units, such as independent-dependent or intellectual-emotional. Together these polarized halves formed a whole personality in the romantic dyad, but each individual alone was incomplete. Whereas separately the two lovers could not sustain an integration of regulatory functions, self-experiences, and interpersonal expectations, together they could. Therefore, the integration that powerfully underwrites romantic love may occur on a dyadic level as well as on an individual level.

To achieve romantic space, internalization and subsequent integration are essential. However, sustaining romantic love is more complex and involves a counterpoint that is often overlooked. Romantic space appears to evolve from the simultaneous presence of distinct modes of relatedness. In other words, there is a counterpoint to the internalization and subsequent integration associated with staying in love. Integration by definition is informed, negated, and preserved by fragmentation. Internalization, therefore, has a counterpoint in projection. One process could not have meaning without the other.

To elucidate this complexity, Ogden's formulations about the dialectically constituted nature of experience are heuristically useful (1992a). He grappled with the interface between the intrapsychic and the interpersonal and concluded that no static boundary separating internal subjectivity from external reality could be established. This vantage point is especially compelling when considering the personal desires each lover brings to the shared experience. In the absence of such absolute self-defining boundaries, Ogden described how the shape of internal subjectivity depends on the dialectical interplay of the depressive and paranoid-schizoid modes of experience. His reformulations of these Kleinian positions has liberated them from Klein's instinctual anchoring, through a fresh focus on the subjective aspects of attachment. Ogden's emphasis is on two contrasting modes of relatedness that paradoxically coexist within a dialectic tension. Each has characteristic defenses, anxieties, symbolization, and object relations. Because paranoid-schizoid and depressive elements of experience inform, negate, and create each other, internal subjectivity is "forever decentered from static self-equivalence" (Ogden 1992b, p. 624).

More to the point in describing the counterpoint to internalization and subsequent integration in romantic love, there is a maturational bias in much of psychoanalytic writing that tends to overvalue the depressive mode of relatedness and thus forecloses appreciation of the significant contribution made by paranoid-schizoid phenomena. Love's poetic rhythm is created by graphically distinct paranoid-schizoid and depressive phenomena that have a simultaneous effect on subjectivity.

Just as a poem's richness cannot be dissected and linearly arrayed, a description adequately capturing the contradictory, synchronous layers of romantic love is difficult to make. One may state, in a highly oversimplified way, that what is integrated in the depressive position is broken up and created anew in the paranoid-schizoid position. Singular emphasis on the lover's capacity for concern and guilt neglects the buoyant merger and intolerance of separation that also fuel ongoing love. Accordingly, to separate out descriptively, the integration underlying depressive functioning allows the lover to respond lovingly to the beloved despite hateful feelings. The fragmentation inherent in paranoid-schizoid functioning springs from the lover's reaction to momentary passion. With respect to staying in love, the stability of the relationship is informed, negated, and preserved by its spontaneity. One cannot have meaning without the other.

Although both modes of relatedness are continuously present, the relative impact on the lovers' experience may ebb and flow. At times, both depressive and paranoid-schizoid phenomena will be equally influential. However, the impact of one mode of relatedness inevitably will become attenuated as the other surges to predominance. The lovers' capacity for relatedness consequently will shift along a continuum between poles of paranoid-schizoid and depressive functioning.

Using Ogden's (1986, 1989, 1994) synthesis of Klein, Bion, and Winnicott, the interplay between the depressive and paranoid-schizoid modes of relatedness can be traced through qualitative shifts in the lovers' object relations, cognition, leading anxieties, and process of internalizations. Table 1–1 distinguishes between the relative contributions of depressive and paranoid-schizoid phenomena.

As a result of the integrative forces inherent in depressive functioning, the lover's effort is to establish familiarity and recapture a feeling state. Object relations are organized around the capacity to be alone, together with a discrete sense of self and other. Love, which is given freely to the other, vicariously results in the pleasure of receiving tender concern. The partner is perceived as a true companion who has participated in the joint creation of a narrative tracing the development of their relationship. The ups and downs of the romance are cognitively mediated through a realistic appraisal of the abilities and

Table 1–1. Romantic Space

Paranoid-Schizoid Mode		Depressive Mode
part	←object relations→	whole
persecutory/ annihilation	←anxiety→	depressive
perception as reality	←symbolic capacity→	"as if"
splitting & projective identification	←defenses→	manic/repression
fragmentation		integration
freshness		joint narrative
coercion		capacity to think one's own thoughts
idealization		capacity for concern

(Wilkinson & Gabbard, 1995)

limitations possessed by each partner. Disappointments arising between the lovers are interpreted based on an appreciation of the enduring nature of the relationship. The primary anxiety that must be negotiated is a fear of harming the other. The process of internalization is identification that results in empathy for the partner's wishes, strengths, and shortcomings.

In the depressive mode of relatedness, the lover acts as an interpreting subject who can separate thought from that which is thought about (Ogden 1986). The capacity to mediate experience through symbols allows the lover to refind a previously lived sense of connection. For example, the beloved may be an appealing figure because of the feeling of familiarity evoked by the beloved's presence. The experience is one of recognition and companionship. Continuity is lent to the lovers' experience due to the capacity to symbolically represent qualities of earlier relationships. Separation from the actual infantile object is managed through the hope and expectation that the object can be discovered again and again in familiar experiences. Thus in the depressive mode, freedom from the actual past is achieved through the hope of refinding its essential elements in the future.

Hope, as the enduring expectation that some element of the past can be matched in the future, supports the lover's capacity to be an interpreting subject. Assured that the *we* established in the past can be expected in the future, lovers are free to think their own thoughts about what is transpiring between themselves and their beloved in the present moment. Symington (1990) pointed out that the freedom to think one's own thoughts is dependent on whether the mode of relatedness between the two individuals is *responsive* or *reactive*. When urgent feelings and inchoate ideas cannot be contained by the lover, projective identification is employed *reactively*. The beloved is coerced into some sort of containing role through projective identification, thereby preventing both partners from thinking their own thoughts. They simply react.

As Symington (1990) cogently argued, the ability to suspend a reflexive reaction allows one person to respond genuinely to another. The response is dependent on lovers reaching deeply into their own thinking-and-feeling center. If they are free to think their own thoughts about what they encounter there, they gain access to the essence of their experience in that moment. Despite the highly personal beginning, it is in such moments that the lover is available to the deepest intercourse with the beloved.

Thinking one's own thoughts leads to integration,

resolution, and containment, yet if unopposed, it results in closure, stagnation, and deadness (Ogden 1986). The divide-and-unite processes cease to complement each other and the interplay between different modes of experience is unnaturally halted. Delusion is penetrated. Secrets are exposed. Curiosity is abandoned. Jealousy is disarmed, and the romantic relationship is stripped of its hints of amorous sin (Viederman 1988). The bond between the lover and the beloved is cemented solely by companionship without benefit of a passionate imperative. Absolute trust, predictability, and repetition anchor the partners in everyday routines where their joint longing is for a comfortable life rather than for each other (Viederman 1988). Their minds, full of memories and hopes, offer little toward the immediate area of their experience and the immediacy of being together in the present. They have prematurely or defensively employed the containing function (indicated by resolution, integration, and thinking one's own thoughts) to mute the impact of emotional reality in their relationship. Consequently, their memory and understanding become dissociated from their emotional reality and arrogantly closed off. Spontaneity and aliveness are lost because of an allegiance to internally represented objects.

To reclaim spontaneity and aliveness, the integration, resolution, and containment of the depressive position must be broken up by the splitting of linkages and opening up of closures afforded by the paranoid-schizoid phenomena. Elements that previously appeared to have no logical connection are brought together in such a way that their connection is displayed and an unsuspecting coherence revealed (Bion 1963).

The paranoid-schizoid mode of relatedness draws on qualitatively different forms of cognition, object relations, anxieties, and internalization. Due to the fragmentation underlying paranoid-schizoid functioning, relatedness evolves in the moment rather than from an effort to refind earlier satisfactions. The lack of symbolically mediated history results in the lovers' cognitive grasp of the relationship being unidimensional. Without an awareness of the past or a hope for the future, each moment the lovers share feels timeless. Perception and interpretation are experienced as one and the same. The concreteness of thought causes the beloved to be defined by how he or she is perceived. The ups and downs of the romance are explained by the illusory conclusions that the beloved is all good or all bad.

Such appraisals occur spontaneously and with great conviction. Object relations are established through a sense of merger. Indeed, the height of sexual passion typifies the paranoid-schizoid mode of relatedness. Because of the dependence on the beloved to complete some aspect of the lover's own self, separation is considered intolerable. The beloved is desired as a container for the most precious as well as the most despised elements of the lover's self-experience. Thus, although lovers give of themselves to their beloved, their goal is to use love as an agent of change in the lover's internal world. The leading anxieties are that the lover will disappear into the beloved or become transformed into a terrifying persecutor. The process of internalization is introjection. In the paranoid-schizoid mode of relatedness, the lovers are riding the tide of a compelling experience without thinking their own thoughts. The opportunity for the certainties born of the depressive position, to be re-created in the paranoid-schizoid mode, may be perceived as one of unlimited potential or unfettered catastrophe. In contrast to the intuitive responsiveness of depressive functioning, a reactive chain may be set mindlessly in motion (Symington 1990).

The mindless reactions sparked by catastrophe are met by the mindless receptivity inherent in faith. Although what is unnameable and invisible in the lovers' experience may provoke a catastrophic reaction, it may also invite unimagined growth. In the absence of expectations, memory, and hope, the lover is simply open to the beloved in faith (Eigen 1985).

The term *faith* is used here in a descriptive effort to frame an expectant, ineffable aspect of the lovers' romance. Faith is not bound by time, infantile signs, facts, or proscriptions. Its alert readiness and alive waiting is in stark contrast to the resolution and containment characteristic of the depressive mode. Familiarity is offset by an ineffable sense of being possessed by thrilling, chaotic, meaningless, timeless, engulfing relational currents. In such moments the lover and the beloved are left with little else but faith that the relationship will carry them toward a true meeting of each other's innermost self. Consider that through faith the lover has the chance to meet, create, and discover in the beloved what is yet to be met, created, and discovered in the self.

Through the relative contributions of depressive and paranoid-schizoid functioning, a powerful interplay exists between refinding and faith. The dialectical interplay simultaneously includes hope, speculation, drama, interpretation, imagination, and memory (all depressive elements), as well as faith, illusion, uncertainty, and fragmentation (all paranoid-schizoid elements). The dynamic interplay underwrites the efforts of the lover to learn who the beloved is and who the lover is when with the beloved. On one hand, there is familiarity with a certain quality of object relationship. On the other, there is a suspenseful meeting with what is yet unknown in two people facing each other (Green 1973).

Neither mode of experiencing the relationship is absolute and exclusive. One intersects the other, thereby informing, negating, and creating the other. It is not that memory and hope are lost with faith. There is both a starting over and a continuous history. The interplay between refinding and faith permits both the past and present to influence the ongoing romantic space.

In defining romantic space as constituting the dialectical interplay of two distinct modes of relatedness, Wilkinson and I (1995) suggested that it is the intermediate area between the lover and the beloved, unchallenged with respect to its belonging to inner or external (shared) reality. It is a place where the lover can both evoke the past and move beyond it. The degree to which the beloved is subjectively cast into the role of an earlier object, and the degree to which the beloved objectively invites an inconceivably new way of being for the lover, cannot be scrutinized. The beloved is perceived as offering a relatedness that is reassuringly familiar as well as abruptly fresh. Paradoxically, the lover's refinding of the past allows for transformation in the present—just as transformation in the present allows for refinding of the past.

If one examines any particular romantic couple, one can observe that at times paranoid-schizoid and depressive phenomena may be coequal elements of the lover's experience, while at other times, one mode of relatedness may predominate. When each partner is functioning in a predominantly depressive mode at the same time, both have a greater freedom to respond to their own internal world while appreciating the impact of that response on the other. More specifically, there is a conscious grasp of their interpersonal exchanges. When both partners are functioning in a predominantly paranoid-schizoid mode, intrapsychic elements that cannot be contained ricochet back and forth between them. Each individual is more likely to be coerced into reacting to the other, whether in erotic passion, tenderness, jealousy, or anger. The amount or viability of romantic space established in the immediate area of their experience depends on the nature of the link between them.

When depressive processes are most prevalent, the nature of the link between the lover and the beloved is primarily psychological (Ogden 1986). Identification allows the lover to perceive, understand, and experience the gestures of the beloved. Through trying on one identification first, then another, the lover empathically plays with the idea of being the beloved while knowing otherwise (Ogden 1986). Lovers retain the freedom to think their own thoughts while cultivating an appreciation of the beloved's personal hopes and desires. The lover may then create a joint narrative with the beloved, enlisting the subjective experience of both partners. The historical account of the relationship catalogues the ups and downs they have endured, acknowledges their mutual efforts, and values their individuality. The constancy and reliability of the relationship they have built together is symbolically contained by their joint narrative. Their ability to entertain a range of personal meanings both within and between themselves is indicative of the symbolic link established in depressive functioning.

When the paranoid-schizoid processes are most prevalent, the nature of the link between lovers is both psychological and interpersonal (Ogden 1982, 1986). Through projective identification, the lovers unconsciously fantasize that part of the self (or an internal object-representation) has been deposited in the beloved. The lovers then exert interpersonal pressure to engage their beloved in an interaction congruent with the projected fantasy. The element of themselves that lovers have imparted to their beloved may contain specific meanings. However, the effort to communicate remains unrecognized as the lover and beloved mindlessly act out their respective roles. There is such a powerful sense of inevitability about their feelings state that they do not consider it to be a subjective state; rather, it is treated as reality (Ogden 1986).

In such instances, lovers are using their beloved as an interpersonal container; as long as the beloved is coerced into reacting to the lover's projective identification, the focus of the link between them remains interpersonal. However, when the beloved are able to regain the capacity to think their own thoughts, the inevitability of the situation can be transformed into an experience having personal meaning. The patterns of the interactions can be recognized. The focus of the link between them becomes psychological, and the projected elements of the lover's self can be reclaimed. The receptivity inherent in faith provides the tolerance necessary for the theme of the lover's actions and the beloved's reactions to be identified. The daring uncertainty of faith makes possible the telling of a new joint narrative. The beloved's interpersonal tolerance helps the lover to meet, create, and discover aspects of the self that have previously been unknown.

Idealization of the beloved is essential to maintain a sense of romantic space in a relationship. Person (1988) pointed out that it is much more durable than many critics have contended. Idealization may be altered over time, but it does not necessarily dissipate. Person even suggested that sustained idealization may be more central to the feeling of being in love than either passion or a sense of mutuality.

The foregoing conceptualization of romantic space lends itself to an understanding of the pathology of romantic relationships as well. A couple entrenched in the depressive mode, lacking the excitement and renewal of the paranoid-schizoid mode, may find themselves sinking into deadly comradeship (Viederman 1988). When both partners are fixed in the paranoid-schizoid mode, communication occurs via projective identification. There is no authentic dialogue because there is no freedom to think one's own thoughts and share them with each other. Every interaction is coerced. The marriage of a narcissistic man to a masochistic woman is a common example of this pathological form of relatedness, in which the woman allows herself to be used as an extension of the man. These marriages may be stable but are rarely described as loving.

The most conflict-ridden relationships are likely to be those in which one partner is fixed in the paranoid-schizoid mode while the other partner is locked into the depressive mode. Chronic tension arises out of the depressive individual's refusal to be coerced into functioning the way the paranoid-schizoid individual demands. This form of coupling is likely to be experienced by both partners as a mismatch.

LOVE IN THE TRANSFERENCE

The concept of romantic space provides a reference point—perhaps an ideal state—from which a myriad of other forms of love depart. Based on a relative loading of paranoid-schizoid and depressive elements, transference love may resemble any variation of love that occurs outside of the treatment situation. Bolognini (1994), for example, has proposed a classification involving erotized, erotic, loving, and affectionate transferences. In this classification, the affectionate transference, on the opposite end of the continuum from the erotized, is one in which the depressive mode of experiencing the analyst is predominant: "The matrix of this internal attitude is, in my view, often an adequate negotiation of the depressive position, whereby the subject has been able to work through the experiential process of separateness" (p. 83).

Confining the focus to the feelings of the patient, however, is misleading. The concept of romantic space must incorporate both intrapsychic and interpersonal aspects to be fully explanatory. In contemporary psychoanalytic thinking, analysis must be viewed as both a two-person and a one-person enterprise—it is both intrapsychic and interpersonal/interactive (Coen 1992, Gill 1994). Two persons are in the room when an analysis takes place, and both bring their habitual patterns of relating and loving to the analytic work. As Gill (1993) has noted, "To say that the same falling in love will occur in some other kind of treatment or in real life is to minimize the specific realities of the particular two-person analytic situation. Transference love is specific to this *particular* analytic situation" (p. 117). In this regard Freud was not entirely accurate in his 1915 paper when he implied that the personal characteristics of the analyst have nothing to do with the transference love and that exactly the same template will be repeated again and again. Moreover, depending on the subjectivity of the analyst, transference love may be reciprocated (or completely unreciprocated) to varying degrees. This response will in turn influence the nature of the patient's love for the analyst. Hence, a unique dialectically constituted, decentered subject is created (Ogden 1994).

From the standpoint of a one-person psychology, in which we focus on the patient's intrapsychic world as it manifests itself in the transference, the type of *loving* that the patient reveals in the transference resembles the forms of loving the patient manifests in extra-analytic relationships. Given the assumption that transference love is not monolithic in nature, we can recognize that Freud's (1915b) position that the patient will inevitably fall in love with the analyst is perhaps oversimplified. Many individuals find it difficult to express love to a spouse, a parent, or any other significant figure in their lives. They will similarly experience difficulty expressing their love to the analyst. In other words, they may reveal no overt sign of falling in love in the transference, but rather a host of defenses against it.

Consider, for example, the following exchange between a 35-year-old married woman patient whom I had seen for about a year and me:

Patient: I don't believe that you actually care about me.

Analyst: Can you say more?

Patient: Well, I imagine that you might dislike me less than my previous analyst did. Of course, I don't believe that I would find any analyst particularly likable. I can feel some sense of admiration for you. I can also say that I depend on you at times. But I certainly don't see you as lovable. Frankly, I don't really like other people that much in general.

Analyst: Well, then, I can appreciate that you might feel the same way here.

Patient: I probably insist that you don't like me for my own comfort. I'd certainly be worried about a therapist who was too enthused about me. With my father I could always deal with his attacks and criticisms better than I could when he told me how wonderful I was. Attacks are predictable, and I can defend against them more easily. Praise always strikes me as phony and confusing.

Analyst: I think it's just as hard for you to express positive feelings such as love or tenderness as it is for you to hear those feelings from others.

Patient: The only time I can say "I love you" or hear "I love you" is with my husband.

Analyst: What's different about that situation for you?

Patient: Well, we have a sexual relationship. I can't feel love outside a sexual relationship.

Analyst: So you're really not able to say "I love you" to anyone else?

Patient: No, and I'll tell you why. When I was growing up, I only heard "I love you" when I was being punished and my parents needed to reassure me that they didn't hate me. It never seemed to go along with their behavior or how they looked. I don't trust the love of others.

In this brief vignette, we see how the patient's characteristic pattern of object relatedness carries over into the analytic relationship. We also see her characterological incapacity to delink feelings of love from a sexual relationship. She provides some insight into the situation by clarifying that expressions of love were always heard in a context where they did not seem to belong so that she grew to be distrustful of such feelings.

With other patients, one may see a predominantly hateful transference that is the patient's characteristic way of loving or attaching to others, as will be explored in Chapters 7 and 8. Joseph (1993) has suggested that a more contemporary way of viewing Freud's thesis is that analytic patients inevitably bring their typical and habitual modes of object relatedness into their relationship with the analyst.

The analyst will also bring his or her habitual patterns of relatedness into the analysis, so that the meeting of these two subjectivities offers the potential for a multiplicity of jointly created forms of loving in the space between patient and analyst. For example, the patient may bring a form of *erotized* transference (Blum 1973, Greenson 1967), in which paranoid-schizoid functioning predominates. Often found in borderline patients and those who were incest victims as children, erotized transference presents as a tenacious and ego-syntonic demand for sexual gratification. The distinction between external and internal realities becomes blurred, and these patients fervently believe that sexual consummation with the analyst is necessary if they are to be healed. In such scenarios, patients have placed an idealized part of themselves in the analyst through projective identification and have become convinced of the reality of their perception of the analyst as the idealized rescuer/lover. The "as if" nature of the transference is lost, so the transference is not viewed as a subjective state requiring analysis. Rather, it is viewed as a realistic perception and must be gratified. These patients were described by Freud as "accessible only to the logic of soup, with dumplings for arguments" (1915b, p. 167).

In an analogous manner, the analyst may also function in a predominantly paranoid-schizoid mode that one can conceptualize as *erotized countertransference* (Gabbard 1994b, 1994c, 1994d). In this state the patient becomes the projected idealized object- or self-representation that will rescue the analyst from despair. The "as if" character of the countertransference is lost, and in the most egregious cases the analyst embarks on a sexual relationship with the patient (Gabbard 1994d, Gabbard and Lester 1995). When erotized transference is reciprocated with erotized countertransference, one observes a *folie à deux*, in which the purpose of analysis is lost to both parties and the depressive mode of mental functioning is overridden by the sheer intensity of the "love" between patient and analyst.

In many other cases, of course, the analyst recognizes the countertransference nature of the loving feelings and engages in a systematic self-analysis in the service of maintaining the analytic purpose. In still other cases, the patient's erotized transference may be responded to with a variety of negative feelings, including contempt, hatred, alarm, irritation, or indifference. Regardless of the analyst's internal responses to the patient's love, the activity that is crucial to the process is that the analyst must analyze the transference love. Indeed, if one were to attempt to identify the primary difference between love in the analytic situation and love in all other settings, the key would be the way the analyst deals with the love. As Freud (1915b) so aptly put it, "The course the analyst must pursue . . . is one for which there is no model in real life" (p. 166). The reciprocity implied in the concept of romantic space may be felt in the analytic setting but cannot be articulated by the analyst in the same way. The analyst neither ignores the patient's love nor responds with mutual professions of love. Instead, the analyst treats the love as material to be understood in all of its current and historical ramifications and meanings.

It is perhaps unfortunate that Freud goes on in the same passage to emphasize the "unreal" nature of transference love. As Ms. S taught me in the vignette described in the Prologue, patients are not likely to agree with an analyst who emphasizes that their love is unreal. A more contemporary view would be that the love is both real in the sense that it involves a unique current relationship and unreal, or displaced, in the sense that it has elements of past object relationships that have been internalized and then reactivated in the analytic dyad (Gabbard 1994b, Schafer 1993). It may well be that Freud's discomfort with being loved influenced him to make a strong case for erotic transference as repetitive and independent of the person of the analyst (Coen 1994, Schafer 1993). Analysts today often share Freud's discomfort with powerful feelings of transference love, and as I have argued elsewhere (1994b), our excessive focus on distinctions between love in the transference and outside of it may serve as an obsessional defense against our own distress when feelings of love arise in treatment.

Modern analysts have come to expect that passionate feelings of love (and hate) will often be stirred in the analytic crucible. The true significance of these feelings as resistance is that they may compel analysts and/or patients into nonreflective action (Friedman 1991). Hence the analyst's task is to set the conditions in both parties for a dual state of consciousness in which active participation is balanced by reflective observation. Friedman has noted that implicit in Freud's paper, "Observations on Transference Love" (1915b) is "the principle that treatment requires a simultaneous conscious activation of repressed wishes and a cool contemplation of their significance, so that they are experienced both as wishes and as objective features of the conflicted self" (Friedman 1991, p. 590).

It is the task of the analyst through management of the analytic framework and through interpretation to provide conditions wherein the patient may dare to transform what is "unthought," that is, what is enacted rather than verbalized and contemplated, into a personally meaningful experience (Bollas 1987, Ogden 1986). The state of romantic space may be approximated in the relationship between analyst and analysand, but unlike the analytic dyad in the throes of erotized transference and countertransference, this analytic couple maintains some functioning in the depressive mode and reflects on what is happening between them. In fact, the systematic process of analyzing the love present in their relationship ultimately transforms romantic space into what has come to be known as *analytic space*. Ogden (1986) defines analytic space as:

> the space between patient and analyst in which analytic experience (including transference delusion) is generated and in which personal meanings can be created and played with. . . . Within analytic space fantasy and reality stand in a dialectical relationship to each other. The capacity for mature transference (as opposed to delusional transference) involves the capacity to generate an illusion that is experienced simultaneously as real and not real. [pp. 238–239]

Given this goal of achieving analytic space from the raw mixture of passions in the analytic setting, the analyst's role can be described as one of establishing symbolic links where mindless actions previously prevailed. Hence, although the analytic work is fueled by the interplay between paranoid-schizoid and depressive functioning in the patient's experience, the strengthening of the patient's observing ego that is part and parcel of the analytic work draws on the integration and internalization inherent in the depressive mode.

In the analytic space, then, the depressive mode predominates as the patient creates and examines personal meanings with the help of the analyst's focus on what is happening between them. We can therefore construct a conceptual continuum characterized by the erotized dyad on one end functioning predominantly in a paranoid-schizoid mode. As we move toward the depressive end of the continuum, we encounter romantic space, which is based distinctly on the capacity of both partners to function simultaneously in both modes of relatedness and flexibly shift between the two. Moving further toward the depressive end, we encounter analytic space, wherein there is greater emphasis on the depressive mode because of the specific analytic task of reflection on and contemplation of passionate feelings. Finally, at the depressive end of the continuum, we would encounter a state of analytic deadness, in which no passion exists in the analytic couple and the process seems empty and lifeless.

It should also be understood, of course, that much of the time analyst and patient will find themselves at different sites along the continuum. These "out-of-synch" periods may be extremely useful to the process. They may approximate aspects of intimate relationships outside the analytic setting, where one partner is operating in a depressive mode and the other in a paranoid-schizoid mode. Also, when the patient is experiencing erotized transference in a full-blown paranoid-schizoid state, the analyst can probably manage the situation optimally if he or she is "out of synch" in a more depressive mode of functioning.

In an optimal analytic process, the analyst's love for the patient is ultimately processed and metabolized into what Loewald (1970) referred to as "analytic love." Although Loewald himself did not elaborate on this concept in his writings, Schafer (1992) has proposed that Loewald was referring to the idea that the analyst believes in the potential of the patient to grow through the process of analysis and safeguards the future of the analysand in the trusting analytic relationship so that development can take place. As Loewald observed at one point in his writings, "It is impossible to love the truth of psychic reality, to be moved by this love as Freud was in his life work, and not to love and care for the object whose truth we want to discover. . . . In our work it can truly be said that in our best moments of dispassionate and objective analyzing, we love our object, the patient, more than at any other time and are compassionate with his whole being" (1970, p. 297).

As any analysand in the process of terminating an effective analysis will tell you, a sense of being loved is an integral component of the analytic process. As Hoffer (1993) has stressed, genuine neutrality involves being engaged and actively loving toward the patient in the sense that the analyst has a profound respect for the patient's autonomy, rather than imposing his or her own biases on the patient. Analytic love of this variety is not free from the encroachment of passion fueled by the analyst's needs, but it harnesses that passion in the service of a higher goal. Indeed, Lear (1990) suggested that the latent content of Freud's remark about cures of love is that psychoanalysis promotes individuation. "In that sense," Lear concluded, "psychoanalysis itself is a manifestation of love" (p. 28).

By way of conclusion, we might say that love in the analytic setting has far more similarities than differences from love in nonanalytic settings. It uses the same metaphors, wears the same masks, and elicits the same variety of responses in others. The analyst is a forbidden object just as mother or father was forbidden in childhood, but also in the same way that the spouse of a friend, a boss, or a coworker may be forbidden *outside* the analytic setting. Patients will relate to the beloved figure of the analyst in much the same way they have related to others toward whom they have similar feelings. The primary difference lies in the analyst's approach, which is toward reflection, contemplation, and analysis, rather than action. As Phillips (1994) has noted, "In psychoanalysis love is a problem of knowledge. . . . Lovers are like detectives: they are trying to find something out that will make all the difference. And the stories that psychoanalysis tells about love tend to confirm a traditional progress narrative about the acquisition of wisdom (wisdom, of course, is always counter-erotic)". (p. 40).

2 ON HATE IN LOVE RELATIONSHIPS: THE NARCISSISM OF MINOR DIFFERENCES REVISITED

> The music at a wedding procession always reminds me of the music of soldiers going into battle.
> —Heinrich Heine

In myths and fairy tales the redemptive and healing power of love is a pervasive theme. The analytic process of healing is often construed in similar terms by both analyst and patient. Patients typically enter analysis with an unconscious (or conscious) fantasy that the unconditional love of the analyst will repair the damage done by the imperfect parents of their childhood. Similarly, a common unconscious determinant of the career choice of psychoanalysis is the hope that providing love for patients will result in the analyst being idealized and loved in return (Gabbard 1992, 1995a). As an analysis progresses, however, both parties soon learn that love is never uncomplicated in the analytic process. On the coattails of love ride expectations that can never be fulfilled. Frustration, contempt, and hatred are always just beneath the surface.

Perhaps the most famous historical experiment with love occurred in the clinical work of Sándor Ferenczi. Bitter after his analytic experience with Freud, Ferenczi became convinced that the emphasis of analysis on the role of fantasy was seriously misplaced. He maintained that many patients had actually experienced sexual trauma as children. As a consequence Ferenczi argued, the analyst needed to supply the love to the patient that the parents had failed to provide, even to the point of hugging and kissing the patient (Gabbard 1992, Gabbard and Lester 1995, Grubrich-Simitis 1986).

Ferenczi's wish to be loved by his patients to make up for the harshness of his own mother in childhood led him to the practice of mutual analysis, in which he would analyze the patient for an hour followed by a role reversal in which he allowed the patient to analyze him for an hour. He tried this technique with four American female patients, one of whom was referred to as R.N. In his diary (Dupont 1988), Ferenczi revealed that his attempts to love his patient were contaminated by repetitions of his internalized object relations from childhood: "In R.N. I find my mother again, namely the real one, who was hard and energetic and of whom I am afraid. R.N. knows this, and treats me with particular gentleness; the analysis even enables her to transform her own hardness into friendly softness" (p. 45). In a later entry, he acknowledged that his own childhood feelings of aggression and hatred toward his mother were often displaced onto his patients. Through a tremendous effort he was able to develop what he termed an "intellectual super-kindness" in an attempt to overcome such feelings and be as loving as possible toward his patients. Despite his earnest attempt, R.N. nevertheless told Ferenczi that she experienced feelings of hate coming from him. In a diary entry on May 5, 1932, Ferenczi acknowledged the accuracy of the patient's perception: "The patient's demands to be loved corresponded to analogous demands on me by my mother. In actual fact and inwardly, therefore, I did hate the patient, in spite of all the friendliness I displayed" (Dupont 1988, p. 99).

Ferenczi's historical experiment has undoubtedly influenced the way modern analysts think about technique. Nevertheless, it floundered when he learned that hatred, sadism, and aggression are ubiquitous forces in love relationships. As Brenner (1982) noted, "That love is invariably mixed with hate and vice versa is a matter of empirical observation, not a matter of logic or of definition. It is a practical matter with practical consequences for analytic work" (p. 206.) Brenner even went so far as to suggest that the term *erotic transference* should be discarded because every transference includes both aggressive and libidinal drive derivatives. In this regard, the phenomena that we label erotic transference refers to the *surface* or the phenomenology of the patient's attitude toward the analyst. It is the manifest content only, and the analyst must always recognize the distinction.

Stoller (1985) observed that even in the most loving relationships, a measure of hostility is an integral part of sexual arousal. I would submit that the hostility that emerges in loving sexual relations is merely a de-repressed moment when feelings of aggression that are always active—though not always conscious—make their appearance. Raphling (1991) has noted that unselfish concern for one's partner is always competing with aggressive claims of the self to exploit, possess, and dominate the partner.

The notion that aggression and even hatred lie beneath the surface of love should not necessarily lead us to conclude that the purity of a powerfully redemptive affect has been contaminated—and thus ruined—by the dark underside of human nature. Aggression has unfortunately developed a bad reputation in many quarters. It is useful to remember that the etymological origins of the word lie in the Latin *aggressere*, the intransitive verb form of which is *aggredi*, meaning "to approach" (*Oxford English Dictionary* 1971, p. 47). Aggressive forces are instrumental in the bonding of love relationships. Kernberg (1991) has made the following observation: "A man and woman who discover their attraction and longing for each other, who are able to establish a full sexual relationship that carries with it emotional intimacy and a sense of fulfillment of their ideals in the closeness with the loved other, are expressing their capacity not only to link unconsciously eroticism and tenderness, sexuality and the ego-ideal, but also to recruit aggression in the service of love" (pp. 46–47).

THE EVOLUTION OF HATE IN PSYCHOANALYTIC THOUGHT

Freud ultimately noted that love and hate are inextricably bound together in our most intimate relationships. This view is captured in his famous comment that the opposite of love is indifference rather than hate (1915a). However, Freud seemed to have difficulties in accommodating hate into his theory of the mind. He first discussed hate in "The Interpretation of Dreams" (1900), when he referred to hating one parent and loving the other as essential constituents of the impulses formed in childhood that later give rise to the symptoms of neurosis. The problem of hate in the oedipal constellation is much in evidence in his famous case histories. In the case of Dora (1905a) Freud noted that his patient hated her mother and wished her dead so she could marry her father. Little Hans's phobia was interpreted by Freud (1909a) as an attempt to solve his conflict of simultaneous feelings of love and hate for his father.

In the case of the Rat Man (1909b) Freud identified a similar ambivalence of the patient toward his father and determined that the coexistence of love and hate is pivotal to the formation of obsessional symptoms. He even speculated that hatred kept suppressed in the unconscious by love was identifiable in *every* neurosis. Freud was frankly puzzled by the fact that the Rat Man's love had not extinguished his hatred. He concluded, "We could only presume that the hatred must flow from some source, must be connected with some particular cause, which made it indestructible" (p. 181).

Freud made no secret of the fact that the phenomenon of hate presented him with vexing metapsychological problems. In "Instincts and Their Vicissitudes" (1915a), he noted, "The case of love and hate acquires a special interest from the circumstance that it refuses to be fitted into our scheme of the instincts" (p. 133). He considered the transformation of love into hate the only instance in which an instinct was reversed into its opposite content. One of the key issues to be resolved was that loving and hating were clearly not instinctual drives—rather they described attitudes that one person held towards another (Compton 1981). Freud realized it was inappropriate to refer to an instinct as "hating" an object, so he clarified that it was the *total ego* that harbored feelings of hate toward objects. He went on to say that the ego hated those objects that produced unpleasurable feelings. He felt that hate was developmentally older than love and derived from the narcissistic ego's primitive rejection of stimuli coming from the external world. These postulated origins of hate linked it intimately to the self-preservative instincts. This formulation enabled Freud to draw a parallel between the antithesis of love and hate and that of the sexual and ego instincts. With the ascendency of the structural model the ego drives became less important, and he shifted his view to see hate as a manifestation of the death instinct when he stated: "For the opposition between the two classes of instincts we may put the polarity of love and hate. There is no difficulty in finding a representative of Eros; but we must be grateful we can find a representative of the elusive death instinct in the instinct of destruction, to which hate points the way" (1923, p. 42).

Freud's first comment on the issue of hate in the transference appears, as noted in Chapter 1, in "Delusions and Dreams in Jensen's *Gradiva*" (1907): "In analytic psychotherapy too the re-awakened passion, whether it is love or hate, invariably chooses as its object the figure of the doctor" (p. 90). In the case of the Rat Man, Freud passingly noted that his patient's hatred of him was a special case of his hatred for his brothers-in-law (1909b). In his autobiographical study (1925), he commented on the extremes of transference feelings, noting that on the one hand, the patient may feel passionate love of extraordinary intensity toward the analyst, while on the other hand, the analyst may be the target of "the unbridled expression of an embittered defiance and hatred" (p. 42).

Analysts in the post-Freud era have come to see hate as having considerable developmental value. As Winnicott (1949) noted, love cannot exist without hate, nor can one reach a state of love if one has not been able to hate. In many patients, hate also serves the function of organizing the ego (Epstein 1977, Pao 1965). It may fend off feelings of disintegration and provide a reason to live, a sense of continuity from day to day. Pao (1965) also noted that hatred can be viewed as an attempt by the ego to assimilate and master rage and destructiveness. Coen (1992) suggested that there is a continuum involving such attempts of mastery. One such method along the continuum is the sexualization of destructiveness into sadism. Another effort involves the transformation of the affects into chronic hate and hateful relationships. Both sadism and chronic hatred may be more adaptive than psychotic disorganization.

The analyst must also be aware that hatred does not always have destruction as its intent. Just as erotized transference may conceal enormous aggression towards the analyst, hateful transferences may conceal longings for love and acceptance. Bollas (1987) has coined the term *loving hate* to describe "a situation where an individual preserves a relationship by sustaining a passionate negative cathexis of it" (p. 118). In patients where this form of hate resides, hate does not exist as the opposite of love but as a substitute for it. This phenomenon may grow out of an attempt to maintain contact with a parent who is chronically hateful. From the patient's standpoint, being hated may be far more preferable to being ignored or abandoned.

Data gleaned from the observations of children also has led to the conclusion that the goal of aggression is not always the destruction of the object. Parens (1979, 1995) deduced that aggression is a universal biological given, that operates in the service of eliminating intense internal feelings of unpleasure. In this regard aggression can be highly adaptive for the developing infant who is learning to regulate his or her environment. Parens also noted that chronically unpleasurable situations in the environment may contribute to aggression becoming a goal in itself where sadistic wishes to destroy the object predominate. In other words, the degree and intensity of unpleasure are the key factors that may transform aggression into what Parens called *hostile destructiveness*. If the unpleasure reaches severe proportions, hate is created as a chronic affective state.

These developmental issues lead us directly into consideration of the differences among aggression, rage, and hatred. The basic disposition toward aggression that is a fundamental component of human nature can be subdivided into rage and hatred. Hatred is developmentally more advanced than rage. Kernberg (1994b, 1995a), for example, has conceptualized rage as the core affect of aggression, analogous to sexual excitement that he views as the core affect of libido. Rage involves raw expressions of aggression that may be ventilated against any external object in the environment that is frustrating. The intensity of rage in reaction to unpleasure, pain, or frustration may vary depending on the temperament of the individual, but it tends to be nonspecific. Hatred, on the other hand, requires an internal object-representation (Gabbard 1991b, Galdston 1987, Pao 1965). To hate is to hold on to an internal object in an unforgiving way. There is no getting beyond the wish for vengeance, the wish to destroy the object. As Galdston noted: "The patient cannot get over it alone because hatred binds him to an object from the past in the grip of an ancient grudge that requires transference for its release" (p. 375). Whereas rage is oriented to present unpleasure, hatred simmers and dwells on the past (Akhtar 1995, Pao 1965). Also, in contrast to rage, which tries to remove the object, hatred forges an unbreakable bond between object and self.

In Kohut's (1972) discussions of narcissistic rage, he described how repeated wounds to the self-esteem can turn into a smoldering resentment or grudge that is ultimately transformed into hatred. In this manner hatred can be seen as a more complex and developmentally advanced derivative of repeated narcissistic rage. Kernberg (1994a) adds that the wish to destroy an internalized bad object can become entrenched in the character of the individual and can also be transformed into a wish to make the bad object suffer. In this transformation hatred becomes a form of sadism that combines aggression and hatred with pleasure. Blum (1995) views these forms of hatred as residing on a continuum with the intent to destroy the object on one end. In the middle is the wish to preserve the object, while making it suffer, and on the other end are milder forms of control and coercion of a subjugated object.

Akhtar (1995) has pointed out that views of hatred vary in direct relation to underlying assumptions about the nature and origins of aggression. He identified five theoretical positions about aggression, ranging from linkage to the death instinct by Kleinians (as well as Menninger, Eissler, and Ferenczi) to the self psychological views derived from Kohut and the "middle groupers" of the British School (Fairbairn and Guntrip) who regard aggression as reactive and in no way connected to instinctual origins. Equidistant between the two extremes would be Kernberg's melding of Fairbairn's emphasis on early object relations in the origins of aggression and Klein's position that instinctual aggression plays a key role, a synthesis that is brought together through ego influences reminiscent of the tradition of American ego psychology beginning with Hartmann. Akhtar stressed that Kernberg's view would regard hatred as a building block of psychic structure, the Kleinians would see it as an irreducible given of existence, and the self psychologists might consider it as part of the tragedy of frustrated human strivings.

In a recent contribution, Mitchell (1993a) has decried the tendency for psychoanalytic writers to polarize in their views of aggression as either a fundamental human drive or a response to frustration in the environment. He viewed aggression as having a central biological basis that is individually constituted and prewired but is also evoked by circumstances that are perceived as dangerous or threatening. From this perspective he suggested that aggression or hatred as it appears in the analytic situation is both subjectively justified from the standpoint that there have been environmental triggers for the response and unjustified from the standpoint that aggression cannot be reduced to simple external causes that have no contribution from the patient's pre-existing internal object relations.

Mitchell's view is close to my own. Although I have been influenced by some Kleinian ideas, such as the importance of the depressive and paranoid positions, I find the death instinct an abstraction that is not securely anchored to clinical observation. The phenomena associated with the death instinct can just as easily be explained by aggression turned inward and self-destructive paradigms of internalized object relations. The advantage of Mitchell's formulation is its "both/and" quality. Neither the hard-wired biological substrate nor the impact of environmental wounds is neglected.

In severe borderline patients, childhood physical and sexual abuse are often the source of the repeated narcissistic wounds that lead to smoldering narcissistic rage and hate-filled internal object relations (Gabbard 1989b, 1991b, Gabbard and Wilkinson 1994, Kernberg 1994a, Paris 1993). The abuser/victim paradigm is repeatedly enacted in the analytic setting. The treatment of these patients will be discussed in detail in Chapter 7, but here I prefer to focus on the more measured doses of hatred that suffuse all love relationships. Indeed, one cannot grow up without inevitable frustrations, narcissistic injuries, and disappointments. The borderline patient's inner world represents an extreme manifestation of self- and object-configurations and defenses that reside within all of us. We are all capable of hate, rage, and even murder given the necessary circumstances.

THE NARCISSISM OF MINOR DIFFERENCES

One of the ironies of intensely loving relationships, whether in an analytic or nonanalytic setting, is that they are ultimately tinged with elements of contempt and aggression. While there are undoubtedly a myriad of motivations that determine our hatred for those we love, I wish to stress here one in particular—the need to find and to exaggerate differences between ourselves and those we love in order to maintain ourselves as autonomous individuals. This point of view receives considerable support from a reexamination of Freud's (1918) notion of the "narcissism of minor differences." (p. 199)

This phenomenon occurs in all intimate relationships, regardless of gender configuration, but in male-female relationships, it is often cast in terms of the presumed innate differences between the sexes. Male-female differences, of course, have been central to psychoanalytic theory since its inception. The development of masculinity and femininity, in Freud's view, grows out of the discovery of genital differences by little boys and little girls. The little boy was viewed as developing castration anxiety in reaction to his discovery that little girls appeared "castrated," while the little girl developed penis envy as a reaction to her discovery of genital differences.

Modern studies of gender identity have led psychoanalysis to reevaluate the significance of the perception of anatomical differences. Stoller (1968) deduced that gender identity is solidified much earlier than Freud had thought and derives from the assignment of a specific gender to children by their parents. Tyson (1982) argued that although the perception of genital differences functions as a psychic organizer, "femaleness stems largely from early identifications with the idealized mother-ego ideal" (p. 77). Blum (1976) has observed that to continue to regard penis envy as the principal organizer of femininity is reductionistic and a distortion of the developmental data available. In Person's (1983) words, "Anatomical differences, while important, are no longer seen as *determining* per se" (p. 632).

Revisionist views of female psychology have grown in concert with reconsiderations in society at large of traditional gender roles. As women have grown increasingly assertive in love relationships and men have developed greater comfort with being sensitive and emotional, psychoanalysts have begun to question the traditional differences assigned to men and women in the way they approach love relationships. Fundamental similarities between the sexes may well have been masked by great attention to relatively minor differences, which have been exaggerated and mythologized (Renik 1991).

Why have we analysts tended to exaggerate and mythologize male-female differences? I would suggest that our tendency to overplay these differences is directly analogous to a similar tendency among men and women involved in love relationships. Although the anatomical differences have received greater attention in the literature, I think the *self-preservative* function of the narcissism of minor differences in love relationships has not been given its due.

As Freud struggled with the phenomenon of love, he developed the view that the self can be taken as a love object via projection of the ego ideal (1914). Hence, the beloved may be viewed as an idealized version of what one would like to be, making the fantasy of a blissful merger with the object highly desirable. This fusion fantasy carries with it the potential to have one's value as a person confirmed through merger with an idealized other. However, the paradox of this ubiquitous fantasy is that the loss of boundaries entailed in such a merger threatens loss of one's identity as a separate individual. Hence, to deal with this anxiety involving the dissolution of oneself, one must seek out and exaggerate differences between oneself and the idealized love object in the service of preserving one's separateness and individuality. In this manner, love is resisted through a measure of hatred.

This view allows us to identify an underlying motivation that ensures that the differences between lover and beloved will be noted, magnified, and experienced as disillusionment. Obviously, a lover is disappointed when the beloved inevitably does not measure up to the idealized version of the lover's own self that has been projected. Awareness of the separateness and distinctness of the love object dashes the fantasy of being perfectly mirrored. But it also preserves the lover's crucial sense of individuality and autonomy.

I think our psychoanalytic theories of male and female psychologies may well be influenced by this aspect of the narcissism of minor differences in love relationships. While Freud's elucidation of anatomical differences in gender identity formation has been given extraordinary attention by revisionists, both from within psychoanalysis and from outside disciplines, his ideas on our reactions to small differences have been neglected. As I will elaborate in more detail, the essence of Freud's observations lay in two related themes: (1) there is a narcissistic injury inherent in the perception of even small differences between ourselves and others, and (2) there is a fundamental need to maintain cohesion within a community or a group by displacing aggression and contempt on other groups who possess essentially minor differences. While these contributions are certainly worthwhile in and of themselves, they strike me as somewhat incomplete. I am suggesting here that Freud's ideas can be extended by recognizing the fundamental narcissistic need to preserve a sense of oneself as an autonomous individual.

The concept of the narcissism of minor differences actually appears three times in Freud's work, but he coined the phrase in his 1918 paper "The Taboo of Virginity." After reviewing anthropological data on the separation of the sexes in primitive tribes, Freud concluded that a taboo exists in such societies based on the dread of women and an associated hostility stemming from the differences between the sexes. Freud suggested that sexual intimacy carries with it a male fear that the act of coitus will weaken the man and rob him of his strength. After commenting on Crawley's notion of the taboo of personal isolation that separates individuals from one another, Freud (1918) made the following remark:

> It is precisely the minor differences in people who are otherwise alike that form the basis of feelings of strangeness and hostility between them. It would be tempting to pursue this idea and to derive from this 'narcissism of minor differences' the hostility which in every human relation we see fighting successfully against feelings of fellowship and overpowering the commandment that all men should love one another. Psycho-analysis believes that it has discovered a large part of what underlies the narcissistic rejection of women by men, which is so mixed up with despising them, in drawing attention to the castration complex and its influence on the opinion in which women are held. [p. 199]

At this point in his thinking, Freud applied the concept primarily to certain feelings connected with castration anxiety that men harbor toward women. However, when he returned to the notion in "Group Psychology and the Analysis of the Ego" (1921), he regarded the narcissism of minor differences as a more universal and generalized phenomenon that is relevant to virtually all forms of human discourse. In this context he noted that "almost every intimate emotional relation between two people which lasts for some time—marriage, friendship, the relations between parent and children—contains a sediment of feelings of aversion and hostility, which only escapes perception as a result of repression" (p. 101).

Freud went on to comment on the tendency of neighboring towns and neighboring countries to develop rivalries with one another. He noted that intense enmity had developed between the Spanish and the Portuguese, the English and the Scots, and the South Germans and the North Germans. Freud remarked that when this form of hostility develops in relationships involving love, it is commonly regarded as ambivalence, which is generally explained in far too glib a manner as connected to conflicts of interest that arise in intimate relations. He then offered an alternative view:

In the undisguised antipathies and aversions which people feel towards strangers with whom they have to do we may recognize the expression of self-love—of narcissism. This self-love works for the preservation of the individual, and behaves as though the occurrence of any divergence from his own particular lines of development involved a criticism of them and a demand for their alteration. We do not know why such sensitiveness should have been directed to just these details of differentiation; but it is unmistakable that in this whole connection men give evidence of a readiness for hatred, an aggressiveness, the source of which is unknown, and to which one is tempted to ascribe an elementary character. [p. 102]

In this remark Freud clearly suggested that a fundamental form of hatred arises from the awareness of
differences. Specifically, small differences in one's love
object may be experienced as a narcissistic injury to the
lover. Unconsciously, the lover experiences these differences as an implied criticism. An immediate assumption
is that what the other has is somehow better, which leads
to envy, defensive devaluation, and contempt. One infer-
ence that can be made from Freud's discussion is that
men and women often enter love relationships with the
fantasy that they will be redeemed in finding a mirror
image in their love object. Novelists and poets have
clearly been aware of this fantasy in their musings on love
relationships. For example, the celebrated Czech author
Milan Kundera made the following observation in *The
Book of Laughter and Forgetting* (1980):

> *Litost* is a state of torment caused by a sudden insight into
> one's own miserable self.
>
> One of the standard remedies for personal misery is love.
> The recipient of an absolute love cannot be miserable. All his
> faults are redeemed by love's magic eyes, which make even
> uncoordinated thrashing and a head jerking back and forth
> above the water look charming.
>
> The absolute quality of love is actually a desire for
> absolute identification. We want the woman we love to swim
> as slowly as we do; we want her to have no past of her own
> to look back on happily. But as soon as the illusion of
> absolute identity falls apart (the girl looks back happily on
> her past or picks up speed), love turns into a permanent
> source of that great torment we call *litost*. . . .
>
> *Litost* works like a two-stroke motor. First comes a feeling
> of torment, then the desire for revenge. The goal of revenge
> is to make one's partner look as miserable as oneself. The
> man can't swim, but the woman cries when slapped. It
> makes them feel equal and keeps their love alive. [p. 122]

Freud's final comment on the narcissism of minor differences appears in "Civilization and its Discontents" (1930), in the context of reflecting on the elemental instinctual nature of aggression:

> It is always possible to bind together a considerable number of people in love, so long as there are other people left over to receive the manifestations of their aggressiveness. . . . I gave this phenomenon the name of "the narcissism of minor differences," a name which does not do much to explain it. We can now see that it is a convenient and relatively harmless satisfaction of the inclination to aggression, by means of which cohesion between the members of the community is made easier. [p. 114]

In this passage Freud was perhaps naive in reaching the conclusion that the perception of small differences is basically innocuous. Only a decade later, the Holocaust would persuasively demonstrate that the awareness of small differences between peoples can lead to the most egregious and ghastly manifestations of hatred and contempt.

DEVELOPMENTAL CONSIDERATIONS

Reactions to the perception of difference in adult love relationships are, of course, recapitulations of earlier developmental experiences. Many of the psychodynamic tensions discussed in the psychoanalytic literature on development, while consequential in their own right, are consistent with the need to exaggerate differences in the interest of preserving autonomy, even though they may be considered with differing emphases. The ambivalence inherent in the oedipal renunciation is decisive in coloring all subsequent love relationships with a degree of hatred. In addition to giving up the fantasy of having the *real* opposite-sex parent for oneself, the resolution of the Oedipus complex also involves renouncing an idealized version of the self as a partner of an idealized version of the opposite-sex parent. A crushing disappointment, associated with lingering bitterness, accompanies the resignation to the reality that such a relationship will never exist.

Another aspect of the oedipal resolution is the acceptance by children that they cannot "have it all," (i.e., they cannot have all qualities of both males and females). Disillusionment with love relationships, as well as feelings of contempt and disappointment toward one's partner are often related to this inherent limitation. One is ultimately either male or female.

The seeds of this disappointment are sown long before the transition to the oedipal phase. Child observational data (Galenson and Roiphe 1976, Roiphe and Galenson 1981) suggest that awareness of anatomical genital difference occurs in both boys and girls during the rapprochement subphase of separation-individuation (Mahler et al. 1975). The little boy may have strong identifications with his mother prior to this discovery. As Freud (1921) noted, identification is the mechanism of the first emotional tie to the object. The boy child may master the rapprochement crisis by exaggerating the differences between himself and his mother in the service of disidentifying. The feelings of contempt and hatred toward his mother may be used adaptively to take flight from symbiotic yearnings, to deal with his envy of her procreative capacities, and to assert his own masculinity (Greenson 1968, Stoller 1973). This developmental task is accomplished largely through identifying with his father and devaluing femaleness and what his mother has to offer. Even in the healthiest of love relationships, people experience echoes of this anxiety about losing their own boundaries in a merger with a love object and an associated need to reestablish their separateness.

Discovery of anatomical genital difference arrives at a time in the development of little girls when they are struggling to emerge from an all-consuming mother–child relationship as persons in their own right. Like boys, girls may look to their fathers as objects of identification (Benjamin 1991). This identificatory love in relation to the father serves two purposes—it assists them in the development of separateness, independence, and a sense of agency, and it also provides them a pathway to deny the reality of their genitals by asserting an identification and sameness with the father. At this stage of development, gender is not perceived as fixed by children of either sex, and the child imagines that the limitations of gender can be transcended. Obviously, the girl will ultimately be disappointed when her father does not treat her as though she were a boy.

The onset of the oedipal phase puts an end to the relatively unfettered freedom to identify with both parents. Children in the preoedipal phase often believe with conviction that they can have all qualities of both genders (Fast 1984). The oedipal recognition of sexual complementarity precipitates a period of mourning that accompanies the realization that gender entails limits. Repudiation of the opposite sex and a certain rigidity of gender identity often accompanies this recognition. In addition, the little girl is aware that her hatred of her mother jeopardizes the much needed emotional supplies inherent in the mother–daughter bond, so she may displace the contempt and hatred associated with her disappointment in her mother absolutely and categorically to all males. Throughout all these developmental tensions runs a common thread—

the narcissistic need to define and preserve one's separateness.

TRANSFERENCES OF LOVE AND HATE

In Chapter 1, I described how the analysand's typical and habitual patterns of loving others are replicated to some extent in the analytic situation through the externalization of the patient's internal object relations. These patterns are modified, of course, by the participation of the analyst's subjectivity in shaping the ultimate form of the transference love. Similarly, the patient's habitual manner of hating others will also be re-created in analysis. While it is artificial to separate out the transferences of hate from those of love, it is heuristically useful to do so as long as one recognizes that we are focusing on the level of manifest phenomenology.

Transference hate is not a monolithic entity. It may vary greatly in intensity, depending on the patient's and analyst's internal object world and on the phase of the analysis. Transference hate can also be subdivided into two broad categories analogous to the distinction between erotic and erotized transference discussed in Chapter 1 (Gabbard 1991b). In the more benign variety, the patient recognizes that the hate is in part internally derived and therefore requires analysis. The hateful feelings are ego dystonic, so the patient maintains a therapeutic alliance with the analyst in pursuit of understanding the feelings rather than acting on them. In the malignant variant, the "as if" quality of the feeling disappears, and the patient views the analyst not as a figure similar to someone from the patient's past, but rather as a truly malevolent individual *deserving* of hatred, identical, in that sense, to the original object. Analytic space collapses so that the patient is operating in a paranoid-schizoid world that seriously compromises the therapeutic alliance.

In the discussion of romantic space in Chapter 1, I explored the richly textured nature of loving relationships based on the dialectical relationship and tension between the paranoid-schizoid and depressive modes of experiencing, with the ever-present potential to collapse in one direction or another. A similar tension exists within the affect of hate. The pure hating of the paranoid-schizoid position can be a source of passion that counterbalances the more attenuated and balanced depressive mode, and the balance can be disrupted into an analogous collapse in either direction.

Analogous to the erotic-erotized distinction, the malignant variant is more likely to be seen in borderline patients and those with histories of serious childhood trauma. However, neurotically organized patients may also dip into malignantly hateful transferences when they feel severely wounded by the analyst's behavior or interventions. The technical difficulties presented by the patient who hates the analyst relentlessly are formidable and will be discussed in Chapter 7. However, a much more moderated version of hate and aggression serves a self-preservative function in the analysis, just as it does in love relationships outside the analytic setting.

As noted in Chapter 1, Freud (1912) subdivided positive transferences into an unobjectionable positive transference involving affectionate or friendly feelings and erotic transferences that were more driven by intense feelings of love and lust. Guidi (1993) has argued that an unobjectionable *negative* transference, also admissible to consciousness, functions as the counterpart to the unobjectionable positive transference.

The unobjectionable positive transference is one in

which the analyst is viewed as a well-intentioned, helping professional trying to understand the patient's difficulties. The unobjectionable negative transference arises in response both to the analytic situation itself and to the analyst's own subjectivity. Lying on a couch with the analyst out of sight trying to say whatever comes into one's mind may be a frustrating experience. Similarly, the analyst's inflexibility, rules, possible errors, and idiosyncrasies may activate an understandable oppositionalism in the patient. As Gill (1994) has argued, "It is reasonable, indeed desirable, for the analysand to object to objectionable behavior on the analyst's part" (p. 59). If the analyst remains silent for an entire hour, for example, the analysand may well feel distanced and grow irritated with the analyst's lack of activity.

Guidi (1993) has suggested that the analyst must facilitate the patient's capacity to oppose the reality of the analytic setting as a way of helping the patient detach from the analyst's authority and develop a greater sense of autonomy: "Intrapsychically, opposition between a positive transference and an unobjectionable negative transference is manifested in the contrast between the aims of attachment versus self-realization" (p. 108). An ever-present risk in the analytic work is that the analyst may have a countertransference resistance to the patient's oppositionalism that contributes to an unconscious collusion to avoid intrapsychic conflict, negative affects, and all forms of negative transference.

As a corollary to the notion of the unobjectionable negative transference, Guidi (1993) distinguishes assertiveness in the transference from the potential destructiveness of more overtly hateful transferences. Hence mild forms of aggressiveness are viewed as creative and constructive to the analytic process itself. Mitchell (1993a) even suggested that healthy assertiveness and destructiveness have different sources in development because the former derives from a joyful sense of engagement, while the latter derives from a sense of danger or threat. Transferences of love and hate can thus be subdivided by their phenomenological features as shown in Figure 2–1.

Figure 2–1. Transferences* of Love and Hate

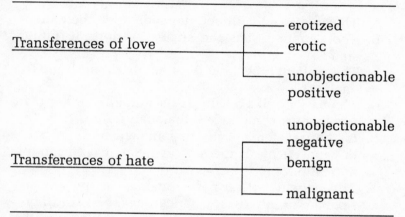

Transferences of love	erotized
	erotic
	unobjectionable positive

Transferences of hate	unobjectionable negative
	benign
	malignant

*The same categories can be applied to countertransference.

Transferences of hate may range from the unobjectionable negative transference to the malignantly hateful transference, while positive transferences may range from moderate feelings of being helped to intensely erotized relatedness.

All of these categories apply equally to the analyst's countertransference, of course, and the analyst must be prepared to allow these various experiential modes into consciousness. In his classic paper on countertransference hate, Winnicott (1949) noted that, "The mother, however, hates her infant from the word go." (p. 73) In this eloquent passage, which was a bit shocking for its time, he went on to enumerate eighteen reasons why a mother might hate her baby right off the bat. In thinking about the analyst's unobjectionable negative counter-transference, we can, by analogy, think of a variety of reasons that some measure of hate might be there from the start simply because of the structure of the analytic setting:

A. The analyst's livelihood depends upon the patient.
B. The patient resists the analyst's efforts to understand.
C. The patient's agenda is often different from the analyst's.
D. The patient, like a baby, insists that his or her own needs must come before the analyst's.
E. In the transference the patient will falsely accuse the analyst of all the sins associated with mother and father.
F. The patient will stir up longings in the analyst, sexual and otherwise, that can never be gratified.
G. After developing an intense relationship with the analyst, the patient will terminate and disappear from the analyst's life.
H. The patient will undoubtedly detect many of the analyst's shortcomings and wound the analyst's self-esteem by parading them in front of the analyst.

In the discussion of romantic space in Chapter 1, I noted the tendency to view paranoid-schizoid phenomena pejoratively as more primitive, more psychotic, and more problematic from the standpoint of object-relatedness. I think Kernberg's view of mature love relations (1995b) contains such a bias. Passions of the most "primitive" nature will inevitably be stirred in the crucible of the analytic process, and the analyst must contain and understand such feelings rather than take flight from them (Coen 1994, Gabbard 1994b,e).

Although the analyst's ultimate goal is to restore an analytic space that involves a depressive mode of experiencing, an analyst firmly ensconced in such a mode may conduct an analysis that is deathly dull. The analyst who can only talk about passions but cannot experience them is reminiscent of the anecdote about the music critic who could read the notes on the page but couldn't play the keyboard.

There is considerable value in allowing oneself to bask in the powerful emotions generated by the analytic process. With many patients the necessary depth of understanding is not reached until one has sat for a sustained period with searing hatred or painful longings. At such moments, the internal self-and-object world of the patient may suddenly (or gradually) present itself in bold relief so that the analyst finally recognizes both the repetition from the past and the new contributions in the present.

3 SEXUAL EXCITEMENT AND COUNTERTRANSFERENCE LOVE IN THE ANALYST

The notion that the lover experiences a fundamental solitude is reflected upon by McCullers (1951) in *The Ballad of the Sad Cafe*:

> He feels in his soul that his love is a solitary thing. He comes to know a new, strange loneliness, and it is this knowledge which makes him suffer. So there is only one thing for the lover to do. He must house his love within himself as best he can; he must create for himself a whole new inward world—a world intense and strange, complete in himself (p. 24).

McCullers might well have been describing the experience of the analyst in the throes of erotic longings for a patient. Analysts face an inordinate challenge when forced to contain such feelings and translate them into the currency of the psychoanalytic enterprise.

Freud himself acknowledged the formidable nature of this task in a letter to Jung, who had transgressed sexual boundaries in his analytic relationship with Sabina Spielrein. In that letter, Freud clearly recognized that erotic countertransference was a challenge for the analyst and noted, "I have come very close to it a number of times and had a narrow escape" (McGuire 1974, letter 145F, p. 230).

While all analysts must struggle with loving and sexual feelings toward patients, until recently the psychoanalytic literature was, with few exceptions (Field 1989, Samuels 1985, Searles 1959), surprisingly silent on this subject. Then, in 1992 a panel was held at the fall meeting of the American Psychoanalytic Association entitled "Love in the Analytic Setting," with presentations by Otto Kernberg (1994b), Estelle Shane, and me. This panel was followed by a similar event at the Division 39 meeting of the American Psychological Association in April 1993, where Hirsch (1994), Davies (1994b), and Tansey (1994) described detailed clinical vignettes involving erotic countertransference.

This opening up of a once forbidden area parallels contemporary developments in our understanding of the analyst's role. The demise of the analyst/surgeon, who remains detached, remote, and objective in relation to his patient, is now widely accepted in all quarters. Analysts bring their own needs and wishes to the analysis. Classical analysts and those who work from an object relations or relational perspective are converging on a consensus that countertransference enactments are ubiquitous, probably unavoidable, and potentially useful (Aron 1990, Chused 1991, Coen 1992, Davies 1994a, Gabbard 1994a,b, 1995b, Greenberg 1991a, Hirsch 1993a, Hoffman 1983, 1992, Jacobs 1986, McLaughlin 1991, Mitchell 1988, Renik 1993, Roughton 1993, Sandler 1976, Tansey and Burke 1989). Sexual and loving feelings, in particular, are likely to impel us into action (Gabbard 1994a,b). Such feelings are powerful, immediate, and compelling in their tendency to override the steady reflectiveness of the analyst.

To help clarify the mechanisms of sexual excitement and love in the countertransference, it may be useful to first review two key concepts—projective identification and countertransference enactment.

PROJECTIVE IDENTIFICATION

The relative contributions of patient and analyst to the countertransference experience are regarded differently, depending on one's theoretical perspective. Kleinians tend to view countertransference feelings as reflections of what the patient has deposited in the analyst via projective identification. British Kleinian analysts have understood Klein's usage to reflect her conceptualization of projective identification as an intrapsychic fantasy (Segal 1964, Spillius 1992). Some contemporary American contributors to the literature on projective identification (Ogden 1979, 1982, 1994, Scharff 1992) have called attention to a footnote in Klein's 1946 paper in which she stressed that she prefers to conceptualize the projected contents as going *into* rather than *onto* the mother. This attempt at clarification by Klein may be viewed as possibly signalling an interpersonal dimension to the process. This perspective is further bolstered by the usage of projective identification in her subsequent 1955 paper, "On Identification." Ogden (1994) pointed out that in the novella, *If I Were You*, by Julian Green, which is the centerpiece of Klein's paper, there is a clear implication that the target of the projection is transformed by the process.

On the other hand, Spillius (1992) did not interpret this usage to imply a change in the external object as an integral part of projective identification. To the extent that the analyst was influenced by the patient's behavior,

Klein understood it to reflect countertransference in the narrow Freudian sense, implying that the analyst needed further analysis. Spillius also argued that Klein was not enthusiastic about the broadening of the concept to include the analyst's emotional response to the patient's provocative behavior, as Heimann (1950) suggested. She was concerned that such a connotation might allow analysts to blame their patients for their own counter-transference difficulties.

The ambiguity in the usage of projective identification by the Kleinians is also reflected in Segal's (1964) some-what contradictory definition of the term. Although she generally regarded it as an intrapsychic fantasy, she also had acknowledged that the person targeted by the projec-tion may identify with that which has been projected through the process of introjective identification (Scharff 1992).

The interpersonal dimension of projective identifica-tion was made explicit in the 1950s by a small group of British analysts including Rosenfeld (1952), Bion (1955), and Money-Kyrle (1956). Bion (1957, 1958, 1959, 1962a,b, 1970), in particular led the way in redefining projective identification in a manner that is now common in con-temporary psychoanalytic parlance.

Bion linked projective identification with his container–contained model. In other words, the infant projectively disavows affects and internal states that are intolerable and thus facilitates their containment by the mother. These feelings are "detoxified" and metabolized by the mother and reinternalized by the infant, who is able to experience them more fully through means of identifica-tion with the mother. Bion was explicit in stressing that an interpersonal interaction occurs above and beyond the projector's unconscious fantasy. He stressed that in the analytic situation, the analyst actually feels coerced by the patient into playing a role in the patient's fantasy.

Elaborating on Bion's construct, Ogden (1979, 1982), in his early writings, described three aspects of projective identification: (1) an aspect of the self is projectively disavowed by unconsciously placing it in someone else; (2) the projector exerts interpersonal pressure that coerces the other person to experience or unconsciously identify with that which has been projected; and (3) the recipient of the projection (in the analytic situation) processes and contains the projected contents, leading to reintrojection by the patient in modified form. In his later contributions, however, Ogden (1992b, 1994) stressed that these aspects should not be construed in a linear sequence of steps, but rather should be conceptualized as creating a dialectic in which the patient and analyst enter into a relationship in which they simultaneously are separate but also "at one" with each other. A unique subjectivity is created through the dialectic of interpenetration of subjectivities. From this perspective, the three-step process could be viewed as overemphasizing the separateness of the psychologies of the two individuals involved.

Modern Kleinian analysts have widely accepted that the analyst's countertransference may reflect the patient's attempt to evoke feelings in the analyst that the patient cannot tolerate. Such feelings can therefore be regarded as an important communication. Joseph (1989) observed that patients often attempt to "nudge" the analyst to act in a manner that corresponds to what the patient has projected. She suggested that analysts must allow themselves to respond to such pressures in an attenuated way so that they become consciously aware of the projected contents and can bring their feelings to bear constructively through interpretation. Spillius (1992) has noted that, in practice, the analyst is always influenced to some degree by what the patient is projecting, a view shared by Ogden (1982). She pointed out, though, that virtually everyone agrees with Klein's caveat that patients should not be "blamed" for all the feelings experienced by the analyst. In this regard she emphasized that analysts may well confuse their own feelings with the patient's and that ongoing psychological work by the analyst is necessary to differentiate feelings that originate in the patient from those that originate in the analyst.

In light of the broad agreement that projective identification relies on interpersonal pressure or "nudging," rather than mystical exchange of psychic content, there is a growing consensus that the process requires a "hook" in the recipient of the projection to make it stick (Gabbard 1994b,c,e). In other words, the preexisting nature of intrapsychic defenses and conflicts, as well as self-object-affect constellations in the internal world of the recipient, will determine whether or not the projection is a good fit with the recipient. Even when the countertransference response is experienced by analysts as an alien force sweeping over them, what is actually happening is that a repressed self- or object-representation has been activated by the interpersonal pressure of the patient. Hence, the analyst's usual sense of a familiar, continuous self has been disrupted by the emergence of these repressed aspects of the self. Symington (1990) has described this process as one in which the patient "bullies" the analyst into thinking the patient's thoughts rather than the analyst's own thoughts.

In considering the notion of a "hook" or "fit" between what is projected and the target of the projection, however, we must recognize that this conceptualization primarily addresses one pole of the dialectic described by Ogden. In other words, this model highlights the sepa-

rateness of patient and analyst rather than their simultaneous state of being "at one" (analogous to the Winnicottian
construct of the mother–infant). The analyst must attempt to hold both poles in dialectical tension with each
other.

Racker (1968) divided the analyst's reactions into con-
cordant and complementary countertransferences. The
former involves an empathic link between the analyst and
patient; in other words, the analyst identifies with a self-
representation within the patient. Complementary countertransferences involve the analyst's identification with a
projectively disavowed internal object-representation of
the patient, which Racker regarded as an instance in
which the *analyst's own conflicts* were activated by the
patient's projections. Grinberg (1979a) made a further
distinction in the analyst's response by using the term
projective counteridentification. He argued that Racker's
complementary countertransference reaction is always a
function of the patient's projection corresponding with
certain aspects of the analyst's own unconscious conflicts. On the other hand, in projective counteridentification he proposed that the analyst introjects an affective
state associated with the patient's object-representation
that comes almost entirely from the patient.

Grinberg's (1979a) view would be considered extreme
by many contemporary thinkers. Although many would
agree that an introjective identification process takes
place in the analyst, if a "good fit" is not present, feelings
and internal representations projected by the patient may
be shaken off by the analyst as alien (Gabbard 1995b,
Scharff 1992). Hence the analyst's valency (Bion 1959) to
respond to a certain projection must be taken into account. Ogden (1983) would appear to agree with this
notion:

It is my experience that projective identification is a universal feature of the externalization of an internal object relationship, i.e., of transference. What is variable is the degree
to which the external object is enlisted as a participant in the
externalization of the internal object relationship (p. 236).

Some critics (Kernberg 1987, Porder 1987, Sandler
1987) of the broadened conceptualization of projective
identification have felt that the original Kleinian notion
has been extended too far and distorted in the process.
Kernberg (1987) argued for a narrower definition that
includes projecting intolerable aspects of intrapsychic
experience onto the analyst, maintaining empathy with
the projected contents, attempting to control the analyst
in the service of defensive efforts, and unconsciously
inducing feelings in the object that correspond to what
has been projected in the here-and-now interaction with
the analyst. He felt that extending it to include the
analyst's intrapsychic elaboration of the projected contents and the return of what has been projected in the
form of an interpretation is unwarranted.

Writing from an ego-psychological perspective, Porder
(1987) believed that projective identification can be alternatively conceptualized as an example of identification
with the aggressor. In his model, the patient unconsciously turns passive into active by casting the analyst in
the role of the bad child, while the patient takes on the
role of a demanding, critical, masochistic, or sadistic
parent. Porder has suggested that rather than something
being projected into the analyst, an affect is *induced* in
the analyst because of the patient's "acting in."

Sandler (1987, 1993) cautioned that it is extremely
risky to assume a one-to-one correspondence between
what goes on in the analyst and what is in the patient's
mind. He regarded projective identification as a defensive

process involving two steps: First, there is an intrapsy-chic projection of a split-off and unwanted aspect of a self-representation into an object-representation, and sec-ond, the object-representation (revised in fantasy to in-clude the unwanted aspect of the self) is externalized via an actualization process in which the analyst is pushed (through unconscious verbal and nonverbal maneuvers) to play a particular role vis-à-vis the patient (Sandler 1987).

Sandler's (1976) original concept of "role responsive-ness" is closely related to the contemporary view of projective identification. Consider Sandler's observation in his classic paper:

> Very often the irrational response of the analyst, which his professional conscience leads him to see entirely as a blind spot of his own, may sometimes be usefully regarded as a compromise-formation between his own tendencies and *his reflexive acceptance of the role which the patient is forcing on him* (p.46).

Sandler conceptualized the patient as unconsciously *ac-tualizing* in the transference an internalized object rela-tionship, in which the analyst is playing a role derived from the patient's intrapsychic world. Spillius (1992) has characterized Sandler's concept of actualization as a colloquial term for the same process described by Joseph (1989), in which the patient unconsciously induces feel-ings in the analyst and nudges the analyst into acting in concert with the projection. Sandler (1993) regarded this form of identification with the fantasied object as more or less the same as Racker's (1968) notion of complementary countertransference. He distinguished it from a process of *primary identification*, an automatic mirroring process that underlies analytic empathy. Sandler underscored that any intense emotional reaction by the analyst to the patient's words or behavior is not projective identification *"unless it is unconsciously intended to evoke such a reaction in the analyst"* (p. 1105, italics original). In this regard he sharpened the definition to avoid a tendency in the literature to ascribe any intense countertransference feeling to a state that is induced by the patient.

COUNTERTRANSFERENCE ENACTMENT

Among classical analysts associated with the ego-psychological perspective, the concept of enactment has stirred a great deal of interest over the past decade. However, usage of the term varies, and full agreement on a specific definition has not been reached (Panel 1992). Jacobs (1986) was instrumental in introducing the term as a way of understanding subtle instances of interlocking transference–countertransference dimensions that operate outside of conscious awareness, often through non-verbal means, such as body postures. In an elegant review of the term, McLaughlin (1991) noted the roots of the word in the notion of playing a part or simulating, and in the notion of persuading or influencing someone else in the interpersonal field. He defined *enactment* broadly as "all behaviors of both parties in the analytic relationship, even verbal, in consequence of the intensification of the action intent of our words created by the constraints and regressive push induced by the analytic rules and frame" (p. 595). He also offered a more specific definition: "those regressive (defensive) interactions between the pair experienced by either as a consequence of the behavior of the other" (p. 595).

When enactments are narrowed further to a focus on *countertransference* enactments, the connection to projective identification becomes clear, as in Chused's (1991) definition: "Enactments occur when an attempt to actualize a transference fantasy elicits a countertransference reaction" (p. 629). Boesky (Panel 1992) noted the similarities between enactment and projective identification and he suggested that detailed study of enactments might allow for a better understanding of how projective identification works. Chused (Panel 1992) stressed that implicit in the notion of projective identification is that any analyst would respond in approximately the same manner to specific behavior or material in the patient. Countertransference enactments, on the other hand, assume that the intrapsychic meaning of an interaction in the analysis could be entirely different for different analysts, who might then behave differently when presented with the same material by the same patient. McLaughlin (1991, Panel 1992) suggested that in projective identification the analyst is viewed as virtually empty and is simply a receptacle or container for what the patient is projecting.

The distinctions made by Chused and McLaughlin may be more apparent than real. As noted previously, modern Kleinians such as Spillius (1992) and Joseph (1989) share the same concern that it would be inappropriate to assume that all of the analyst's feelings derive from the patient. They would agree with Chused's perspective that individual variations in the analyst might result in different countertransference enactments or different variants of projective identification.

It is true that more classical analysts, when writing about enactments, often focus to a greater extent on countertransference in the narrow sense, i.e., experiences from their own past that are revived in the interaction with the patient (Jacobs 1986). However, most would agree with the Kleinian notion that the analyst's countertransference may convey important information about the patient (Abend 1989). As Jacobs (1993a) has noted, "The inner experiences of the analyst often provide a valuable pathway to understanding the inner experiences of the patient" (p. 7). Similarly, Renik (1993) described a countertransference enactment in which he felt immobilized and emphasized that the enactment was partly determined by his own childhood wish to save his mother and partly by his patient's need to elicit a rescue response in him.

Roughton (1993) also regarded countertransference enactments and projective identification as strikingly similar. He made a distinction, however, between an enactment, which simply involves putting an experience into behavior, from *actualization*, which he sees as

> subtle forms of manipulation on the part of the analysand that induces the analyst, often unknowingly, to act or to communicate in a slightly special way or to assume a particular role with the analysand that silently gratifies a transference wish or, conversely, defends against such a wish. This interactive aspect might also be called an enactment which has an actualizing effect. [p. 459]

He acknowledged that this view of enactment as actualizing a countertransference response in the analyst is virtually the same as Sandler's (1976) role-responsiveness and Ogden's (1979) understanding of projective identification. He noted that the principal difference may be that the common usage of projective identification is in the context of more primitive patients who are in somewhat regressed states during analytic treatment.

By way of summary, this review suggests that modern usage of projective identification among those analysts influenced by Klein (and by the British School of object relations) and the usage of countertransference enactment by classical or ego-psychological analysts both involve an understanding of the analyst's countertransference as a *joint creation* by patient and analyst (Gabbard 1994a,b,d, 1995b). The analysand evokes certain responses in the analyst, while the analyst's own conflicts and internal self- and object-representations determine the final shape of the countertransference response.

A consensus is emerging that such countertransference enactments are inevitable in the course of psychoanalytic treatment. What is less consensual is the extent to which such enactments are useful to the process (Chused 1991). Eagle (1993) presented a case vignette in which a transference–countertransference enactment in and of itself appeared to cure a symptom. He invoked the mastery-control theory of Weiss and Sampson (1986) as an explanatory framework, assuming that the patient disconfirmed a core unconscious pathogenic belief, which in turn led to symptom remission without insight.

Chused (1991) has noted the value of enacting certain impulses within the analytic frame, only to catch oneself and retrospectively examine what happened. She stressed, however, that the value for the analysis is not in the enactment itself but rather in the observations and eventual understanding that derive from those enactments. Jacobs (1993b) has taken a middle course by saying that both experience and insight operate together and cannot truly be separated.

Renik (1993) argued that countertransference awareness always emerges *after* countertransference enactment. He shares Boesky's (1990) view that analysis may not proceed unless the analyst gets emotionally involved in ways that he or she had not intended. Renik has embraced a technique that allows for spontaneity of the analyst even though a certain degree of the analyst's subjectivity inevitably works its way into interventions.

In this regard, he has aligned himself with constructivists such as Hoffman (1983, 1992, 1994) who recognize the inevitability of bringing subjectivity to bear in understanding the analytic interaction. The constructivist view also acknowledges that to some extent the analyst's behavior is shaped by influences from the patient. Both transference and countertransference would be regarded as joint creations within this view.

Relational theorists, such as Mitchell (1988, 1993b), Aron (1991), Hirsch (1993a, 1994), Tansey (1994), and Tansey and Burke (1989), have arrived at similar conclusions about the inevitability and usefulness of countertransference enactments. Mitchell (1988), for example, in pointing out the similarities between his view and those of Sandler, Gill, Racker, and Levinson, has made the following observation:

> The analyst is regarded as, at least to some degree, embedded within the analysand's relational matrix. There is no way for the analyst to avoid his assigned roles and configurations within the analysand's relational world. The analyst's experience is necessarily shaped by the analysand's relational structures; he plays assigned roles even if he desperately tries to stand outside the patient's system and play no role at all. [p. 292]

He went on to emphasize that unless the analyst enters into the patient's relational world, the analytic experience will not be optimal.

INTERSUBJECTIVITY

There is now widespread recognition that two subjectivities are operating in the analytic enterprise. Revisionists of self psychology, such as Stolorow and Atwood (1992) have proposed that an "objective" position for the analyst is an impossibility. Writing from a deconstructionist tradition, they have stressed that the analyst's subjectivity contributes to an interpersonal field that profoundly affects the perception of the patient and the psychoanalytic process itself. Their emphasis, however, is on attempting to discern the patient's subjective point of view rather than looking at how their own subjective reaction may be partially induced by the patient's behavior. Similarly, Natterson (1991) has differentiated between countertransference and the therapist's own subjectivity. He preferred the language of intersubjectivity because of its emphasis on how the therapist initiates behaviors and affects as well as reacting to what the patient does in the analysis.

Bollas (1987), influenced by thinkers associated with the British School of object relations, principally Winnicott, also regarded the analytic process as involving two subjectivities. However, he regarded the countertransference as offering a unique window into the patient's internal world: "In order to find the patient we must look for him within ourselves. This process inevitably points to the fact that there are two 'patients' within the session and therefore two complementary sources of free association" (p. 202).

Ogden (1994) has extended our understanding of intersubjectivity further. He noted that contemporary psychoanalysis has moved beyond a positivist frame where analyst and analysand can be regarded as separate subjects. The core of the analytic process, in Ogden's view, is the dialectical movement of subjectivity and intersubjectivity. Just as Winnicott (1960) noted that an infant cannot be conceptualized apart from a maternal environment, Ogden (1994) has made a similar point regarding analysis: "There is no such thing as an analysand apart from the relationship with the analyst, and no such thing as an analyst apart from the relationship with the analysand" (p. 63).

Projective identification, then, in Ogden's view, serves to create an interpersonally decentered subject, *an analytic third*, as he has called it, and the analysis takes shape in the interpretive space between the analysand and the analyst. In this context, Ogden has argued against the totalistic view that countertransference refers to everything the analyst thinks or feels. For the concept of countertransference to be meaningful, it must be viewed as constituting a dialectic between the analyst as a separate entity and the analyst as a joint creation of the intersubjectivity of the analytic process. Ogden has stressed that there are actually three subjectivities involved in psychoanalytic work: the subjectivity of the analysand, that of the analyst, and that of the analytic third. Projective identification, then, negates the subjectivity of both analysand and analyst while simultaneously reappropriating both subjectivities to create a newly integrated "third," a new "subject" of the projective identification process. A clear implication of this view is that a mutual projective identification process is going on in both parties. Another implication is that the portion of the analyst's psychic reality occupied by the countertransference is to a large extent a *new* creation.

THE COMMON GROUND

In recent years there has been a growing awareness of a convergence between classical analysts and contemporary Kleinians. Practitioners from both schools of thought pay serious attention to the role of unconscious fantasy, share a common understanding of the organization of unconscious mental life, and devise interpretative strategies that include aggressive themes (Richards and Richards, 1995).

Another area of convergence is the manner in which countertransference has come to be regarded. While analysts associated with the more classical position (Abend 1989, Chused 1991, Coen 1992, Jacobs 1993a, McLaughlin 1991, Porder 1987, Renik 1993, Roughton 1993, Sandler 1976) have moved away from a strict adherence to the Freudian view of countertransference as *only* the analyst's transference to the patient, those associated with Kleinian and object relations views (Joseph 1989, Ogden 1994, Scharff 1992, Spillius 1992) have moved away from the totalistic or broad view of projective identification in which the analyst makes no contribution to the emotional reaction induced by the patient.

The perspective that the countertransference represents a joint creation that involves contributions from both analyst and analysand is now endorsed by classical analysts, modern Kleinians, relational theorists, and social constructivists. Although differences do exist, most contemporary analysts would agree that at times the patient actualizes an internal scenario within the analytic relationship that results in the analyst's being drawn into playing a role scripted by the patient's internal world. The exact dimensions of this role, however, will be colored by the analyst's own subjectivity and the "goodness of fit" between the patient's projected contents and the analyst's internal representational world.

The similarities between projective identification as it is used in contemporary psychoanalytic writing, role-responsiveness, and countertransference enactment have been observed by a number of authors (Gabbard 1994a,b,c, McLaughlin 1991, Roughton 1993, Spillius 1992). Even

Kernberg (1995b), who has objected to Ogden's view of projective identification, nevertheless has recognized the induction of countertransference responses by the patient and has acknowledged that part of his approach to interpretations of projections and projective identification is to diagnose in himself the characteristics of the self- or object-representations projected onto him.

To be sure, differences between the concepts may be identified. For example, projective identification is a term usually associated with more primitive patients with severe personality disorders and psychoses. This usage reflects the analyst's experience of being overcome by an ego-alien force that feels highly unfamiliar. To be more precise, repressed aspects of the analyst's internal world are brought into conscious awareness that clash with the analyst's usual self-experience. Hence projective identification generally connotes aspects of the patient being activated in a powerfully coercive way in the analyst. By contrast, classical analysts writing about enactment tend to imply greater contributions from the analyst's unconscious conflicts, although most would acknowledge that these may be evoked by the patient's behavior. Certainly both groups would agree that the experience of the analyst is not an exact replica of the patient's projected internal self- or object-representation. The analyst's subjectivity lends a new element to the re-creation of the past and the present, what Ogden (1994) would call the "analytic third."

Another difference between enactment and projective identification is that the former implies an action. Theoretically, at least, projective identification could involve a countertransference feeling induced in the analyst that is not carried into action. However, if one includes the subtle shifts in tone of voice, body posture, use of silence, and so forth described by Jacobs (1986) and McLaughlin

(1991), the line between inducing feelings and action influenced by those feelings is a narrow one. Hence one could conceptualize countertransference as involving a gradient or continuum with projective identification on one end, enactment on the other, and considerable overlap in between.

What is more controversial is whether and how countertransference enactments are useful. Carpy (1989) believed that the inevitable partial acting out of the countertransference is what allows patients to gradually reintroject aspects of themselves that were previously intolerable.

Other analysts (Abend 1989, Chused 1991, McLaughlin 1991, Renik 1993) have stressed that it is the interpretive working through of the enactment that ultimately helps the patient to change. Still others (Cooper 1992, Jacobs 1993b, Ogden 1989, Pulver 1992) have argued that it is not an either/or proposition. The events occurring in the relationship and the interpretations resulting from those events work synergistically to produce psychic change.

While there is a growing consensus that countertransference enactments are inevitable (and perhaps useful), a caveat is in order. Concepts like projective identification and countertransference enactment can be misused to justify egregious boundary violations and gross instances of countertransference acting out. One analyst who became sexually involved with his patient reported that through projective identification he had become the patient's incestuous stepfather and was simply not acting like himself. Another analyst justified a string of sarcastic and contemptuous comments toward her patient by saying that the patient had to reenact the mother–son relationship to work it through. Integral to the notion that countertransference enactments are useful is the understanding that analysts must catch themselves in the midst of the enactment when it is manifesting itself in an *attenuated or partial form.*

An examination of the converging views of countertransference illuminates some of the major controversies in contemporary psychoanalysis. A gradient not dissimilar to the one applied here to countertransference could be applied to the entire psychoanalytic situation. On the one end are analysts who view themselves as primarily "objective" and relatively free from the patient's direct influence. Interpretations are provided from a detached, neutral perspective, and the mutative forces are explanatory/interpretive rather than relational in nature. At the other end of the continuum are analysts who conceptualize analysis as a two-person process in which mutual influences are ubiquitous. Within this conceptualization there is no objectivity in the positivist tradition, and the emphasis is on interpenetration rather than separateness. These analysts recognize the inevitability of the analyst's subjectivity as an influence on their interventions and regard the relationship itself as an important mutative force.

My own view is that the convergence we are witnessing in the area of countertransference reflects a movement within the field toward analysis as a two-person process in which the intrapsychic and interpersonal are inextricably linked. Passionate feelings such as love and hate arise in both parties as a result of mutual influence. Insistence on the view of the analyst as an objective blank screen may reflect difficulties some analysts have in tolerating wishes and feelings that arise in the crucible of the analytic setting.

Longings for love and sexual gratification elicit countertransference enactments that occur along a continuum from overt sexual relations between patient and analyst at one end, to subtle forms of enactment involving partial transference gratifications of a verbal or nonverbal nature within the boundaries of the analytic frame. In any countertransference enactment, analysts must strive to determine the relative balance of their own contributions versus the patient's contributions. A key part of that reflective process is determining which role, if any, one is playing in the patient's internal cast of characters. Sexual arousal in the analyst is frequently connected to one of these characters that has been thrust upon the analyst by the coercion of the patient's behavior in the analytic setting. A common role is that of an incestuous object in the patient's past, for one aspect of what is sexually exciting is what lies in the realm of the forbidden (Coen 1992).

More primitive roles may be enacted as well. Welles and Wrye (1991) have described how the maternal erotic countertransference may be highly disconcerting to the analyst. Both analyst and patient may experience simultaneous terror of and longing for fusion with the other. This primitive wish to merge may be particularly frightening for male therapists. While erotic phenomena may not be experienced as organized genital sensations, they may become manifest in diffuse and nonspecific bodily sensations. Davies (1994a) has noted also that somatically encoded and physiologically based feelings that are the counterparts to verbally encoded cognitive operations must be monitored and processed as part of the systematic examination of the erotic countertransference. Hirsch (1993a) has provided an account of how the role identifications vary with external characteristics, such as age and gender of analyst and patient.

In the rest of this chapter I will share some observations about the origins of sexual excitement in the analyst and the multiple determinants of these sexual longings. Erotic countertransference is often, but not always, associated with feelings of love, so observations about countertransference love will be woven into the discussion when appropriate. I shall also offer some hypotheses about the differences between those who engage in extreme enactments and those who confine their countertransference feelings to constructive limits.

COMMON THEMES IN EROTIC COUNTERTRANSFERENCE

Psychoanalytic investigation of sexual fantasy is not undertaken for its own sake. Erotic fantasies are gateways to a panoramic vision of the interior world, including conflicts, defenses, object relations, and self structures. A systematic examination of the multiple determinants of and recurrent themes in the analyst's sexual excitement will illustrate this principle.

LOSS OF THE "AS IF" NATURE OF TRANSFERENCE AND COUNTERTRANSFERENCE

Although transference and countertransference are the cornerstones of psychoanalytic work, analysts who are infatuated with their patients commonly view their "in love" state as transcending transference-countertransference considerations. For example, Fromm-Reichmann (1989) reported the following experience with her patient: "You see, I began to analyze Erich. And then we fell in love and so we stopped. That much sense we had!" (p. 480) Intimately related to this denial of transference is the analyst's wish for exclusivity, the wish to be "the only one" for the patient. Embedded in the notion of transference is the idea that the love for the analyst is in part a derivative of a childhood wish for someone else and that the patient is trapped in a repetitive pattern that will recur with other analysts. Especially at times of great personal stress in the analyst's life, the need to take at face value the patient's erotic longings may be irresistible for the needy and beleaguered analyst. As I noted in Chapter 1, Freud presented transference love as both "real" and "unreal," but he argued that it should nonetheless be treated as though it is unreal, a dictum that may appear confusing. Greater clarity might derive from viewing transference love as both a real experience with a new object (the analyst) and *displaced* feelings from an old object (Gabbard 1994a). Neither analyst nor patient is likely to believe that the feelings are "unreal."

As I observed in Chapter 1, analysts may also lose their bearings under the pressure of intense expressions of love and lust and develop *erotized countertransference* (Gabbard 1991c, 1994a). In such states, the analyst views the patient's feelings as *only new* or *only real* rather than connected with past relationships. Many analysts enter this realm transiently as part of a countertransference enactment with the patient, only to regain their bearings and reenter an "analytic space" (Ogden 1986) in which the dual awareness of the analyst as both a participant in and an observer of the patient's immediate experience is restored.

HOSTILITY AND CONTEMPT

The phenomena of erotized transference and countertransference lead us directly into another significant source of sexual arousal in the analyst. Erotized transference may be associated with a patient's tenacious and ego-syntonic demand for sexual gratification, a demand that is tinged with sadism and aggression. Indeed, Goldberger and Evans (1985) suggest that the aggressive underpinnings of such florid sexualized transferences should lead them to be referred to as "overly instinctualized" rather than erotized. The same underlying aggression can be observed in the erotized countertransference (Gabbard 1991d, 1994a,d,e; Searles 1979; Twemlow and Gabbard 1989). Therapists and analysts who have actually become sexually involved with their patients often experience themselves as "lovesick," and the hostility is entirely outside conscious awareness.

Stoller (1979) hypothesized that the desire to harm or to degrade is at the center of most erotic excitement. Sexual excitement in the analytic setting is no different in that regard. He observed that the hostility that generates sexual excitement is "an attempt, repeated over and over, to undo childhood traumas and frustrations that threatened the development of one's masculinity or femininity" (p. 6). He recognized that this hostility exists on a continuum, at one end of which affection coexists with the hostility.

Contempt may also provide a self-preservative function, as I described in Chapter 2. Analysts who fall in love with a patient may view that patient as an idealized version of themselves, creating fantasies of a blissful merger. The anxiety thus generated by concerns about the loss of one's identity as a separate person may cause analysts to regard their patients with contempt as a way of exaggerating the differences between themselves and their patient, in order to preserve their separateness (Gabbard 1993b). In this manner love is resisted through a measure of contempt and even hatred.

THE PERCEPTION OF DEFICIT

Kernberg (1994b) has observed that masochistic female patients who work at generating powerful rescue fantasies in their male analysts may also stir sexual feelings in those analysts. Often at the core of such rescue fantasies is the perception that these patients suffer from a deficit condition that must be repaired by providing them with the love they did not receive as children from their parents (Gabbard 1994d). Both Field (1989) and Tansey (1994) have described sexual countertransference feelings in response to a female patient's tears. In Field's account, he recognized that when his woman patient suddenly broke down in a flood of tears, he experienced her weeping as a sudden capitulation or an act of submission. He noted that his own arousal was related to a male triumph accompanied by a sense of conquest and sadomasochistic excitement.

In Field's courageous and forthright self-analysis, one can see the frequent linkage between hostility toward the patient and the perception of deficit. A subtle form of contempt underlies the view that the patient is unable to do things for herself and needs to be rescued by the love of the analyst. Benjamin (1988) has observed that as children develop, dominance becomes connected to males, while submission becomes associated with females. Erotic love may become erotic domination for some males.

Stoller (1979) suggested that one of the principal childhood traumas that adults attempt to undo in their erotic lives is humiliation. Men may humiliate women in an effort to turn trauma into triumph and undo the humiliation they suffered in childhood at the hands of women. A female patient who appears helpless and overwhelmed may generate sexual feelings because the male analyst unconsciously experiences the woman as humiliated, while he himself retains a powerful and strong position. One male therapist who had been charged with sexual misconduct came to realize in his analysis that his choice of becoming a psychotherapist had been influenced by his wish to frustrate women's sexual desires in the same way he had experienced frustration of his own sexual desires by his mother.

DEFENSE AGAINST LOSS AND MOURNING

The termination phase of analysis is a particularly high-risk time for sexualized countertransference enactments. The loss of the relationship with the patient triggers a painful mourning process in the analyst that may activate powerful defenses (Gabbard 1994e, Searles 1959). As Coen (1992) has stressed, sexualization may transform one's perceptions and feelings from bad to good. It may defend against wishes to surrender, intense neediness, and feared destructiveness. A patient's grief may be just as disturbing to the analyst, and some analysts will unwittingly offer transference gratifications to avoid making the patient face the pain associated with the grief. This countertransference aversion to grief may begin with words and eventually lead to hugs, kisses, and sexual involvement. Finally, sexualization may also defend against feelings of love (Gabbard 1994b), which are relatively more difficult for many analysts to acknowledge than lustful feelings.

Having outlined some of the themes commonly found in countertransference love and sexual excitement, I will now present some clinical material that illustrates how these themes may appear in the analytic process. This case will also demonstrate the central role of counter-transference enactments in revealing the meaning of the analyst's responses.

CLINICAL EXAMPLE

The paucity of reports in the literature on intense erotic countertransference reactions is undoubtedly related to the reticence of most analysts to expose such feelings. While a wide range of other countertransference feelings have been shared in clinical reports by analysts of all persuasions, a taboo persists in the area of sexual feelings, that is probably linked to the incest taboo. Some time ago I was presented with a unique situation in which a female colleague asked for a series of consultations to help manage her intense erotic feelings toward a male patient. In fact she encouraged me to write up the process, knowing that her anonymity was assured, in the interest of helping others who may struggle with similar feelings.

Dr. A was a 44-year-old analyst who had completed her training ten years prior to seeing me. Mr. B was an extraordinarily attractive 44-year-old professional man. When he first came to see Dr. A, the analyst's initial reaction was tinged with contempt: "Some men are too attractive," she thought to herself. "I don't trust them. Life is too easy for them. Power is too easy. Manipulating people is too easy." The initial contempt, however, soon gave way to other feelings. Mr. B's wife had just left him, and he desperately wanted her back. Dr. A thought to herself, "I want a man like that—someone who loves me so intensely, someone so eager to understand me." Dr. A had been married for eighteen years to a fine man whom she loved. She also knew that her husband loved her, but she realized that he was no longer fascinated by her, and she longed for it to be otherwise.

Dr. A felt smitten, like an adolescent with a crush. She found herself worrying about her appearance each day before the appointment with Mr. B. Her pulse quickened when she saw him in the waiting room. She felt like collapsing when a session ended, and found herself preoccupied with Mr. B away from their sessions, even to the point of daydreaming about running off with him. At the same time, she became aware of a calm, objective observer inside her who noted that her feelings were potentially dangerous and that she needed to arrange for a consultation to head off disaster.

Mr. B told Dr. A about his relationship with his wife, Claire (not her real name). Dr. A noted (to herself) that Claire was also her mother's name. Mr. B recounted how Claire would tell him that he was "controlling, manipulative, and angry" and that he "used her as a sexual toy." Mr. B could not understand how she could perceive him in that manner. He poignantly recalled how every Saturday they would get up early, go for a run together, drink champagne, and make love all afternoon. Dr. A listened and found herself enraptured as she thought, "What wouldn't I give for just one Saturday like that with a man who adores me?" That same week, she happened to see the film *Sleeping with the Enemy*. She found herself appalled when she kept making connections between the monstrous, paranoid, controlling, and violent character in the movie (portrayed by Patrick Bergin) and Mr. B.

As the analysis continued, Mr. B learned from a friend that Claire had been having an affair for the last year and was simply stringing him along and using him. He was devastated and enraged. He turned to Dr. A as though he were a vulnerable child. He was intensely anxious, unable to sleep, spent many hours crying, and dreamed of himself as a pathetic little boy with a shriveled penis. Dr. A found herself amazed at the extent of his vulnerability. She longed to hold him in her arms and comfort him, reassuring him that he was desirable. She felt profoundly empathic and continued to have the fantasy that she was the woman who could make him happy. She felt like a rescuer or a healer who could finally provide him with what he needed.

Much of her fantasy and daydream material involved episodes in which she was free from the constraints of the consulting room. Each time she boarded an airplane, she imagined she would see him sitting in first class as she walked back to her coach seat. He would come back and invite her up for a drink. Much of the excitement came with creating a scenario in which the power balance shifted in his favor. Dr. A noted that as a daughter of patriarchy, she would like it better that way and found herself feeling like a hypocritical feminist. She also imagined that she would create the *occasion* of sin, but not the sin itself. She imagined jogging in his neighborhood and running into him, apparently by chance. They would stop and walk together and eventually end up in bed. She noted that the details of the sexual activity did not seem to be so important to her—it was the moment of the boundary breach that was most exciting.

Another fantasy that recurred involved a scenario in which she would be crying in her chair after a session with him. Mr. B. would then unexpectedly reappear in her office to get his briefcase. He would see her in an emotional state, understand immediately, and come over to comfort her. She noted that the reality was distinct from the fantasy, because one day she was having exactly that fantasy while relaxing in her chair after a session. Mr. B reappeared to ask about changing an hour, and she handled herself with admirable professionalism. Another fantasy that came to mind was curling up next to him or lying on top of him on the couch. However, these imagined scenarios were not nearly as compelling as the wish to meet him on different turf, particularly *his* turf, where the power differential shifted in the relationship.

As Dr. A engaged in a self-analytic process, she recognized the connection between Mr. B and other forbidden objects. She noted that his body was long, lean, and muscular and that he reminded her of her 17-year-old son. She had always thought of her son as her "sweetheart." She reflected on how her son was now taller than she was and no longer wanted to hug her. She marveled at his strength and his beauty. There was a good match between Dr. A's internal world and what was being evoked by her patient. Mr. B had always been the apple of his mother's eye. His mother had been disillusioned with her husband and made that clear to her son. Mr. B was the center of his mother's universe, and he viewed his mother's love as a secure but suffocating reference point. He assured himself that he was masculine and autonomous by constantly moving away from her. Clearly, this countertransference enactment involved a convenient fit between Mr. B's transference experience of himself as her son and Dr. A's perception of Mr. B as similar to her own son. (This convergence is viewed as an *enactment* rather than a simple countertransference *feeling* because it led to an inhibition in the analyst regarding her capacity to interpret the transference, as will be discussed later.)

In Dr. A's continued self-analytic observations, other connections came to mind. She observed that Mr. B looked like her father had when he was 30 years old. She specifically recalled a picture of herself with her father when she was only 3, and she noted how handsome he was before he became bald and paunchy. She also recalled old rivalries with her mother (Claire) and with her sister, who she felt was her father's favorite. She desperately wanted to be part of the discussions her sister used to have with her father on topics ranging from politics to religion.

Dr. A's fantasies about Mr. B were not bound by strict considerations of gender. Once, while observing him on the couch, she noted that he was almost beautiful and graceful in a feminine way. His smile reminded her of her sister's, the sister her father loved better than her. She then flashed onto the idea that Mr. B. could be her, the second daughter, who was supposed to be her father's son. She pondered the possibility that she was falling in love with an idealized male version of herself.

In the midst of her musings, Dr. A realized that it was exactly because the relationship was *not* overtly sexual or social or romantic that it could be what it was. She had never been more vividly aware of the nature of the tradeoff in analysis—that she could only be special because she was willing to relinquish all other possibilities of special relationships. She also recognized that the forbidden nature of the relationship made it highly enticing. Mr. B himself was fascinated by the forbidden and was a rule-breaker, and Dr. A got a vicarious thrill out of his breaking rules. She reflected that if they actually had a sexual relationship, Mr. B would probably not report it to the state licensing board, because he was a man who would not feel victimized by her.

Mr. B manifested no overt erotic transference for some time in the analysis, but Dr. A continued to share with me her concern that she might be colluding with his resistance to the awareness of the erotic transference. She felt unable to deal with it, so she did not actively interpret it. To her surprise, it was a great relief when the overt erotic transference did develop. In one session Mr. B. reported two dreams from the previous night. In the first, he was in a bedroom with his mother. He was going to make love to her, but he stopped when she took off all her clothes because he did not want to make love after all. In the second dream, he was making love to Dr. A and noted that she had a magnificent body. He remembered how responsive she was to oral sex. In his associations to the dream, he chuckled over the realization that he was equating the analytic relationship to a form of "oral" sex.

Dr. A drew his attention to the fact that he was finally bringing all of the disappointment with his father, the overstimulation by his mother, and the erotized battles with his ex-wife into the relationship with his analyst. As she offered interpretative interventions, Dr. A noted that instead of feeling uncomfortable or overwhelmed, she felt a strange sense of calm that his sexual feelings were finally out on the table so that they could be analyzed. She also sensed that part of her relief was related to her no longer worrying about being rejected by Mr. B.

Once Mr. B. became aware of the erotic transference, he became more preoccupied with work and found many reasons to miss analysis. He talked about wanting to be in control of his emotions and not wanting to be dependent. He thought of himself as being the "little king" in relation to his mother. Dr. A recalled that Claire had told Mr. B that she did not feel loved by him, and Dr. A began to understand what she had meant. But she could not yet put it into words. She continued to feel excluded by him and tried to help him analyze his distancing. He acknowledged that he was making himself unavailable to her and complained that everybody wanted a piece of him.

Dr. A asked, "What does it seem I want from you?"

He said, "I'm afraid you want to use me for your own purposes. I'm powerless to prevent that overtly, but covertly I'll let you know that you can't have what's inside me." She asked for further elaboration on how she might want to use him. He replied, "This is a relationship, but it really isn't. It's very personal, but completely one-sided. I disclose everything, but I know nothing about you. I don't even know if you want me to call you by your first name or Dr. A. There's an imbalance of power. I must have reacted to my mother this way." He also said that he imagined that Dr. A wanted him to talk about his sex life, but he wanted to guard his privacy. He reflected that he was protecting his inner feelings from Dr. A in the same way he had protected them from his mother. He felt his mother would take over his feelings and appropriate them as her own. He wondered if he was inviting Dr. A to use him. Dr. A recognized her own wish to take him up on his invitation, and I pointed out to her in my consultation that this was yet another form of transference-countertransference enactment. Mr. B recognized a theme in his life: He allowed himself to be used by a woman, only to hold part of himself in reserve and grow resentful as a consequence.

Dr. A was grateful for the opportunity to consult with me. She told me that the analysis was no longer a secret relationship that went on behind closed doors. She felt that engaging a third party as a consultant fortified her against acting more overtly on her feelings. She had recently been deeply troubled by a colleague who had transgressed sexual boundaries with a patient, and she could now recognize how such sexual involvement could occur.

DISCUSSION

This vignette illustrates a number of features common to erotic countertransference. The undercurrent of contempt and sadomasochistic excitement was evident from the beginning when Dr. A viewed Mr. B as a narcissistic man who got whatever he wanted and was further confirmed by her association of the patient with the Patrick Bergin character in *Sleeping with the Enemy*. The perception of deficit was exemplified by the intensification of her sexual longings when he revealed himself to be vulnerable and even pathetic, and she viewed herself as the all-giving, seductive mother who could make up for his maltreatment at the hands of his wife and the overstimulating relationship with his mother.

It is noteworthy in this regard that as Mr. B got back on his feet and became romantically and sexually involved with other women, he became less attractive to Dr. A. In Freud's 1915 paper on transference love, he noted, "It is not a patient's crudely sensual desires which constitute the temptation" (1915b, p. 170). Indeed, it is not necessarily patients who have overtly erotic or erotized transferences who are most likely to create sexual excitement in the analyst. In Dr. A's case, her patient's vulnerability in reaction to a crushing loss created more sexual arousal. When Mr. B's erotic transference became overt, she found her own sexual excitement significantly decreased. Perhaps after the patient regained his equilibrium and was actively dating, the sexualization ceased to perform its defensive function of avoiding the painful, vicarious feelings of grief associated with his loss.

One pattern that appears to be gender-related in female analysts is the sexual excitement associated with a man who, like Mr. B, is a rule-breaker. Dr. A noted her vicarious thrill at his boldness in violating rules and boundaries, and the thought of breaching such boundaries herself was highly arousing. In lovesick female therapists who have actually become sexually involved with male patients, the attraction to these noncomforming males is a key factor in their infatuation and ultimate boundary transgression (Gabbard 1991c, 1994d).

While gender-specific patterns may occur, there are more similarities than differences between male and female analysts in the determinants of their erotic countertransference patterns. In fact, in one study (Pope et al., 1986) therapists were asked to identify what it was about patients that seemed to elicit sexual feelings. Male and female therapists did not differ in the frequency with which they named patient characteristics in nineteen different categories except for two items—male therapists were more likely to mention "physical attractiveness," while female therapists were more likely to identify "successful" as an important stimulant. Rescue themes are prominent in the erotic countertransference responses of both male and female analysts. The case of Dr. A and Mr. B nicely demonstrates how the rescuer–victim paradigm grows out of a jointly created enactment.

More striking than any narrowly construed gender-specific responses in Dr. A's situation is the gender fluidity inherent in the rapidly changing view of her patient as representing forbidden objects of both genders: son, father, sister, and even an idealized male version of the analyst herself. Blum and Blum (1986) noted, "Although the actual gender of the analyst and patient are treatment variables, human bisexuality introduces the complexities of dispositions and identifications of both sexes in both analytic partners" (p. 183). Just as Torras de Beà (1987) noted that a male patient can experience passive homosexual conflicts with a female analyst, a female analyst can experience passive homosexual striv-ings with a male patient.

A number of authors (Benjamin 1988, Davies 1994a, Dimen 1991, Fast 1984) have proposed a phase that might be termed "transitional oedipal play" in which children of both genders experience fluctuating identifications and kaleidoscopically shifting erotic fantasy with parents of both sexes. This period of experimentation precedes consolidation of a firm gender identity and the ultimate renunciation of bisexual omnipotence (i.e., the wish to be both male and female and "have it all"). Davies (1994b) has stressed that one of the analyst's tasks is to reopen this transitional arena and create an analytic space in which this "play" can be resumed. In an analogous manner, analysts must be open to this transitional do-main within themselves. They must function as a recep-tacle for the self- and object-representations projected into them by the patient, while also paying close atten-tion to the contributions from their own internal world.

As Dr. A recognized, erotic countertransference creates varying degrees of anxiety in the analyst. In extreme situations, the analyst may regress to what Kumin (1985) has termed *erotic horror*. Much of this distress relates to anxiety about dissonant gender configurations in the analytic dyad. Renik (1990) has noted that transferences in which a male analyst is treated as a genitally respon-sive female homosexual elicit anxiety that can influence the analyst's technique. Most analysts are much more comfortable with countertransference enactments that are "in gender" (Hirsch 1993b, Shapiro 1993).

In Dr. A's consultation process with me, she was somewhat embarrassed to acknowledge her wish to shift the power balance into traditional male/female gender roles. While fantasies of this nature may reflect Ben-jamin's (1988) observation regarding the link between dominance/submission, gender, and erotics, we can also understand the direction of these fantasies as a defensive effort to stabilize the shifting gender identifications into more stable and familiar configurations as a way of diminishing Dr. A's anxiety. She also commented to me that, in her view, erotic submission to Mr. B was one way of dominating him.

This vignette illustrates as well the value of engaging in a consultation process when one feels swept off one's feet by an attractive patient. The forbidden and secretive quality of the analytic relationship is transformed by the enlistment of an objective third party to assist the analyst in understanding the dynamics of the situation. Erotic countertransference becomes less mysterious and compelling when exposed to the light of day and discussed as a matter of rational discourse between analyst and consultant.

A common difference is reflected in this example between those analysts who are able to contain and process their erotic countertransference feelings and those who act on those feelings in a manner that is destructive to both the patient and themselves. In writing on perversion, Meyers (1991) has postulated an impairment in the development of the cognitive ego function of fantasizing. While high-level neurotic patients may use conscious fantasy to contain conflict, patients with impaired fantasy functions may be limited to narrow and stereotyped fantasies and be prone to action rather than reflection. In many cases that I have seen of frank sexual enactments with patients, an analogous impairment is present (Gabbard and Lester 1995). Because these analysts lack the capacity to play in a symbolic realm, there is a direct equation between the symbol and what is symbolized. In this form of concrete thinking, paranoid-schizoid functioning predominates, and the object is concretely identified as a projected part of the subject. Through the medium of projective identification, the analyst relates to the patient as though the patient is part of the self, without benefit of the reflective, contemplative faculties associated with the depressive mode. Whereas Dr. A could allow herself a variety of fantasied scenarios to metabolize her sexual feelings and could channel her wishes into a consultation process that constructively dealt with them, other analysts may not feel they have that option.

For example, one female psychotherapist referred herself to me after she had ended a sexual relationship with a man who had been her patient. She knew that she had made a serious error and had sought out psychotherapy with me to avoid repeating the transgression with future patients. She found herself rather constricted in the psychotherapy and was unable to talk freely about a relationship she was forming with another professional man (not her patient) she had met recently. As I explored this difficulty in talking about her relationship she told me that it was much easier to speak with her lover than with me. She commented that she knew he was sexually interested in her and that I was not. She went on to say that she had always felt she had to have a sexual relationship with a man to be able to speak openly. I asked what it was about sex that facilitated the feeling that she could talk openly. She said it had something to do with feeling loved. She said she could not get close to women and speak as openly with them because there was no sexual relationship with them. She said that unless I could assure her that I was interested in her sexually, she was not sure she could talk to me. She also noted that this same problem made functioning as a psychotherapist difficult for her because so much distance existed in the psychotherapy relationship that it was hard for her to expect much from the patient.

This therapist was telling me in so many words that she could not think about or verbalize the erotic aspects of her transference relationship with me. She had to *actualize* them, if not with me, then with an extratransference object. There was no symbolic realm of fantasy where loving, caring, and sexuality could be discussed but not acted upon. Acting had to precede any fantasy or discussion.

Another difference between those who act on their sexual feelings with patients and those who do not involves the extent of self-destructive and masochistic propensities (Gabbard 1994d, Gabbard and Lester 1995). While countertransference love inevitably entails a measure of torment for the analyst, some clinicians are more prone to carry their suffering to self-destructive extremes.

In drawing these distinctions between therapists who become sexually involved with patients and those who do not, a caveat is in order. These differences may be eroded in times of great stress in the personal or professional life of the therapist. In the context of divorce, death of a loved one, major professional adversity, or even adult developmental crises related to aging, any therapist may potentially succumb to the fantasy that a patient may satisfy his or her intense emotional hunger. Maintaining gratifying personal relationships should be a high priority for those working in the mental health professions.

CONCLUDING COMMENTS

Erotic countertransference enactments are unavoidable and potentially useful aspects of the analytic process. Systematic examination of the relative contributions of patient and analyst to these enactments is a fruitful and essential analytic strategy. Myriad factors contribute to sexual excitement in the analyst. These include hostility and contempt toward the patient, the perception of a deficit state in the patient with a corresponding fantasy that the analyst can fill the void left by others, and denial of the reality of transference and countertransference connected with a wish to be the patient's exclusive love object. The defensive aspects of sexualization should also be investigated, particularly in regard to the avoidance of grief and loss in both analyst and patient. The forbidden nature of the analyst as a love object may represent both oedipal and preoedipal reenactments that involve a variety of gender configurations. More primitive and disorganizing dimensions of erotic countertransference may only be experienced in physiological reactions that cannot yet be cognitively grasped.

Powerful sexual feelings toward patients can compel us into action and bring us perilously close to the abyss of unethical transgressions. However, only by tiptoeing on the edge of that abyss can we fully appreciate the internal world of the patient and its impacts on us. The value of consultation with a colleague cannot be overemphasized. Analysts must never feel that they are all alone in their struggles with the patient. Most of us do not avail ourselves of consultation as often as we probably should.

I close this chapter with a few lines from Peter Everwine's (1991) poem, "Speaking of Accidents":

The trick is to risk collision,
then step back at the last moment:
that ringing in your ears
might be construed as the rush of stars.
We all want stars, those constellations
with the lovely names we've given them blossoming

in the icy windblown fields of the dark.
Desire is always fuming into radiance,
though even a drunk can't hope to ignore
some fixity underfoot, some vivid point
closer to home where all the lines converge—
scars, I mean,
not stars.

4 THE ANALYST'S CONTRIBUTION TO THE EROTIC TRANSFERENCE

At the May 1991 annual meeting of the American Psychoanalytic Association, I chaired a panel called "Hate in the Analytic Setting." During my opening comments, I introduced the four panelists as "the most hated men in psychoanalysis." At the conclusion of my introduction, Merton Gill stood up in the audience (even though I had not yet opened the meeting for questions), and said, "Dr. Gabbard, you offended me." My heart sank as I contemplated the embarrassing spectacle that was about to unfold. Gill then went on to say, "Why wasn't I included in the most hated men in psychoanalysis?" A hearty round of laughter in the audience broke the uncomfortable silence, and the panel proceeded.

Although Gill's assessment of himself was perhaps exaggerated, it is nonetheless true that his writing did often inflame the passions of the more conservative psychoanalytic thinkers. Gill was a major contributor to the shattering of the objectivist, logical positivist view of the psychoanalytic situation. Just as Copernicus enraged his fellow astronomers by asserting that the earth was not in fact the center of the solar system, Gill (1982, 1994) suggested that the facts within the analytic process are not objectively observed in an authoritative manner by the analyst but rather are a matter of agreement between the analyst and analysand. Consider the following statement: "The classical definition of transference is false even on purely logical grounds. For it is the analyst who declares what the transference is, and surely a basic tenet of psychoanalysis is that we can never be unequivocally certain of our own motivations. His declaration therefore must be a construction; that is, he has participated in its formation" (p. 36, 1994). In declaring the participation of the analyst in the patient's transference as inevitable and irreducible, Gill had a profound impact on subsequent developments in modern psychoanalysis. There is now widespread acceptance of the notion that psychoanalysis is at least in part a two-person psychology.

Two major elements of constructivist thinking derived from Gill and his colleague Hoffman (1983, 1991) are that (1) the patient's transference perception of the analyst is to some degree based on the *real* behavior of the analyst, and (2) "the personal participation of the analyst in the process is considered to have a continuous effect on what he or she understands about himself or herself and about the patient and the interaction" (Hoffman, 1991, p. 77). As Levine (1994) has noted, these developments have led us to think about analytic data as a "continual stream of jointly created events" (p. 669). The psychoanalytic school of thought known as constructivism borrows its name from the philosophical school known as social constructivism, which adheres to the view that reality is not an objective entity "out there" but a subjectively constructed one. In a similar vein, the psychoanalytic constructivists regard "objectivity" as a myth. There is no objective transference "out there," only a subjectively constructed one created by the two members of the dyad.

One implication, already implied, of the constructivist view is that the epistemological dimensions of the analytic situation become increasingly complicated. How analysts know what they know was, of course, never clear to begin with, but the idea that the analyst's observations are inevitably altered by the irreducible subjectivity of his or her participation confounds it even further. Analysts must harbor a certain degree of skepticism about what they are observing at a particular time because their perceptions of the patient's intrapsychic world are influenced by the interpersonal process between the two parties. In this regard, the intrapsychic and interpersonal, although acknowledged as separate by constructivists, are irrevocably intertwined and difficult to disentangle.

In this chapter I will illustrate the relevance of constructivist thinking to how we conceptualize erotic transference, while also providing a critique of what I regard as problematic extensions of constructivist thought. I will also attempt to illustrate with clinical material how the analyst's countertransference inevitably influences the specific characteristics of the patient's transference longings.

THE EROTIC TRANSFERENCE

If we turn the lens of constructivist thought onto the phenomenon of erotic transference in clinical psychoanalytic work, we find that to a large extent the analyst serves as a collaborating architect in designing the ultimate shape of the patient's transference desires. I approach this conclusion not only from the standpoint of one who has dealt with the vicissitudes of love and desire in the analytic setting, but also as one who has spent a good deal of his professional career involved in the evaluation and treatment of therapists and analysts who have gone to the tragic extreme of actually engaging in sex with their patients (Gabbard 1989c, 1994d, 1995a, Gabbard and Lester 1995). These extreme cases, of course, are particularly informative, because they reveal underlying dynamics that occur in more attenuated form in everyday practice.

In light of contemporary thinking about the analyst's contribution to the patient's transference love, we must revise Freud's classical view (1915b) that the personal charm (or characteristics of the analyst) have nothing to do with transference love and that exactly the same template will be repeated again and again. In Chapter 1, I observed that from the standpoint of a one-person psychology, we can be sure that analytic patients will inevitably bring their typical and habitual modes of object relatedness into the relationship with the analyst. However, the other person in the room, the analyst, also brings characteristic patterns of loving into the relationship, so that the "love" experienced by both patient and analyst is jointly constructed to some extent.

In my view, though, the constructivist pendulum has swung a bit too far in placing so much emphasis on the current situation between the analyst and patient while undervaluing the cumulative impact of a lifetime of specific interactions with objects in the environment as well as the intrapsychic fantasies arising in context with those interactions. Although it is true, as Hoffman (1991) has stressed, that no stage directions and dialogue are scripted in advance for the analytic couple, the patient's internalized object relations have a life of their own and will make themselves known in one way or another despite the analyst's influence (or interference). In other words, the patient must ultimately make the analyst into the transference object. The analyst's subjectivity may have an influence on the exact dimensions of that transference object, but that influence is limited by the finiteness of the patient's actual life history and internal object world.

To continue with the metaphor of drama, although the play has not yet been written, there are nevertheless certain key characters (contained within the patient) who will emerge on stage in due time. The analyst's involvement will undoubtedly influence how the dialogue of the characters unfolds, the order in which they manifest themselves, and to some extent the nuances of the characters themselves. Indeed, the analyst is more than a script consultant. The key point here, though, is that the patient is likely to present the same basic cast of characters to other analysts as well.

Another aspect of the constructivist model that I think has been overstated is the deconstruction of the analyst's authority. As long as an analyst is charging a fee for a service based on specific knowledge of how the mind works, the abdication of authority is somewhat disingenuous. Moreover, even though absolute objectivity is not possible for the analyst, there are certainly periods of *relative* objectivity in which the analyst can observe the patient's intrapsychic processes in a manner that is much less accessible to the patient. I also think that few patients would agree to a complete deconstruction of the analyst's authority unless they were indoctrinated by the analyst in a manner that could only be called authoritarian.

Having established my reservations about some of the more extreme assumptions of the constructivists, I nevertheless think it is of heuristic value to identify key aspects of the analyst's subjectivity that play a role in the evolution and shape of the patient's erotic transference. These would include the analyst's expectations, the analyst's needs, the analyst's theory, the analyst's obvious characteristics (gender, physical appearance, and age), the analyst's flexibility, the analyst's anxiety, and the analyst's countertransference. In attempting to catalog some of these dimensions, I do not mean to imply that the list is complete or that these specific elements can be teased out from one another in the complex matrix of the analytic experience. These factors converge in a variety of ways so that the analyst's participation may *encourage* erotic transference feelings, *squelch* them, or *shape* them into a specific pattern. Each of these aspects of the analyst's influence on the patient's transference will be discussed in the following passages.

THE ANALYST'S EXPECTATIONS

Although Bion's injunction to approach the patient without memory or desire is sometimes held up as an ideal towards which the analyst should strive, the analyst's expectations cannot be factored out of the equation (Renik 1995a). Analysts expect their patients to show up for appointments, to lie down on the couch (in most cases), to say what comes to mind, to resist saying what comes to mind, to pay their bills, to refrain from violence toward the analyst or the analyst's property, and to leave the office when the hour is over, just to name a few of the obvious expectations.

Most germane to our discussion, some analysts may even expect their patients to fall in love with them. Indeed, the psychoanalytic method was historically steeped in such expectations. In Chapter 1, I cited Freud's early communications to Jung, in which he made it clear that erotic transference was the cornerstone of the psychoanalytic cure, as far as he was concerned. He was also aware that the analyst creates an optimal climate for the patient to fall in love with the analyst.

As Modell (1991) has commented, "Where in everyday life can you find persons who, for an agreed upon period of time, will place their own needs and desires to one side and be there only to listen to you and who are more than usually punctual and reliable and can, for the most part, be counted on not to retaliate and to be free of temper tantrums?" (p. 25). Certainly such a person might elicit loving feelings in the patient.

We now know, of course, that not all patients develop a transference that corresponds to the usual phenomenology of falling in love, nor do all patients experience sexual desire toward their analyst. In some cases hate is the most manifest affect in the transference, while in patients who come to analysis because they cannot fall in love, we find that the same problem presents itself in analysis.

Nevertheless, in discussions with colleagues, I have learned that many analysts today continue to conceptualize the analytic process as one in which the patient will progressively fall in love with them. In addition, other analysts imply that the patient *should have* sexual feelings by repeatedly introducing that agenda into the flow of the psychoanalytic dialogue. Patients may comply with such suggestions, or they may dig in their heels and become oppositional in the face of what they view as the analyst's wishes, or they may submerge such feelings for fear that the analyst is too eager to solicit them.

At times the analyst may unwittingly convey the expectation, as in the case of a beginning analytic candidate who made an embarassing parapraxis: In his first meeting with a prospective control case, he said, "Of course, when we begin the analysis, we will move from these chairs over to the bed." The patient responded, "Isn't it called a couch?" The flustered young analyst inquired, "What did I say?" The patient replied, "You said 'bed.'" The analyst then corrected himself, "Oh, no, no, no. It's referred to as a couch, not a bed."

THE ANALYST'S NEEDS

While to the casual observer the analytic set-up may appear like a situation in which the analyst's needs are set aside to facilitate serving those of the patient, the analytically sophisticated observer is not so naive. All analysts enter the profession for a variety of unconscious motivations stemming from their own childhood experiences (Gabbard 1995c). One of these may be a desperate desire to be idealized and loved (or sexually desired) by the patient. In this way the analyst may stabilize a tenuously held self-esteem, deny sadism, repair damaged internal objects, or otherwise address personal agendas through the vehicle of psychoanalytic work.

The analyst's need to be desired may arise in the context of an impoverished personal life often related to losses, such as death of a loved one, divorce, or to marriages or partnerships that no longer meet the analyst's emotional or sexual needs. In other instances, the needs of the analyst for love are longstanding and characterological rather than situational. In still other cases, the analyst may be beleaguered by a persisting deadness in the transference and countertransference (Ogden 1995), a problem that is much more common than perhaps most analysts would like to believe. The analyst may desperately attempt to cut through the deadness by interpreting it defensively as the patient's resistance to the awareness of erotic transference. Sensing that the deadness is intolerable for the analyst, the patient may need to comply by fabricating such feelings for the analyst's benefit. One female analyst with whom I consulted after she had begun to kiss her male patient during the sessions told me that the kisses seemed to breathe life into her. She felt a profound sense of deadness that was remedied in a literal concrete way by the patient's kisses, as though the kiss had been transformed into a form of mouth-to-mouth resuscitation.

Parentified children, in particular, who have had to shore up their parents' self-esteem by providing love and adoration (or even sexual gratification) throughout childhood, may find that the situation repeats itself in the transference-countertransference setting of the analysis. These patients are quick to tune in to the analyst's desperate wish to be loved and desired.

A striking historical example of this kind of attunement can be found in Sándor Ferenczi's relationship with his patient Elma Palos. Ferenczi, while intending to marry Gizella Palos, undertook the analysis of her daughter Elma only to fall passionately in love with her. He eventually found it impossible to remain abstinent in the face of his fiery passion, and he began to express and act on his love for his patient. In a revealing letter to Michael Balint written in 1966, Elma Palos described the experience:

> So, after a few sessions (on the couch), Sándor got up from his chair behind me, sat down near me on the couch and, obviously carried along by passion, kissed me and in a state of great excitement told me how much he was in love with me and asked me if I could love him. I don't know if it was true or not, but I answered him "yes" and I hope that I really believed it. . . . I don't remember for how many days or weeks Sándor came daily to have lunch with us as my fiancé,

before I realized that already I loved him less than I had thought during the analysis (Dupont 1995, p. 830).

Although in this instance the analyst's needs were carried into an extreme form of enactment, Elma's compliance with Ferenczi's needs in an effort to respond to the analyst's desperation is seen routinely in much more moderated forms. One female patient told me that her previous analyst, who was not prepossessing in appearance, conveyed to her that she must view him as sexually desirable, so she agreed in order to prevent "hurting his feelings." She noted that on several occasions when she had told the analyst that she wanted him to be a father to her, the analyst had responded, "Or a husband." Although I heard only one side of the story, she came to perceive that it was important for the analyst to know that she had sexual longings for him.

THE ANALYST'S THEORY

Analysts cannot practice without a theory of how the mind works. Those who think they can transcend theory are simply not aware of the theory by which they are guided (Gabbard 1991a). Schafer (1992), in what Hoffman (1992) has termed a "limited constructivist view" (p. 290), has noted how the analyst's theoretical biases lead to the shaping of the patient's narrative in a particular direction. Erotic transference can be deconstructed in a variety of ways depending on the analyst's favorite theory. Through the interpretive process, the analyst contributes to the patient's conceptualization of what he or she feels toward the analyst. For example, Kohut (1984) argued that the sexualization accompanying the classical oedipal transferences is a breakdown product reflecting problems with the developmentally earlier self-selfobject bond. Hence a patient receiving such an interpretation might come to understand that the transference feelings were not "really sexual" but were rather a kind of genitalization of more primitive wishes.The rigidly classical analyst who insists that longings in the patient are *only* sexual or predominantly sexual in nature may miss the wishes for fusion and the terror of separation that may also characterize the patient's experience.

In a discussion of the impact of theory on the analyst's approach to transference-countertransference enactments, Hirsch (1994) has stressed that the phenomenology of the transference is variously interpreted according to the analyst's theoretical orientation. He has emphasized that different theories are likely to make a distinction between whether a patient needs to renounce infantile wishes or, rather, cannot move forward until certain early needs are met. If patients are viewed from a developmental arrest model, they may then be seen as children in adult bodies. The loving feelings transpiring between analyst and patient are not viewed as sexual in nature, and the love supplied by the analyst is viewed as facilitating a continuation of development that has been stalled since childhood. Hirsch pointed out that this model discourages optimal awareness of romantic or sexual love by stressing nonsexual love instead.

Another problem with this paradigm is that the "adult body" part of the picture is often underappreciated. The patient may not understand the theory and be surprised to learn that his or her sexual feelings are actually longings for parental holding. Indeed, the analyst cannot reduce genital arousal in the patient into "mere" wishes for love simply by fiat. A rose regarded as a tulip is still a rose (Gabbard 1994a). Analysts may engage in similar forms of self-deceit regarding their own feelings. I saw a borderline patient in consultation who was seeing her therapist seven times a week for "reparenting." She informed me that she would frequently sit on her male therapist's lap during the sessions, and the therapist would stroke her hair and tell her he loved her. When I phoned her therapist to ask for corroboration of this story, he acknowledged that her account was true, but he clarified that there was "nothing sexual" about it. Rather, he was functioning as a mother providing a "holding environment" for a child. The patient, however, had perceived it quite differently. Although the external supplies that the therapist was attempting to provide were not intended to be sexual in nature, the patient herself had mature adult genitals and they were responding as though the interaction was indeed genital. In fact, she confided to me that she hoped her therapist would leave his wife and marry her.

Sexual longings in the transference stir up anxiety in the analyst, and theory is probably most useful when the analyst is discombobulated by intense countertransference feelings. Nonetheless, analysts must always be wary of imposing theory on the patient's material as a way of soothing their own anxiety. It seems to me that endless debates about whether a phenomenon is oedipal/genital versus pregenital are really of little clinical value. Love and desire almost always have components of both developmental experiences just as in romantic love, paranoid-schizoid and depressive elements exist side by side (Wilkinson and Gabbard 1995). As Kernberg (1995b) has stressed, the search for symbiotic fusion is always present in erotic desire. From a technical standpoint, the analyst must be mindful of conveying to the patient the full complexity of transference love. Of course, at times interventions will be directed more at the genital aspect of the longings, while at others, earlier longings will be most germane. Nevertheless, the analyst must convey over time that it is not an "either/or," but a "both/and" proposition.

GENDER, PHYSICAL APPEARANCE, AND AGE

Some of the quotidian aspects of the analyst may also contribute to the presence or absence of erotic transference, as well as its texture and intensity. Obviously, some patients will have more overtly erotic feelings toward one gender than the other. Similarly, a strikingly beautiful or handsome analyst may activate yearnings in the patient that are different from those for a less attractive analyst. But the importance of the physical appearance transcends aesthetics. An analyst who looks like the patient's father may contribute to a stronger or weaker sense of desire in the patient. Another analyst may resemble the patient's mother or a former lover, thus influencing the patient's longings in a way that is resonant with the patient's feelings for the mother or the lover. In this context, one must include the analyst's age as another characteristic that clearly influences the erotic transference.

Sexual orientation also must be taken into account. A heterosexual male analyst may, for example, interpret his female patient's yearnings as emblematic of a genital sexual wish toward father/analyst. The possibility of a homoerotic longing may be less accessible to the analyst's conscious formulation of the case and therefore less likely to be interpreted. As a result, the patient's erotic transference may be sculpted in a specifically heterosexual direction. While engaging in a self-analytic process involving a dream, McDougall (1995) discovered long-repressed homoerotic urges directed toward her mother. She reflected on the fact that her two male analysts had never interpreted homosexual longings in the course of her treatments. (She also acknowledged the possibility that she contributed to the omission by not offering material for interpretation.) Analogously a homosexual analyst may be more inclined to regard a same sex patient who is experiencing sexual feelings toward the analyst as having homosexual rather than heterosexual feelings.

One caveat is in order when discussing gender, sexual orientation, and similar matters. There is an unfortunate tendency in the literature to generalize about the nature of the transference based on the gender constellation of patient and analyst. For example, Person (1985) has suggested that erotic transferences are rather uncommon in dyads with two males because of shared homosexual anxieties in both parties. She has also noted a tendency in male patients to resist awareness of the erotic transference when they are seeing female analysts, a point of view shared by Lester (1985). These generalizations can become self-fulfilling prophecies when the analyst enters the treatment with such preexisting notions. In fact, in my opinion, there is considerable gender fluidity in the roles played by both analyst and patient in the analytic drama, and if these are allowed to emerge without premature foreclosure, a variety of transferences may appear that involve both homosexual and heterosexual longings (Gabbard 1994e).

THE ANALYST'S FLEXIBILITY

Modell (1991) observed that transference love presents a situation that is paradoxical in the sense that real feelings are generated in an unreal situation. An interplay between two levels of reality, one the transferential reality and the other the reality of everyday life, is a fundamental component of the analytic process. The ability to playfully move between these two levels of reality is important for both analyst and patient to establish what we think of as the optimal analytic dialogue (Bollas 1994). The analyst who is rigidly abstinent may convey to the patient that this form of "play" in the transference is dangerous and thus may discourage further elaboration of transference fantasy.

Analysts may, on the other hand, promote the full flowering of the erotic transference by holding the paradox of the feelings as both real and unreal. One of the surest ways to suppress an erotic transference is to fail to maintain the paradox and insist on the feelings as only a displacement from past objects or as only real and relevant to the current situation.

THE ANALYST'S ANXIETY

The analyst's anxiety is probably the most powerful factor in squelching the developing erotic transference. Analysands are acutely sensitive to the analyst's response when feelings with incestuous valence are brought into the open. Any sign of discomfort in the analyst may be viewed as an indication that the analysand should shut up about his or her sexual feelings. The anxious analyst may prematurely interpret the expressions of love or desire as "resistance" to the analytic process. The analyst may also fall silent for a prolonged period of time, which the patient may interpret as a reflection of the analyst's difficulty in handling erotic feelings. A female analyst may be anxious about the potential aggressiveness in her male patient's sexual wishes and effectively castrate the male patient through zealous interpretation of the hostile component of the wishes. A male analyst with a male patient may react to the expression of erotic desires in the transference as so disconcerting that his interpretive strategy is to desexualize the feelings into a longing for a father.

The analyst's anxiety may also derive from passionate countertransference feelings. As Mayer (1994) has noted, some analysts have internalized a caricature of abstinence in the course of their analytic training which has led them to the conviction that passionate feelings of love or sexual desire are not part of the analytic role. If such feelings are deemed unacceptable and as an unnecessary interference with the analyst's task, they may be projectively disavowed and seen in the patient rather than in the analyst. Indeed, I have consulted on a number of cases where "as if" analyses were being conducted in which the analyst insisted on the patient's erotic transference while the analysand continued to be convinced that sexual feelings were not present.

THE ANALYST'S COUNTERTRANSFERENCE

By saving the analyst's countertransference as the last aspect of the analyst for consideration as a potential contributor to the erotic transference, I am also stressing that it is perhaps the most crucial element. In fact, I believe that in the shift towards psychoanalysis as a two-person enterprise, it is generally more clinically useful to consider transference and countertransference as a unit rather than to artificially cleave them. As I pointed out in Chapter 3, the subject of countertransference has been emerging as a common ground for groups as diverse as the modern Kleinians, the American ego-psychologists, the relational theorists, the "middle groupers" of the British School, and the constructivists. This consensual view involves an awareness that countertransference is generally a joint creation involving contributions from both patient and analyst.

This framework suggests that erotic transference is shaped in an ongoing way by the enactments between patient and analyst in the intermediary space between them based on the interlocking of two separate templates of internal self and object experiences brought to the table by both participants. From the standpoint of projective identification, certain of the patient's self- and object-representations projected into the analyst will be a "good fit" with those residing in the analyst's internal world, while certain others will not. Those that take hold will lead to patterns of enactments that are mutually influential in shaping both transference and countertransference. A clinical example will illustrate this process.

CLINICAL EXAMPLE

Ms. D, a never-married, 30-year-old attorney, had developed an intense erotic transference during the first two years of her analysis with me. She was convinced that I was the kind of man that she had been looking for all her life. My unavailability to her as a lover because of my analytic role infuriated her. Hence her professions of love and sexual desire toward me often gave way to equally intense expressions of anger at my insistence on maintaining an analytic relationship with her. So while her predominant transference expressions were erotic in nature, these feelings were frequently suffused with frustration, anger, and even hatred. On Wednesdays she had her session at the end of the day after I saw another patient. Ms. C started her session ten minutes late because I felt unable to get off the phone with a colleague from Europe who had a pressing problem he needed to discuss with me. My late start resulted in my ending Ms. C's session late and calling for my next patient, Ms. D, immediately after. After about ten minutes of silence, Ms. D began by saying, "I know it's ridiculous, but I can't help feeling that you staged that. You're hardly ever late. I think you wanted me to see your other patient leave your office so I would be jealous. She saw me and looked shocked, like she had been caught doing something forbidden. It reminds me of other situations with E (her ex-lover) where he had other women involved with him and sneaky things going on."

I replied, "So you felt that I would deliberately engineer such a situation to make you jealous."

With an edge to her voice, she said, "You must have known I'd have a reaction to it. You know how much I love you. You know how important you are to me. You knew it would make me jealous. I have this terrible sense of being displaced. I immediately thought she was probably your favorite patient. I bet she does everything right. She looks like a real charmer, just like F (her sister). She probably charmed you the way that F charmed Dad."

Ms. D began the session the next day by saying, "I felt like sobbing when I left yesterday. That's why I'm late today. All of my life I've felt like a worthless piece of shit."

I said in response to her self-denigration, "Your sense of worthlessness today seems to be based on a conviction that I staged your encounter yesterday and that I undoubtedly like her better than you, thus re-creating with me the situation with your dad and F."

Ms. D reflected for a moment and told me that there was something she didn't like about what I was saying. She said my use of the term *conviction* suggested to her that she was distorting something. She felt that I was failing to acknowledge the reality of the situation, and she told me it was hard to give up the idea that I was basically cruel.

Over the course of the next several sessions I continued my interpretive strategy of helping her to see how the situation served as a nidus for the re-creation of her childhood rivalry with her sister for her father's affection and attention. At the same time I acknowledged that my lateness had indeed contributed to the encounter with the woman she viewed as her rival. I did not acknowledge that I was cruel or that I had indeed staged it. Yet, there was a nagging concern within me that she had correctly discerned an unconscious hostile intent towards her that had a component of revenge in it. As I sat in session after session with her, engaging in my own process of reverie and self-inquiry, I had a persistent feeling that she was dangerous, that she somehow wished to destroy me, and that I had to be on my guard with her.

A dream she brought into the analysis just before a one-week absence of mine shed further light on what was transpiring between us. In the dream Ms. D was standing in a shower washing male genitals that were unattached to a body. In her associations to the dream, Ms. D commented that she had read in the *New York Times* that police were arresting prostitutes in Manhattan and then printing the names of the men who visited them. She then told me, "I have a fantasy of taking you to the cleaners." She went on to say, "It must be related to literally castrating you. I can see you standing around missing your vital parts. But I don't want to leave here feeling I damaged you. I want to make sure everything's in its place. I don't want to be castrating towards you. I'm terribly afraid I'll damage you and lose you, especially when you're about to be away for a week. I'm already feeling left behind."

I replied, "I wonder if there is a wish in the dream, namely, that if you have the man's genitals, it assures that he'll come back for them."

Ms. D then began to cry. "My father always said no man would put up with me. What I fear is that you'll see that behind my wish to seduce you and to become your lover is a desire to bring you down. I derive such a sense of power over men when I have sex with them. I feel like I literally bring them to their knees. I reduce them to my level."

I said that I thought she was terribly concerned that the analysis would be a fulfillment of her father's prophecy that no man would have her, and that she was convinced that when her motives became clear, I would abandon her and never come back.

The patient's dream and her associations had made it clearer to me why I felt a sense of danger and needed to be on my guard with her. Ms. D had, I think, correctly identified an unconscious hostility I harbored toward her. In retrospect, I decided that I could have ended the phone call with the colleague in Europe and called him back at the end of the day, but something compelled me to stay on the line, quite at odds with my usual punctuality. By unconsciously setting up the encounter with my other patient, I had enacted a countertransference scenario in which I had become the patient's father who was the object of a rivalry between the sisters. However, I was not merely an empty container into which the patient's internal representation of her father was projected. I, too, had grown up as one of two siblings, like the patient, and always had a significant rivalry with my brother for my mother's affections. It occurred to me that I had turned the tables by creating a rivalry of two women for me, thereby simultaneously gratifying a wish for revenge against both my mother and my brother. In this regard there was a good fit between the patient's projections and my own internal object world. Moreover, the real aspects of the patient, i.e., her wish to castrate me and "bring me down," were factors in the patient's presentation of herself to which I was reacting. By unconsciously arranging for her to see a rival, I think I also intended to convey to her that she did not exclusively possess me and would not be able to have a pyrrhic victory by gaining me for herself.

Gill's (1982, 1994) observation that the analyst's real characteristics may be accurately depicted in the midst of the patient's convictions, levels the playing field for the analyst. As Greenberg (1991b) has stressed, there is a certain degree of vulnerability that accompanies the awareness of being the target of the patient's observations. With Ms. D, clearly I was not only responding to her wish to destroy my effectiveness as an analyst in the act of seduction, but also to *her* perception of real hostility in me that was enacted in the course of the analysis. The patient's associations and dreams suggest that she, too, was concerned about my vulnerability and my potential to retaliate like her father, and she feared she would lose me because of her destructiveness. My observation that washing and holding the genitals in the dream might suggest a wish that the man might return to get them seemed to make her feel understood because I recognized both the longing and the hostility in her fantasy.

The case of Ms. D also reflects how the mixture of contempt, sexual desire, and longings to be taken care of often constitute an admixture under the umbrella term of erotic transference. Indeed, to label a transference so complex as "erotic" is analogous to identifying only the manifest content of a dream while not looking at the undercurrents below the surface. The analyst's countertransference may first respond to latent themes rather than to the manifest sexuality.

Countertransference love may be an equally potent influence on the patient's erotic transference. The erotized countertransference of the lovesick analyst may frighten the patient with its intensity and result in professions of love as it did with Elma Palos and Ferenczi. Alternatively, the patient may shut down any erotic feelings for fear that the analyst is out of control. In still other cases, the analysand may reciprocate, leading to a full *folie à deux* where little analytic work is done at all.

SELF-DISCLOSURE

Analysts who accept that their real characteristics and influence must play a role in the patient's developing transference towards them will naturally be curious about how their patients are construing that role. Hence, it is useful to inquire about the patient's fantasies of the analyst's countertransference, or more generally, the analyst's subjectivity (Aron 1991, Greenberg 1991b, 1995, Hoffman 1991, Mitchell 1993b, Renik 1995a,b). This inquiry may lead to curiosity on the patient's part regarding what the analyst *actually* feels. When the patient is curious about whether the analyst has erotic feelings for her or him, the analyst's decision regarding direct self-disclosure presents a dilemma in which the analyst must negotiate a veritable minefield.

Let us return to Ms. D once again to illustrate one form

of this common dilemma. We pick up at session 814 of an analysis that lasted a little over 1,000 sessions.

When Ms. D entered the office, she said, "For a long time I didn't want to let you know about my longings for you because I thought it would lead to your clarifying that I could never have you. Now I recognize that I'm going to have to terminate one of these days and that I'm not going to have you. Now that I know I can't have you, I still want you to say, "I think you're sexually attractive and I would be interested in you under ordinary circumstances, but I'm your analyst so I can't.""

I remained silent at this point. Ms. D continued talking, "I have this terrible feeling of unworthiness, and I want to be rid of it. Don't you understand that for me seduction isn't really sexual? It is wanting some validation. My father would never give me validation. During my promiscuous period earlier in my twenties, I was angry at Dad. I figured I would get even by getting men to validate me since he wouldn't. But it didn't work. I felt worse."

At that point, I noted, "And of course you would also have felt worse if you had been able to seduce me."

Ms. D replied, "Yes, I would. I'm relieved that you're un-seducible. I should have known that you wouldn't actually tell me if you found me sexually desirable. I think if you had, I would have started worrying about you in the same way I used to worry about Dad. One time when I was about 16 I woke up from a nap in my bedroom, and he was lying next to me with his body pressed closely to mine. I always felt *I* had to be the one to set limits on him or he would keep going farther and farther. If I had gotten you to admit that you are sexually interested in me, it would have been just like seducing you. I would have corrupted you only to have the dilemma of then controlling you and preventing you from going any farther. I also think the reason I would have felt terrible is that it would have been a confirmation of my destructive effect on men."

A long silence ensued. Finally she said, "You've been good for me. I can imagine other analysts who wouldn't have been as patient and would have gotten more tangled up with me. Somehow you've stayed disentangled. I needed for you to be incorruptible, and you were."

I bring up this vignette to point out the advantages of refraining from self-disclosure of sexual feelings toward the patient. While this point of view was long held to be a common sense perception in psychoanalysis, in an era where spontaneity is in and anonymity is out, the wisdom of keeping one's sexual feelings to oneself needs to be reiterated.

As I have written elsewhere (Gabbard and Wilkinson 1994), I think self-disclosure can be extremely useful in some specific situations where the patient needs to hear about the impact he or she is having on the analyst. Indeed, as Renik (1995b) has pointed out, since all of the analyst's activity involves some form of self-disclosure, the challenge in the field is to develop guidelines about what information should be explicitly communicated to the patient. In my view, a line needs to be drawn at the disclosure of sexual feelings. As a consultant to other analysts, I am aware that it is not uncommon for an analyst to express his or her sexual feelings toward the patient as a way of attempting to shore up the patient's shaky self-esteem. I have also heard it said that the patient can probably sense it anyway, so why not admit it?

The analyst who acknowledges sexual feelings to the patient, however, collapses the analytic space or "play space," so that patient and analyst may find it difficult to continue talking about the issue in a symbolic realm. What should remain symbolic has become concrete. As Modell (1991) puts it, "Gratification at any one level of reality leads to paradoxical frustration at another" (p. 26). By analogy, a father would not tell his daughter that he had sexual feelings for her, even though the daughter might sense such feelings through interactions with her father. The fact that the father does not disclose his feelings toward his daughter allows her to engage in an important developmental task involving elaborated fantasy about him as a love object, knowing that there is an aura of safety to do so, created by the boundaries and limits the father sets. If the father were to disclose such feelings, the disclosure would shatter the sense of safety and very likely shut down the daughter's capacity to fantasize about her father. A corollary to this point is that explicit verbal self-disclosure is far less ambiguous than subtle nonverbal enactments, which leave more room for fantasy.

Analysts (Davies 1994b, Knoblauch 1995) who have argued that disclosure of their sexual feelings toward the patient may be useful have asserted that it makes sense in a well established treatment to systematically examine and understand the inevitable countertransferences that will develop. Why should sexual feelings be excluded? They also may argue that inaction or projective disavowal is a far worse alternative. In fact, however, there is a vast middle ground between explicit verbal self-disclosure and projective disavowal or inaction. Even Ehrenberg (1994), who has advocated limited self-disclosure by the analyst in specific situations, argues that revelation of one's sexual desire for the patient is actually counteranalytic. To be fair to the constructivists like Gill and Hoffman, they also suggest limiting direct self-disclosure of the analyst's feelings (Hoffman 1991), and the controversy around disclosure of erotic feelings largely reflects the views of constructivist extenders.

Sexual feelings are fundamentally different from other countertransference feelings (Gabbard 1994a, Maroda 1991). As implied earlier, by invoking the analogy of the father–daughter situation, disclosure of sexual feelings toward a patient is perilously close to violating the incest taboo. Reports in the literature involving self-disclosure of such feelings suggest that there is something intrinsically overwhelming in hearing that one's analyst is having countertransference sexual excitement (Gorkin 1985, 1987, Maroda 1991), and patients in these reports have generally responded quite poorly, often with terror and confusion. Another dimension of the problem may be that sexual feelings (more than other feelings) may imply some form of action, at least from the patient's point of view. Hence, disclosure of such feelings might jeopardize the patient's sense of safety in the analyst–patient relationship.

Returning to Ms. D, it became clear that if I had disclosed my sexual feelings toward her, she would have experienced it as a repetition of a role reversal from her childhood and adolescence. She would then have felt that my capacity to stay in the analytic role was jeopardized and that she would have to be the one to maintain the boundaries of the relationship. Of course, I cannot state with certainty that such a reaction would have occurred if I actually had disclosed my feelings toward her, and even if it had, one might argue that that specific impact could then be the focus of the analytic work. I am skeptical, though, about the analysand's capacity to continue analyzing after such a breech has occurred, because the climate of safety necessary for analytic work may have already been compromised. Moreover, in some instances disclosure may fuel the patient's sexual desire to the point that no analytic work can be accomplished. I once treated a female patient who had been told by her previous male analyst that he found her sexually attractive. He went on to reassure her that he would not act on such feelings because it would be unprofessional and unethical. The patient told me that she held on to those words for many months and could think of nothing else. As far as she was concerned, the analytic work stopped at that moment (Gabbard 1994a).

Self-disclosure of countertransference feelings of love or affection can also be highly problematic. Analysts certainly reveal much of how they feel about a patient inadvertently by reacting spontaneously in the myriad of transference/countertransference enactments that occur in the course of analysis. However, a conscious decision to disclose loving feelings to the patient is more complicated. I would want to know what my own agenda was in making such a disclosure. The *conscious* intention might be to suppress negative aspects of the patient's transference toward me. Of greater concern would be my unconscious intent in revealing such feelings. Would I be attempting to be the good father or mother, designed to make up for the damage caused by the parents? Would I be involved in a seduction of the patient to make him or her love me? Would I be reacting to difficulty in accepting the level of the frustration experienced by the patient? Many frank self-disclosures of love have an unconscious sadistic or hostile intent, which can readily be gleaned by the patient's devastating reaction to such disclosures. An analyst who *does* decide to disclose loving feelings to the patient is, of course, revealing only a partial truth. To say one loves the patient is to reveal a manifest content at one particular point in the analysis. Love in the analytic setting is always a compromise that is suffused with a variety of other feelings, and, as the constructivists remind us, derives from a subjectivity that the analyst cannot fully understand at any one moment.

In lovesick male analysts who are passionately infatuated with their female patients, a consistent finding is that the hostility and control underlying the "love" is completely split off and disavowed. What they fail to see is that their love is a controlling love, like James Stewart's obsessive love for Kim Novak in Alfred Hitchcock's *Vertigo*, the aim of which is to reshape the woman into a fantasy object of desire, while denying the woman her subjectivity and autonomy.

In this acting out of the positive countertransference that I have termed *disidentification with the aggressor* (Gabbard in press), the analyst is drawn into the fantasy that a transcendent love, cleansed of hate, will heal the patient. The patient soon learns that aggression is not welcome in the transference and displaces it elsewhere. Self-disclosure of this variety of love may shift the analytic process into an "as if" analysis where only pure unadulterated love is espoused by both parties.

Hence, one's motives must always be suspect when a decision to disclose love for the patient is reached. The road to hell is paved with good intentions, and many corrupting agenda can lie behind the sincere wish to help the patient. I share Greenberg's reservation about deliberate self-disclosure: "There are always multiple perspectives on the participation of each party. This means that whatever is revealed is simply one person's understanding at a given moment—never (despite the patient's and sometimes also the analyst's hopes) the last word on the subject. . . . I am not necessarily in a privileged position to know, much less to reveal, everything that I think or feel" (1995, p. 197).

Countertransference self-disclosure can certainly have an influence on the nature of the patient's erotic transference. While the analyst's manner may convey a great deal to the patient about countertransference desire, it is important to underscore Modell's (1991) point that the asymmetry in the analytic setting is not an asymmetry of desire but an asymmetry regarding the *communication* of desire. It is this feature that demarcates the analytic relationship from other intimate relationships.

In this chapter I have sought to clarify that the erotic transference, regarded by Freud as the sine qua non of the analytic cure, is subject to a variety of influences from the analyst's participation in the analytic process. As Gill (1994) noted, "The idea of the spontaneous unfolding of the patient's neurosis is a myth" (p. 149). Reality factors like gender, age, physical appearance, as well as the analyst's theoretical orientation, expectations, degree of flexibility, emotional needs, and countertransference dispositions, all enter the equation in the final shape of the erotic transference.

While giving credit to the constructivists' perspective, however, I am also suggesting that they may have overstated their case. The internal object relations of the patient, including those involving desire, will ultimately find a way to express themselves within the treatment setting. In the case of Ms. D, for example, her feelings of hostility, worthlessness, jealously of a sibling rival, and lack of validation by her father would somehow have to make themselves known in the particular variety of erotic transference she brought to the analysis. The fact that certain aspects of my own internal world interacted with hers influenced the timing, the intensity, and the specific tenor of her transference desires toward me. Through projective identification she coerced a particular form of response in me that in some ways matched her internalized father and that also resonated with some of my own past object relationships.

The point I wish to stress is that while the specific enactment involving the other patient and my lateness contributed to her wish to "take me to the cleaners," that wish was present long before my countertransference participation and would have emerged in due time anyway. In other words, the constructivist view may not take sufficient account of the fact that meaning has already been attributed to the patient's internal world and life experiences long before setting foot in the analyst's office. This intrapsychic meaning is then altered to some extent, but not radically rewritten *de novo* because of the influence of the analyst's subjectivity.

In most cases explicit self-disclosure by the analyst of feelings involving sexual desire or passionate love are likely to do more harm than good. If I had gratified Ms. D's conflicted wish for me to tell her that I found her sexually attractive, I would have re-created a dangerous situation from her childhood and adolescence, where she would feel that she had to be the one to control the boundaries between her father and herself. I might also have caused her to shut down full exploration of her longings. As Bollas (1994) noted, "Erotic wishes intensify in relation to the analyst's maintenance of his abstinence of physical contact and erotic suggestiveness, ironically releasing the analysand to a more elaborate narrative expression of desire, which is unique to the psychoanalytical situation and may qualify as an erotic specific to it" (p. 582).

Moreover, I would have spoken only a partial truth. While at times I did feel sexual desires toward her, these were accompanied by a host of other feelings, including hostility and a need to gird myself against her attempts to corrupt me and destroy my analytic effectiveness. Psychoanalysis above all is a perspective that values complexity, and disclosure of sexual desire by the analyst is doomed at the outset because it cannot express the richness of that complexity. Perhaps we should heed the words of Joan Collins, who as far as I know is not analytically trained, but is well schooled in problems of desire: "The secret of having a personal life is not answering too many questions about it."

5   LOVE AND LUST IN THE MALE
ANALYST–MALE PATIENT DYAD

It is widely recognized that female psychology, and in particular female sexuality, represented something of a "dark continent" for Freud. Later psychoanalytic contributions have made great strides in enhancing our knowledge. I think it is relatively less appreciated that our psychoanalytic understanding of male sexuality is rather limited as well. Clinical observations of the vicissitudes of transference have long been the primary source of psychoanalytic data. Information regarding male sexual longings from this source has been rather sparse, because until recently there has been an almost total absence in the literature of clinical reports involving erotic transference in male patients (Bergmann 1985–1986). Person (1985), noting that virtually all reports of erotic transference are focused on female patients, has even suggested that one might erroneously assume that such transferences are a problem of the psychology of women.

Lester (1985) pointed out that the scarcity of reports of erotic transference in male patients with female analysts may simply be a reflection of the general rarity of transference love in analytic dyads with that gender constellation. Lester also noted that the male analysand's anxiety about the female analyst's power may be a formidable resistance. She may be viewed as the preoedipal phallic mother, who makes "penetrating" interpretations. The male patient may thus regard her as dangerous. This view may engender a fear that inhibits the expression of sexual feelings toward a less dangerous and more desirable oedipal mother. On the other hand, genitalization may in some instances serve as a defense against darker fears.

Wrye (1993) has described the horror of the male patient when experiencing early maternal erotic transference. He may feel panic and terror by the added threat of boundary diffusion and loss of separate gender identity posed by the regressive, erotic pull to the preoedipal mother. Transforming the analyst–analysand relationship into a seduction of a "weaker" female by a more powerful male may ward off this terror.

When both members of the analytic dyad are male, Person (1985) has suggested that homosexual anxiety may be activated by the emergence of erotic feelings in the transference or countertransference, so she argues that intensely erotic or erotized transferences are relatively rare in these dyads. Also, some male patients may become anxious when experiencing dependent wishes toward a male analyst and thus become contemptuous or competitive as a defensive way of handling this regressive pull. I do not think erotic transference in male patients with male analysts is a rare phenomenon, but my direct experience as a male analyst, as well as my indirect experiences as a supervisor of and consultant to other male analysts, leads me to the conclusion that both analyst and analysand may have powerful resistances to recognizing its presence.

My impression differs somewhat from Person's notion

that homosexual anxieties are central. I have found that tenderness and loving feelings may present greater difficulties for both men in the analytic dyad than more overtly genital and sexual issues. The emphasis of Freud on the discharge of drive tensions as a primary motivator in the unconscious has been regarded by many as particularly applicable to male sexuality. Because the penis is more visible and accessible than the female genitalia, men are often characterized as more driven by the need for sexual release. A common cultural stereotype, perhaps fueled by the fiction of Philip Roth, John Updike, and others, is that men will indiscriminately engage in sexual relations with any available woman without regard to the nonerotic aspects of the relationship.

In recent years, greater emphasis has emerged, particularly in contributions from the theorists associated with the British School of object relations, on the notion that erotic desire is always connected with conscious or unconscious internal object relations that are linked to sexual urges. In my own experience of analyzing male patients, I have come to believe that the male patient's focus on phallic prowess and lust may serve as a powerful defense against feelings of vulnerability to loss and yearnings for love. The following case example illustrates some of these themes in the male analyst—male patient dyad.

CLINICAL EXAMPLE

Mr. M was a 24-year-old single male who came to analytic treatment with a history of having had no sexual relationships. Solitary masturbation accompanied by a vivid fantasy life was his only sexual activity. He longed to establish relationships with others, but was terrified to take the risks involved. His masturbation often took place in adult book stores where he would rent a "jerk-off booth" and watch both homosexual and heterosexual pornographic movies until he achieved orgasm.

In the opening phase of his analysis, he told me that he had been practicing free association at home while lying on his bed and that he hoped that I would avoid any interruption of the associations. After some weeks of approaching analysis as though it were a soliloquy with no one else on the analytic stage, Mr. M began tentatively to entertain thoughts and fantasies about me. When he found this development disconcerting, I suggested to him that he had been regarding my office as similar to a "jerk-off booth" where he could masturbate without having to engage in a relationship. I commented that his hesitancy in forming a connection with me was mirrored in his hesitancy outside the analysis to relate to others.

As he began to analyze his anxiety about allowing me to play a larger role in his internal drama, he began to express intense fears of punishment by me. It soon emerged that the fear of punishment was in large measure a wish. He described a pornographic movie to which he had masturbated, involving a man who developed an erection in response to being beaten on the buttocks. Mr. M's erotic transference to me was heralded by a dream: "I was lying there on the couch, and when I got up I was pulling my trousers on. I looked at you, and you had some of your clothes off. My T-shirt was inside out over my other shirt. Your clothes were rumpled, and you were tucking your shirt in." In his associations to the dream Mr. M acknowledged a wish to have sex with me. He said that he imagined lying on his stomach on the couch while I mounted him from behind and pumped semen into him. At home he had masturbated to that fantasy while inserting a Coke bottle into his anus. He said it had caused him considerable pain but that it was intensely pleasurable. Day after day he would come to the analysis with fantasies such as the following:

> I imagine myself looking at nude pictures of men with large penises. You come into my room and discover me. You take off your shirt and have rippling muscles. You then tie me up and drip molten wax on my asshole. Then you force me to deepthroat your cock, and I swallow down the semen. The semen is real satisfying, like food, like concentrated masculinity.

The graphic nature of such fantasies obviously was intended by Mr. M to have an impact that carried considerable shock value. Although the fantasies generally contained sexual content of some sort, my own experience of them was often that they were far more aggressive than erotic. At times they involved perverse activities that I frankly doubted entailed much sexual gratification for him. In one particular session, Mr. M got on the couch after following me down the hallway to my office. He told me that he had been watching my buttocks as he walked behind me, and he began to elaborate the following fantasy:

> I thought about how your ass would look if you were shitting, and I imagined that you would get up from your chair, pull down your pants, and straddle me with one leg on either side of the couch. I then imagined you shitting into my mouth and forcing me to swallow the shit.

As Mr. M's homoerotic longing unfolded over the ensuing weeks and months, I offered a number of interpretive comments and invited him to explore some of the meanings of the fantasies. Mr. M did not consider himself homosexual and the pornography he used to arouse himself consisted of an equal number of heterosexual and homosexual scenarios. Nevertheless, in the transference his verbalized fantasies primarily involved himself as a passive recipient of masculinity in the form of semen either through fellatio or anal intercourse. Mr. M seemed oddly lacking in curiosity about his rather entrenched pattern, and I became more and more active in interpreting possible meanings. I found in myself a growing sense of impatience and annoyance with Mr. M. I was concerned that my interventions were being experienced as increasingly forceful and penetrating to Mr. M, thus creating an attenuated enactment of the sadomasochistic related-ness for which he was longing.

A breakthrough came when the patient informed me that he had seen the movie *Little Shop of Horrors*. He told me that one scene had reminded him of the analysis. He recounted how Bill Murray played a masochistic patient who went to see a sadistic dentist played by Steve Martin. He laughed as he recalled how Bill Murray's masochist had thwarted Steve Martin's sadist by enjoying the pain inflicted upon him.

I responded to his association by saying that I could clearly see how he connected that scene with what had been happening in the analysis. I suggested that my efforts to help him understand himself had been experienced as sadistic attacks from which he was deriving masochistic gratification. I also suggested another parallel. The Bill Murray character in the film had no real wish to be cured of a toothache—the infliction of pain was an end in itself. I suggested to Mr. M that, in a similar vein, he was not so much interested in insight and understanding in the analysis. Rather, he wanted to create a stable relationship with me in which he would be the recipient of interventions that he could experience as punitive and sexually charged, while thwarting my analytic efforts to provide understanding.

In response to my comment, the patient became more somber. Reflecting on what I had said, he responded:

> There is a part of me that would like to be just like the Bill Murray character and come here forever to be tortured. That way I would assure a connection with you. I'm always worried about others leaving me. My father left for the Vietnam War when I was only 5. I was convinced he would never return. I was furious at him for leaving me alone with my mother. I blamed my father for not filling me up with maleness, so now I want to be fucked in the ass by you.

While his father was away at war, the patient had become "the man of the house." He said he had found it sexually exciting but also terrifying to be placed in that role. Occasionally, when he woke up at night, he had crawled into his mother's bed and slept beside her. He began to cry and said:

> I had all this power and responsibility and didn't know what to do with it. I wanted my father to come home and beat me up to make me feel less guilty about what I was doing. I want you to be my dad—a dad that won't go away and not tell me where he's going, a dad who won't go to Vietnam. I was so worried that he would die.

Shortly after that poignant session, the patient reported the following dream:

> I am watching television and I see a father masturbating in front of his little boy. Semen is running down the father's penis and the little boy licks off the semen and swallows it. My mother walks in and I'm horrified that I'm caught watching this. Mother switches the channel.

In his associations to the dream, Mr. M said that his relationship to me was much like the little boy's relationship to his father. He compared himself to a little baby wanting to drink my semen. He said he grew up in a military family where his father was always gone, so he never had the kind of nurturing paternal experience he needed. He looked at strong males and longed for what they had and felt envious of them. While his father was away at war, Mr. M used to imagine having sex with his mother while his father had anal intercourse with him. In the fantasy he imagined that he would have the big penis he needed to have sex with his mother. He said he was afraid to become sexually involved with women because he lacked the big penis he should have gotten from his father.

The following day he came to my office and began his associations:

> I didn't want to come today because I feel I'm in love with you and I don't want to talk about it. In pornographic movies the most arousing thing is deepthroating a penis. That's what I'd like to do to you. I want your manhood in my mouth. I want to be fed somehow. On Friday when I left, I did something I'd never done before—I stood and looked at you at the end of the session and asked what time we were going to meet on Monday. It was bold, like I had a nonanalytic relationship with you. I felt I had done something questionable, like having sex with you, or identifying with you. I was also happy because I felt I was growing up.

I responded to the patient's frank confession of love toward me by wondering with him if his experiences during his father's visit over the weekend had anything to do with his feelings toward me. He responded that his dad had hugged him and said, "I love you, more than you know." He then told his father, "I love you, too, Dad." No sooner had Mr. M gotten out these words than he began to cry in deep, heaving sobs. As I sat behind the couch, I felt a growing sense of discomfort. First, I wondered if his sobbing was so loud that my neighbors in the office building would be disturbed by it. Reflecting on my anxiety, I recognized that it was the intensity of the patient's affect that was disconcerting to me. I realized that I had not been comfortable with his expression of love toward me and had changed the subject by asking what happened with his father, an attempt to deflect his feelings away from me onto someone else. I reflected on my own longings for expressions of love from my father, and I felt a strong sense of empathic resonance with the patient. I also became aware of a sickening feeling of being overwhelmed with the grief and longing that Mr. M was stirring up.

When the patient regained his composure, he told me that strong feelings were like the end of the world for him. I, too, was feeling that neither he nor I would be able to bear the pain of the feelings. He associated further to the dream by saying that he always felt his mother had gotten in between his father and him so that he was not able to receive the kind of paternal nurturance he wanted. He said that talking about what he needed in terms of sex was in some ways easier than talking about love. I suddenly recognized that I might have colluded with his avoidance of such expressions because of a counterresistance within me. Homosexual

anxieties and sadomasochistic enactments were uncomfortable, but relatively less threatening than dealing with overt professions of love.

I said to Mr. M that the wish for my penis seemed to
concretize a number of longings for love that were more
difficult to talk about it. He said he preferred to think of
analysis as "a cock up my ass" instead of as a relationship.

After some analytic work had been done on the
loving transference feelings and their origins in his
wish for a more satisfying relationship with his father,
the patient began to risk involvement with women.
After cancelling a session due to illness, I returned the
following day to find that Mr. M had been extremely
worried about my absence. He said he was afraid that I
did not love him. He imagined that I disapproved of his
dating. An image of the Pietà came to his mind. I noted
that the image was a mother and son with no father
present. He replied:

> I imagine being slung across my mother's lap. A virgin
> mother. I'm afraid if I talk about my feelings toward her,
> you'll chop my head off. I was afraid that sleeping with
> my mother was like stabbing a knife into my father's heart.
> I had the image of me having intercourse with my mother
> and then having my father come along and rip her away,
> taking the front part of my body away. If I make an
> attachment, I feel like a part of me is ripped away. I'm
> afraid you'll rip J (his girlfriend) away from me, but I'm
> also afraid that I'll be ripped away from you.
>
> I guess I also want you and me to be like the Pietà, all
> alone with no interference from outside. You could nur-
> ture me like a mother. I imagine that sucking on your
> penis and swallowing your semen would be like what a
> baby gets from breast milk. As a child I ate shortening and
> dough. My mom didn't understand. I needed something

more from her. My mother was afraid to relate to me in a special, intimate way. Now I'm afraid I'll have to terminate because we've gotten to the core of my problems. I'd rather think of sucking men's penises than Mom's breast. I imagine her breast milk could be poison. She was inadequate in her nurturing. Your words are like nurturing breast milk. I need you to sustain me. But I'm afraid that I will suck you dry to try to make up for what I didn't get from Mother.

In reflecting on his wish for me to be a mother who would satisfy his oral longings, I became concerned that he viewed the analysis as an end in itself rather than as a vehicle through which he could understand problems in relationships and then form attachments outside the analysis. I felt a sense of dread connected with a fantasy that Mr. M was expecting me to be both mother and father to him. I imagined him sucking all the life out of me and leaving me an empty shell.

Mr. M said he had always feared that his love was destructive. He imagined that he was so greedy that he would suck out all the life from anyone he loved. He was afraid his love for me had damaged me. He also feared that as he grew older he would become a monster destroying his mother and father. He associated to Yeats's poem "The Second Coming" and said he thought of himself as the monster "slouching towards Bethlehem."

I pointed out that in the imagery of the Pietà and Yeats's "Second Coming," he was implicitly comparing himself to a messiah who had a special relationship with his mother and with me. He acknowledged that he felt incredibly special to me and never wanted to give that up. He imagined that his wish to suck my penis was really a wish to take me inside himself and never lose me. Growing up entailed losing a profoundly special relationship.

As Mr. M moved toward termination, he was able to establish a satisfying heterosexual relationship and overcome his castration anxiety. However, with each step forward, he experienced profound feelings of loss and grief. We came to understand his preference for pornographic movies as a defense against such feelings. The shift from observer to participant carried with it a threat of catastrophic loss. He assumed that I would desert him as would his parents. He had fantasies of premature death. He compared himself to Icarus soaring too close to the sun and imagined he would plummet into the sea and drown. We came to understand that his homoerotic attachment to me served as a means to avoid facing these feelings of grief and loss that accompanied movement into adult heterosexual relationships.

DISCUSSION

Person (1985) has pointed out that the terms *erotic transference* and *transference love* are often used interchangeably. Her definition of erotic transference is "some mixture of tender, erotic, and sexual feelings that a patient experiences in reference to his or her analyst and, as such, forms part of a positive transference" (p. 161). The case of Mr. M illustrates that sexual feelings and loving feelings may not appear at the same time or in the same context. His sexual longings antedated his professions of love by a considerable length of time.

Indeed, the overt sexualization of the transference appeared to serve a variety of defensive functions, one of which was the avoidance of the powerful feelings of love associated with paternal disappointment. The erotized phase of the analysis also involved a prolonged sadomasochistic enactment in which sexual fantasy was expressed without reflection or movement in the analysis. Coen (1992) has noted that certain patients suffering from pathological dependency do not engage in transference repetition for purposes of mastery or integration but rather to preserve the status quo and protect themselves from hidden dangers. Mr. M regarded the repetition as an end in itself rather than a phenomenon subject to analytic scrutiny because it protected him from the painful awareness of separateness from his analyst.

Coen (1992) observed that "patients who use sexualization extensively will tend to reassure themselves that they can transform the analyst by seduction into an idealized, omnipotent paternal object. This illusion reassures the patient against the risk of being left alone with a dangerous maternal introject" (p. 132). As long as Mr. M could involve me in such an enactment, he could avoid the dread of repeating the oedipal experience of being in bed with mother while father was thousands of miles away at war. His posture of masochistic submission also served to suppress his feelings of oedipal triumph with their associated castration anxiety and his destructive feelings of rage at his father for leaving him. Mr. M's resistance to change or movement in the analysis could be reframed as a refusal to abandon his claim on his analyst as a parent.

The enactments in the analysis of Mr. M also illustrate the dual function of erotic transference as resistance that I noted in Chapter 1. In the sense of Freud's original notion of memory retrieval, the erotic transference may have produced a stoppage of movement in the analysis, but it also served as a revelation of a highly significant internal object relationship. The pressure of the transference was toward an unintegrated action that opposed the analytic goals of recontextualization, reflection, and contemplation.

By creating a context in which Mr. M could express his sexual longings, I was also making it implicit that those longings would be frustrated rather than gratified. The paradox in this particular case was that the very frustration of the analytic situation gratified Mr. M's masochistic wishes. The pain of having his longings analyzed and interpreted rather than gratified also provided a form of sadistic pleasure to Mr. M, who was able to thwart the analysis by playing Bill Murray to my Steve Martin by refusing to use my interventions productively.

In the case of Mr. M, we can clearly see how the analysis progressed through a series of transference–countertransference enactments. First, I had unwittingly become a sadist to his masochist. At other points I was cast in the role of the distant father who could not tolerate overt expressions of love and caring as well as the mother who felt "sucked dry" by the patient's seemingly bottomless desires for nurturance. Mr. M shared in common with Fairbairn's (1954) schizoid patients the fantasy that his oral longings were so insatiable that they would end up destroying the persons he loved the most. Fairbairn coined the phrase, "the Little Red Riding Hood fantasy," to capture the dynamics of this fear. In his view of the fairy tale, the little girl finds, to her overwhelming horror, that her grandmother is not home. In her place is the little girl's own projected oral greed in the form of a devouring wolf. At times Mr. M felt that his intense neediness would devour me, while at other times he projected this voraciousness into me and feared that he would disappear in the process of fusing with me. When he overcame his reluctance to express some of these longings openly, I noted a corresponding anxiety in myself. On the one hand, I thought I was being coerced into the role of an all-giving mother who was trying to fill a bottomless pit. On the other hand, at a more primitive level I felt I would be consumed by the depth of his neediness. In retrospect, I think my anxious response to his heaving sobs were very much related to such primitive concerns.

Part of Mr. M's feeling of being "stuck" was related to a wish to be both heterosexual and homosexual, both male and female, a desire to "have it all," as discussed in Chapter 2. McDougall (1995) has observed that the confusion deriving from bisexual wishes in the course of development may have wide-ranging effects on adult life. In particular, the inability (or incapacity) to integrate the wishes to have and be both sexes may result in symptoms, inhibitions, and delayed maturation.

Mr. M's fantasy of being anally penetrated by his father while simultaneously engaging in vaginal intercourse with his mother was in part a manifestation of this nonintegration. In this fantasy we can see several interlocking themes. At one level he was longing to be his father's sexual partner, that is, to become his mother. At another level, he wanted to become his father by appropriating his large adult penis and using it with mother. As McDougall (1995) has emphasized, homosexual oedipal longings have a dual aim—to be the opposite-sex parent and to possess the same-sex parent. These longings, of course, are inextricably connected with the reverse or heterosexual configurations.

Some adult patients have not yet accepted the reality that they can never possess both genders. Much of the analytic work must be geared to dealing with this stark reality and the mourning that accompanies it. McDougall (1995) has noted that conflicts over the wish to have either the father's potency/penis or the mother's creative capacity may inhibit one's ability to put forth symbolic offspring. Accepting the reality of one's limitations while also integrating these dual wishes may free up the patient's creativity.

These observations on the vicissitudes of love and lust in the male analyst-male analysand dyad reflect some fundamental aspects of male psychology relevant to the erotics of the psychoanalytic situation. An overriding focus on the penis and what can be done with and to the penis may obscure other issues that are defended against and contained by this focus. For example, in the case of Mr. M, his longing for a "cock up the ass" symbolized longings for love from father, wishes for the protection of a powerful father as a desymbiotizing force to counterbalance the yearnings to fuse with mother, and a substitute for mother's breast. In the transference, his wish to have my penis inside of him was connected with the fantasy that it would be a way of internalizing me so he would never lose me. In addition, his erotization of the transference defended against profound feelings of loss and grief that accompanied his movement into adult heterosexual relationships.

There has been a trend in psychoanalytic theory to minimize the importance of the preoedipal relationship between father and son. Blos (1991) has stressed that the growing boy's development of trust and a sense of safety is too exclusively attributed to his relationship with the early mother when, in fact, the dyadic father is highly significant in the boy's efforts to break the symbiotic ties with mother. This need to idealize and identify with the father *precedes* full entry into oedipal triangular relationships in which father may be seen as a dangerous retaliatory rival. Blos has argued that the same gender or "negative" oedipal complex is not transformed into psychic structure until adolescence, and the longing for the dyadic father is too frequently assumed to be genital or homoerotic rather than recognizing the developmentally earlier components.

One can also view intensely sexual transference fantasies in male patients (perhaps with female as well as with male analysts) as a form of erotization of early vulnerabilities associated with inadequacy, rage, the potential for abandonment, and the terror of an all-powerful and controlling mother (Maguire 1995, Person 1986). Another manifestation of this defensive pattern is the common male fantasy depicted in both film and literature of an idealized and objectified woman who is always available and always interested in sex. Rather than representing power and control over the man, she is meant to represent dutiful submission. Stoller (1975) suggested that there is a particular triad of conflicts in the male psyche involving a yearning to regress to a symbiotic state with mother, accompanied by a terror of losing one's male identity as a result, and an associated wish to avenge mother for creating the situation in the first place. Male potency, then, may help solidify a stable sense of self and male gender identity to a much greater degree than its female counterpart because it actively defends against these powerful pregenital conflicts.

This point of view regarding male sexuality also raises some provocative questions about the centrality of castration anxiety. There is little doubt that the fear of castration is a common concern that regularly surfaces in the analysis of male patients. In the case of Mr. M, because of his profound guilt related to having his mother to himself while his father was away at war, castration anxiety emerged in some combination of a fear and a wish for punishment. Nonetheless, it clearly blended into more primitive concerns, such as having the front part of his body literally ripped away from his mother, so that separation anxiety, loss of mother's love, and loss of father's love, all were closely linked to castration. The male fear of castration is, in part, a defensive way of dealing with more disconcerting anxieties involving human yearnings for attachment, love, and succor. In tracing Freud's thought, Lear (1990) noted that sex ultimately metamorphosed into love. The evolution in Freud's thinking was not connected to a wish to deny the power of the body and its drives. Rather, it reflected Freud's growing awareness that libido was what invested objects. Sexuality was co-opted in the service of other longings. Freud finally reached the conclusion that what psychoanalysis referred to as sexuality was similar to the all-inclusive love described by Plato.

In the waning years of his life, Freud (1937) contemplated the two most powerful resistances he had encountered in the practice of psychoanalysis. He argued that the wish for a penis in the female and the masculine protest in the male gave the analyst more trouble than any other psychological themes. He noted that when the analyst had reached these issues, he or she had "penetrated through all the psychological strata" and had "reached bedrock" (p. 252). In a footnote, Freud commented that "the 'masculine protest' is in fact nothing else than castration anxiety" (pp. 252–253). There is a broad consensus among contemporary psychoanalysts that penis envy is no longer considered bedrock, and I think we are now recognizing that in an analogous way, castration anxiety is not the endpoint of analytic work either. Like penis envy, it can be deconstructed into component parts that have specific meanings for each individual.

For many analysts the experience of being loved intensely may be far more disconcerting than being lusted after sexually. (For others, the reverse may be true.) Most of us pride ourselves on being able to discern the negative aspects of erotic transference, perhaps because we find anger, envy, and hatred more tolerable than naked expressions of love and affection. In this regard I disagree with Blum's (1995) view that love is easier to tolerate and enjoy than hate. Those of us who become analysts have chosen a field in which we spend the greater part of our day in a posture of professional distance from the most intimate disclosures of others. The intimacy and affective charge entailed in transference love may threaten to break down that carefully constructed distance. The term *erotic transference* has a reassuring clinical ring to it. By contrast, to hear a patient say, "I love you," sounds too personal, too close for comfort. Our obsessional dissection of the differences between transference love and real love may, in fact, reflect a wish to be reassured that the feelings are somehow not "real," not truly intended for us.

6   EROTIC TRANSFERENCE IN THE MALE ADOLESCENT–FEMALE ANALYST DYAD[1]

As I noted in Chapter 5, the psychoanalytic literature on erotic transference has traditionally focused on a male analyst and a female patient. In the last ten years or so, analysts have increasingly turned their attention to the phenomenon of sexual longings by a male patient for his female analyst. Much of the controversy originated when Lester (1985) noted that reports of erotized transferences of male patients to female analysts were virtually absent from the literature because they were rare in clinical practice. She stressed that the emergence of the transference fear of the powerful preoedipal phallic mother tended to overshadow and inhibit the full expression of sexualized impulses directed toward the oedipal mother. She felt that the destabilizing effect of such primitive anxieties on male gender identity contributed to the suppression of intense sexual fantasies in the female analyst–male patient dyad.

---

1. This chapter is based on a paper coauthored by Sarah Atkinson, M.D.

Following the appearance of Lester's contribution, a number of articles by female analysts (Goldberger and Evans 1985, Gornick 1986, Myers 1987) appeared that presented a somewhat different view. These authors felt that erotic transferences were more common than Lester suggested, but Myers, and Goldberger and Evans acknowledged that resistances against the transferences are often powerful. Person (1985) suggested that male patients with female analysts often displace their erotic transferences to extratransference figures, and she agreed with Myers and with Goldberger and Evans that resistances to the awareness of the erotic transference may be formidable.

Tyson (1986) and Russ (1993) observed that the female analyst's psychologically and culturally determined countertransference may inhibit the fully developed erotic or eroticized transference in the male patient. Moreover, they suggested that female clinicians may prefer to remain with early dyadic or preoedipal material not only because of the avoidance of genital sexuality but because of the powerful position it affords.

Much of this newly emerging literature has arisen in concert with the demise of the classical view that the analyst's gender had minimal relevance in determining the nature of the transference. As analysts have become increasingly aware of the significance of the "real" person of the analyst, the gender configuration has become one key element of the interaction between the two members of the analytic dyad (Greenson 1967, Lester 1985, Ticho 1975). As early as 1936, Bibring stated that one of the most influential aspects of the "real" person of the analyst was her gender. The fact that the literature on the erotic transference of male patients to female analysts has only recently come to the attention of clinicians may reflect a confluence of factors. As Russ (1993) noted: "Social

convention says that an empowered man is unambiv-
alently sexually desirable, but for a woman, the sex/
power issue may cause conflict for herself and those
around her" (p. 393).

Ongoing societal changes may result in this perspective
becoming less rigidly held. In the meantime, however,
succumbing to a man's sexual advances, even psychologically, may conjure up a perception of loss of autonomy
and authority, or even of a basic sense of safety for many
women (Benedek 1973, Russ 1993). These concerns may
lead to a premature closure of the unfolding transference.
The analytic relationship between a woman therapist and
a male patient represents a reversal of traditional positions
of power. The woman may be placed in a madonna/whore
paradox of charging for the hour while simultaneously
being viewed as the all-listening, all-giving mother (Russ
1993). The analyst may collude with the patient, unwill-
ing to see herself in both aspects of this paradox, and the
transference may be viewed only as an asexual maternal
transference.

The aforementioned difficulties are compounded when
the patient is an adolescent. The literature is virtually
silent with regard to erotic transference of male adolescent patients to their female analysts. There are several
possible contributing factors to the literature's silence on
this topic. As Russ (1993) and Lester (1985) both cite,
women are hesitant to reveal themselves in the academic
literature as sexual beings especially as they strive to
establish themselves professionally. Society expects adolescent girls, budding into womanhood, to have "crushes"
on older men. These highly charged emotional attachments are generally viewed as benign, or at worst, that the
adolescent is creating a "scene," ostensibly embarrassing
herself and the recipient of her affections. In the reverse
situation, with an admiring adolescent boy and an older

woman (occasionally the mother), the woman may be condemned as a temptress. This theme is replete in classic literature, such as Homer's *Odyssey*, and in popular films such as *The Graduate, Spanking the Monkey, Summer of '42,* and *What's Eating Gilbert Grape?*

Parents and responsible adults have historically attempted to strike a balance between encouraging children toward adulthood and protecting them from the realities of the world. This dialectic is even more strained as brutal, random violence and overt sexuality now permeate every level of our culture, creating a strong impetus for adults to simultaneously educate and shield children from the world. Child analysts with or without the collusion of the child's parents may seek to protect the child from "worldly knowledge" that would launch the child into a genital sexual world of adulthood. This affords the child analyst and even the parents the illusion of working in a neverland where boys remain playful, adoring, and asexual, which may serve to defend against the realization of any potential erotic transference or countertransference material. For the analyst, this stance guards against the psychological violation of incest taboos involving the transferential parent-analyst seducing the child-patient. If the adolescent agrees to maintain his station as a boy in neverland, then the transference is thwarted and the potential for exploration and growth is constrained (Gornick 1986). The exploration of all aspects of the transference, specifically any erotic components within the confines of the analytic boundaries is frequently regarded by male analysts as benefiting their female patients' relationships with a flowering of their sense of femininity (Freud 1915b, Gorkin 1985, Trop 1988).

Acknowledging erotic material in an adolescent's transference may create a level of concern or even fear of parental retaliation should the parents become aware of the material. This potential is especially relevant in today's litigious climate in conjunction with the zealous pursuit of even the most remote adumbration of impropriety. An allegation of sexual misconduct could wreak havoc on the analyst's career. Even in the absence of fears of retribution by society and parents, the child analyst may have concerns that he or she has manipulated the child's thoughts or actions into following a particular course. From these concerns, rather than exploring the material, the analyst may disregard or deny any emerging evidence of erotic transference.

A child may begin analysis in early- or mid-childhood and will as a matter of course mature. The subtle (and not so subtle) cognitive, physiological, psychological, and social development of the child may evoke strong countertransference reactions that may or may not be acknowledged. Analysts may wish, on a countertransferential basis, to maintain an internal sense of being the all-giving, benign, omnipotent and asexual parent figure (Gabbard 1994a,e, Waksman 1986). During this passage of time both analyst and child may attempt to avoid the issues of what the child's maturation means relative to termination of therapy, graduation from school, attaining employment, and the child's no longer being as receptive to the transferential parent-analyst. Some analysts may have qualms about their own aging process that influences how they experience their patient's maturation.

The process of normal and pathological development represents a cornerstone of psychoanalytic theory. Oral, anal, phallic, oedipal, and latency conflicts are integrated and subsumed under a final genital orientation during adolescence. In adolescence the oedipal conflicts come to the forefront once again to be reexperienced not only with parents, but with parent substitutes and older peers. The intensity of aggression shrouding the sexual aspect of relationships may determine the degree to which the manifestations of an erotic transference is consciously and/or unconsciously shunned (Russ 1993).

The reawakening of pregenital urges with the newly acquired genital urges in conjunction with the cognitive and physical capabilities to fantasize and act on the fantasy enhances a sense of dangerous excitement in reexperiencing oedipal issues (A. Freud 1958, Ritvo 1971). The male adolescent is now focused on his body in a way not experienced or exhibited since infancy and toddler-hood (Ritvo 1971). Adolescent boys are preoccupied with multitudinous voyeuristic looking, not only at women's bodies but also at their own bodies and those of other young men (Blos 1962). The actual experience of genital sexuality with partners is preceded by a variable period of intense erotic looking, the dénouement of which is the emergence of the adolescent's identity as a sexual male. These experiences serve to counteract, "the ubiquitous fear that one's sense of maleness and masculinity are in danger and that one must build into character structure ever-vigilant defenses against succumbing to the pull of merging again with mother" (Stoller 1975, p. 149). Russ (1993), Lester (1985), and Karme (1979) posit that the fear of regressive symbiosis with the mother may limit erotic expression in adult males, but for the adolescent patient the voyeuristic looking period that precedes physical genital expression may allow for the discussion of erotic transference issues. Overall, adolescent relationships are characterized by both ardent declaration of emotions and a rather brief duration of such feelings. The intensity and exclusivity of analysis without the brevity typical of adolescent relationships may serve to enhance the devel-opment of an erotic transference in young adolescent boys as they struggle to consolidate their sense of sexual and personal identity. The analytic resolution of the erotic transference may be critical to the adolescent's developing a resolute sense of his own identity and not succumbing to a regressive fantasy of preoedipal merger with mother or mother-substitutes such as the analyst.

Here I present a fragment of the treatment of an adolescent boy who developed an erotic transference to his female therapist. In the course of the discussion, I will review the evolution of the transference, the potential contributions of early mother–child/father–child relations and the developmental period of early adolescence, and the ramifications of an erotic transference on the treatment process.

CASE REPORT

At age 13 Nicholas was a veteran of many forms of psychiatric intervention including brief hospitalization, pharmacotherapy, and therapeutic boarding school. He was admitted to residential treatment with a litany of behavioral disturbances, including smoking marijuana, drinking alcohol, running away from boarding school, and spending large sums of money riding about in taxicabs. Despite his excellent intellect Nicholas had repeatedly failed school. The immediate reason for poor academic showing was that Nicholas attended class and simply sat, refusing to do any work. To remedy this situation his parents transferred him from one private academic institution to another. His first hospital admission occurred after a verbal altercation with his mother that escalated to an exchange of blows.

The parents were from disparate cultural and socioeconomic backgrounds. Father was descended from a western family steeped in prospecting and ranching. Formal education and conformity to social norms were not valued; independence and a taste for adventure were prized. Mother was from a prosperous intellectual and artistic family and was herself an artist of significant repute.

The parental expectations from treatment reflected their own backgrounds. Father wanted to have a better relationship with his son, while mother wanted Nicholas to gain some "self soothing for his inner fire." Father viewed Nicholas as a distant child who was overly dependent on his mother, refused to "have any real discussions with me [father]," and was bullied by his 21-year-old brother. Nicholas had traveled extensively with his mother during exhibitions of her works. Mother saw Nicholas as an extraordinarily sensitive and talented child, whom she had unsuccessfully attempted to teach to draw. He seemed to ". . . fly into a rage whenever I corrected him. He tore up his drawings, even wonderful, beautiful ones."

After a comprehensive psychiatric evaluation, Nicholas was referred for thrice-weekly psychoanalytic psychotherapy. Despite years of psychiatric intervention, he had never had a good trial of expressive treatment, and the evaluating team felt an in-depth exploration of his internal conflicts was crucial.

Although he was rather sophisticated about psychological jargon, Nicholas was a newcomer to expressive treatment. He arrived in the therapist's office dressed as a cross between a conservative school boy and a punk rocker. His clothing was immaculate, precisely coordinated, and costly. On the other hand his hair was partly shaved and partly shoulder length, and he wore a small diamond earring. He stammered and stumbled when his therapist, Dr. Z, asked him what had brought him to the hospital. Blushing, with his head bent so that his hair partially concealed his eyes, he said that he had run away from his latest school. His voice sounded weary and sad, not defiant or angry. The unit staff had described him as an angry, belligerent adolescent, contrary to the young boy who sat before Dr. Z timidly asking if the cookie jar really contained cookies. Nicholas's dress and presentation were in sharp contrast to each other and to his history as a stridently rebellious young teenager.

Over the next month, Nicholas carefully modeled clay roses complete with thorns. He was most concerned about the clay rubbing off onto the table or bits falling onto the floor. After completing each flower he meticulously tidied up, despite being assured that he need not be concerned about the mess. He was remarkably fastidious. He seemed nervous and anxious, like a small boy trying to please his mother. As Nicholas carefully combined various colors to create magenta and corals, Dr. Z commented on his choice of colors. Nicholas beamed, staring deeply into Dr. Z's eyes as he placed each new creation on her desk. His responses sounded like those of a 5–6-year-old child, very warm and yet somehow sensual. Because Nicholas was 13, intelligent, and experienced as a patient, Dr. Z had thought he would be more verbally inclined, but whenever Dr. Z made an inquiry or remark other than about his work he became sullen and mute. So he sat with her at a small table while he modeled with clay and drew sketches. Occasionally, short notes saying "hello," accompanied by a sketch, would arrive via interoffice mail. Dr. Z felt uncomfortable with how the treatment was proceeding and wondered if she should be interpreting more and confronting more of his behaviors. Yet she also felt that being more active would suffocate the blossoming transference. The notes, sculptures, and drawings were like small tokens of affection. There was a flirtatious quality (bordering on seductive) to the single stems of roses and the surreptitiously sent messages.

Despite comments from Dr. Z on the drawings and sculptures regarding the technique used in rendering them and the affects they evoked, Nicholas never destroyed his work, until asked about an upcoming phone call with his parents. He mumbled a reply of "fine" and abruptly destroyed a well-formed rose in full bloom. Dr. Z wondered aloud if she had intruded into his creation. He countered with how talented his mother was and offered to show a photograph of her work. Dr. Z then remarked that her work was that of a mature artist with many years of experience, and he silently repaired the fractured rose. His art was a private affair between the two members of the treatment dyad. He did not draw or paint on the unit or take art in school for his first semester at the hospital school.

For the following session, he arrived scowling and pouting. Angrily he accused Dr. Z of being ". . . like all the others [adults], just like my parents." Perplexed, Dr. Z asked him what had happened. He vehemently replied, ". . . I didn't feel sorry about something I said to staff. What are they there for anyway? They're paid to take care of us. They told me I had to clean my room. I'm not going to do it." Nicholas continued a long monologue of self-righteous indignation, relating how all adults treat children as if they had no feelings, no thoughts of their own, and had no right to their own opinions. As the diatribe continued, his voice softened to a pleading, soulful sound. Dr. Z commented that she had insensitively introduced his parents into his treatment, disregarding how he might feel. Looking rather surprised and sad, he agreed. Play therapy was now over: the two had crossed the bridge from physical objects representing affects and wishes to his being able to express himself verbally. Nicholas drew only once more during the treatment.

Rather than creating objects to express himself, Nicholas began directly discussing how he felt and thought. Dr. Z's attire evolved into a central issue. Nicholas came in, sat down, instantly noticed the length of her skirt and said she looked better in short skirts. Dr. Z's initial response was one of dismay, as she pretended to ignore his comment. While attempting to recover her composure, she inquired about how he was getting on at school. Nicholas was a child, yet he was beginning to mature physically into a young man. His statements no longer had childishly innocent overtones. Nicholas fidgeted, made monosyllabic replies to her inquiries and asked if they could walk outside to a snack shop on the hospital grounds. As they left the office, the highly charged atmosphere in the room gave way to a more relaxed one. Nicholas walked quickly, too quickly for Dr. Z to keep pace. She did not ask him to slow his pace, noting that she somehow felt safer with him a short distance ahead, and he too seemed in better control.

After several sessions of this scenario, Dr. Z commented that he was always observant about her style of clothing. She recognized a countertransference dread that a Pandora's box might be opened by acknowledging his comments and was afraid of what might be enacted in or out of the treatment. Would his feelings and wishes be confined only to words? After all, it was only a few short months ago that he had left her roses. Dr. Z now dealt with a more self-confident, handsome young man who had the braggadocio of someone wooing his first love. He was no longer a little boy playing with plasticine, worrying about a mother's reaction to a mess on the carpet. What would happen if the balance of power tilted, as it had in his family? Dr. Z had maintained the role of observing adult. Now she sensed that she might lose this position.

Nicholas and his mother had engaged in an exclusive, sensually intimate relationship long after his toddlerhood. Although there was no history of overt sexual abuse, Nicholas's every whim was catered to by his mother. He felt smothered and at the same time competitive with her. His tentative attempts to flirt with Dr. Z appeared to parallel his flirtation with his mother that led to the physical altercation and his subsequent hospitalization. The sexual tension had become so intense that Nicholas was forced into physical action against his mother to ward off his own sexual impulses. Furthermore, Nicholas's competence as an emerging young adult could not flourish in the competitive dance in which he and his mother were engaged. He viciously undermined his potential by refusing to discover his assets and weaknesses, as when he refused to do any school work or take art class. By leaving his own competence undiscovered, Nicholas remained an infant, incapable of independent achievement.

Feeling as though she were plunging into torrid waters, but simultaneously wanting to remain in the relatively safe, serene world that had been previously created, Dr. Z started keeping pace with Nicholas as they walked. As her pace increased, he slowed his and began to talk. He said that she was "really beautiful" and that he had not really noticed how pretty she was until six months into treatment. Actually he had first observed Dr. Z's earrings, but said that he felt too embarrassed to let her know how much he admired them. She commented that he had recently pierced his ear for a second earring, so that now both of them had two earrings. Nicholas grinned in agreement, flirtatiously adding that he bet she would not let him borrow the admired pair of earrings. Dr. Z smiled and simply said no. He looked relieved, and she was too.

Sighing, he said he thought a lot about how Dr. Z dressed quite differently from girls his own age. She wondered how he viewed the differences. His pace quickened, then he abruptly turned and said, "You're not like the others." Dr. Z asked him what he meant. Nicholas replied that she treated him like a person with something important to say. She told him that she frequently disagreed with some of his viewpoints. He said that he knew that she would disagree with him, but that he did not feel devalued when she did so. He accurately perceived that she respected his opinions, even when she told him that his views might change with time or be different from her own.

Nicholas rapidly shifted back and forth from emotionally charged issues of his own competence to flirting. He regularly commented that Dr. Z now dressed better and that he liked her hair shorter. His eye for detail was incredible. He noted every nuance of change in hairstyle, make-up, perfume, weight, and wardrobe over the past eight months. Dr. Z began to have a sense of being stalked. She said that it seemed to give him great pleasure to list her outfits. His initial response was a smirked flat denial. She felt stymied and rather undone, perhaps "undressed." He silently spent the next few sessions staring at Dr. Z with a penetrating glare, periodically shifting his gaze from one part of her body to another while simultaneously grinning in apparent satisfaction.

Subsequent sessions were filled with unspoken tension. Unlike many silences with other adolescents, Dr. Z did not feel angry, but she was anxious and unsure of what to do at this particular impasse. Finally, there were angry retorts about how treatment was worthless and how he did not understand how he could ever have wanted to become a psychiatrist. Dr. Z said that this type of relationship was incredibly close, maybe sometimes too close for comfort and perhaps dangerous. Nicholas told her that she was completely wrong, that he had never felt unsafe with her. He also stressed that he was now bigger (indeed he was now taller than Dr. Z). She agreed that he was growing up and would soon be moving into young adulthood. Pausing, he said that maybe he felt like he wanted more than just treatment. Dr. Z asked him what he had in mind. Tersely, he replied that he was 14 and was too young to get married. When she agreed, he visibly relaxed. (So did Dr. Z.)

He spent the next several sessions discussing dating and marriage. Then he had a dream about being forced into marrying an older woman after impregnating her. He appeared extremely distraught when he first mentioned this dream. Initially he walked rapidly away in silence. Later he commented that he always went after the older girls on the unit and the ones who dressed right. Dr. Z talked about how difficult relationships were to maintain over time, even between two mature adults. She also said that the task of adolescence was to find one's identity and purpose. She was letting him know indirectly that no boundaries would be crossed. He was very quiet.

The patient's grades took a dramatic upturn, and he began enthusiastically talking about what he would like to do as a career. He said that he could not imagine her staying home from work. Dr. Z asked him what not working meant to him. He replied that his mother always worked, even after she had children. Dr. Z asked him if he thought *she* would work even if she had children. He nodded his head affirmatively and moved closer. Dr. Z did not move away. She commented that part of becoming professionally successful was knowing when to compromise. He agreed and wondered if he could ever be like his mother's family.

One day it was pouring rain and Dr. Z refused to go for a walk. Nicholas spent a few minutes pouting and then picked up the sketch pad to draw his dream. He suddenly stopped and told her the dream. "I was hoping. I mean thinking. Dreaming that I could marry you." He recalled that when he was around 5 he had crept into his mother's studio where a nude male was modeling. He said how angry he felt, really envious, "like I wanted to kill him." Nicholas looked sad, confused, and frightened. Dr. Z noted how very confusing that must have been for him. He replied that he did not have to share that part of his mother with his father. Dr. Z asked what he meant. He said his father was not an artist, unlike him and his mother. As he spoke, Nicholas sketched a young male nude of 7 to 8 years of age. Dr. Z pointed this out to him. Despite the obvious male genitalia, he denied that it was a boy, insisting that it was a girl.

In the next session, he reexamined the drawing. He quietly stated that he had recognized himself in the picture and had become "too embarrassed to talk" to Dr. Z anymore, saying, "I really thought about not coming here today, especially since I know you keep all my drawings." Nicholas said that he felt "like a tidal wave hit me." He realized that his mother used to draw nudes of him and that he had enjoyed being her special model. The existence of the drawings was confirmed by his mother in a family session with the social worker. He said that he had felt exposed in the previous session; Dr. Z might reject him if she knew of his passionate feelings toward his mother. He elaborated that he thought about "being in bed with you, what it would be like." Dr. Z commented that on some level he may have wondered also what it would be like to have his mother as his wife. Startled, he nodded his head, but said that his feelings toward Dr. Z were much stronger, "So strong that sometimes, well you know, I wake up really hard." Rapidly he added that he was too young to get married. Dr. Z assured him that she had no intention of seducing him, but wondered aloud if he had thought of being both the seducer and the seduced. She said how frightening and exciting it must be for him to think of being with her. Rather than changing the subject, sulking, or otherwise retreating, Nicholas agreed that his thoughts were all of the above and even more. He said that even when he was little (ten months ago!) and was naive about what to do in therapy, he had thought about her "all the time."

He wondered at first if therapists ever adopted their patients. This rapidly took on sexual overtones, similar to his relationship with his mother. He was afraid that if Dr. Z adopted him, she would want him to model. When she asked a question or made an interpretation, especially if it did not reflect favorably on him, he felt vulnerable and exposed, like when he modeled for his mother. At the same time he felt extremely close and intimate, and he wanted to expand the relationship. He said he enjoyed making her feel uncomfortable, and he really liked her figure and her style of dressing. Dr. Z said that she understood how exposed he felt with his mother, despite being her favorite model and special child. He countered that the relationship was not directly parallel to the one with his mother and that Dr. Z seemed to want him to ". . . finish growing up." She asked him to clarify. He said that he wished for the relationship to mature into something even better than therapy. He liked therapy because he could express himself and "work out the problems inside myself," but he also said, "I want to sleep with you." Dr. Z asked him what exactly he meant by "sleep with me." He said it depended on the day. Dr. Z commented that it might also depend on the minute.

He laughed and said she was always clarifying adult time, adolescent time (a month is forever), and children's time (a day is divided into mealtimes) for him. He said it really depended on the day, the school day. If he was interested in school, then he thought that they should ". . . just go off together to sculpt, draw, and write" in some ethereal realm. If school was not going well, then he wanted her to hold him and tell him that she would love him forever, even if he was not brilliant or creative. Dr. Z said, "You want me to accept and love you for you, regardless of what your body looks like or how it changes with time or how you perform sexually, academically, or creatively." He said that he wanted this relationship to be "the one" and then said, "It feels like it should be the right one. You know me better than anyone else and you know that you are attracted to me." He elaborated that the therapist had changed her perfume to one that he liked better (the perfume had in reality not been changed) and that she was now "dressing better" by wearing more colors and different types of fabric—like more silk (no new clothes had been bought). Dr. Z commented that *he* was attracted to *her* and acknowledged that they did share some interests. He looked sad, angry, and embarrassed. Bitterly he asked how much more he had to prove before she would let him get closer. She said that he had himself to face and nothing to prove to her. He seemed utterly defeated at this remark.

Before the next session real roses arrived in Dr. Z's office with a note from Nicholas expressing his love for her and hopes for a continued relationship. Dr. Z was embarrassed, worried how intense the acting out would become, and saddened by his desperation to win her over. He arrived and smiled at the sight of the roses. He said that he hoped they had arrived just before him; indeed, they had arrived less than five minutes before his appointment. Dr. Z asked how he understood sending flowers and what he hoped for in her reaction. He looked angry and then started crying, asking how he could make her love him. Dr. Z told him that the type of romantic, intimate relationship he kept attempting to create was not going to occur with her. He said that he "guessed he had lost." Dr. Z told him that she was never his to win. Again he looked defeated, saying that he had thought that maybe she was not his to win and wondered if he might find someone like her. She reiterated that she hoped he would find someone to share his life with him when he was "old enough." Nicholas agreed that he was definitely not old enough, and added that maybe after graduate school would be a good time to find someone.

DISCUSSION

The foregoing clinical material raises a number of issues regarding the development of erotic transference in male adolescent patients with female analysts. Some features of the case appear to be specific to this particular patient, while others may provide some tentative conclusions that can be applied to other treatment situations with adolescents that involve the same gender configuration.

Nicholas's presenting difficulties were remarkable only in their ubiquity as adolescent complaints. As with many children who are brought to therapy, he was not doing well at school despite more than adequate cognitive abilities. He had failed also to develop his artistic talents noted by his mother. There was intense conflict within his family relationships. Overall, he was rapidly turning toward inferiority at the close of his latency years, rather than developing a sense of industry and self-worth (Erikson 1980). Initially, the transference wish for admiration from an adult woman was a maternal preoedipal transference. As he created precise clay sculptures he sought and acquired praise for his talents from a maternal figure who was not competitive, as he had been with his mother. Even within this transference there was a flirtatious, seductive quality with notes being sent and the sculpture being left on Dr. Z's desk. Her anxious wish to view this as only a nonerotic maternal transference that would repair Erikson's industry versus inferiority conflict was evident by the absence of any interpretations that dealt with the sexual overtones that these tokens carried. Sexualization of the transference was viewed by Dr. Z as implying action rather than reflection. The vantage point of an asexual maternal transference preserves a perception of safety for the therapist and is highly promoted by our culture (Gornick 1986, Russ 1993).

The countertransference struggles that Dr. Z endured are not atypical. Her feelings of being stalked or "undressed" were highly disconcerting. Retrospectively, Dr. Z recognized that Nicholas had turned the tables on her. As an artist, his mother had made him uncomfortable by visually studying him and having him pose in the nude for her own artistic interests. Nicholas had actively mastered passively experienced trauma by looking at Dr. Z in a way that made her just as uncomfortable as he had been as a model for his mother. Another aspect of her counter-transference was to view the transference material as pregenital, which may have been experienced as castrat-ing, in that the adolescent's identity was not confirmed as a phallic male. For this child on the cusp of adolescence, failure to acknowledge the erotic component of the trans-ference material would have consigned him to a role of a nonproductive, inferior person. Furthermore, not to ac-knowledge his emerging sexuality would drive him to-ward a resumption of the symbiosis he had experienced with his mother not long after his infancy. During his toddlerhood and early childhood Nicholas traveled ex-tensively and exclusively with his mother, despite the birth of a brother when Nicholas was 3 years old. His relationship with his mother culminated in violence just at the point when Nicholas was physically maturing. This act may have represented for Nicholas just how endan-gered his own sense of masculinity had become by his symbiotic yearnings toward mother (Stoller 1975).

The role that looking played in the transference is striking in the treatment of Nicholas. While the emerging genital sexuality of the young adolescent boy is always connected with voyeuristic activities, the particular na-ture of the mother–son relationship in this case (particu-larly his serving as a nude model for her) may have heightened the sexualization involved in looking and showing. The clinical material suggests that Nicholas's struggle to define his own masculine identity was inti-mately related to themes of sexualized looking. He would look Dr. Z up and down, studying the contours of her body and attempting to differentiate her anatomy from his own. His sketch of a young male nude with male genitalia was regarded by him as a little girl. While this difficulty may reflect a way of handling his castration anxiety, it may also point to his wish to "have it all" (i.e., have both male and female features and thus avoid dealing with his envy of his mother's procreative capacities).

Jacobson (1951) noted that in male artists and other creative persons, analysis often reveals intensely cathected unconscious feminine reproductive fantasies. Nicholas's envy of his mother's ability to grow and produce children may have been heightened by his mother's artistic profession and her seductive relationship with him in that context. These men, according to Jacobson, may withdraw cathexis from their penis and displace it onto the wish for a baby or other displaced creative pursuits.

When the little boy becomes aware of anatomical differences, he often seeks to undo them in a variety of ways (Ross 1977). The hermaphroditic fantasy that little boys may harbor is often a derivative of the fantasy of the mother as a phallic woman (Bak 1968, Greenacre 1970). In discussing the analysis of adult males, Karme (1979) has stressed that a man treated by a female analyst will very likely have to deal with his transference fear of the analyst as the phallic mother. The patient may worry that his female analyst is more potent and phallic than he, and he may feel the need to "castrate" her by demonstrating that he is more potent than she. Similar issues may arise in the male adolescent patient, resulting in a counterphobic erotization of the transference.

In many cases of male adolescents treated by female analysts, the erotization may be limited to looking. It is possible that the highly incestuous nature of Nicholas's relationship with his mother allowed him to be more forthright in verbalizing his sexual feelings toward Dr. Z. Many male adolescents are too ashamed of their feelings to address them directly with a female therapist. Similarly, some female analysts may deal with their counter-transference distress by effectively "castrating" the young male's emerging sexuality and colluding in the resistance the patient experiences to discussing such feelings openly. The fact that male adolescents are often referred to male analysts—with the rationalization that a strong identification figure is needed—may reflect the female clinician's countertransference anxiety at the potential for erotization of the transference.

While the intensity and sexualization of the mother–son relationship may be unusual in the case of Nicholas, we may speculate that similar factors may be at work in many other cases. Two major societal changes appear to contribute to such dynamics. First, the large number of broken homes with distant fathers may result in excessive closeness between mother and son with an accompanying erotization on both sides of the dyad. Second, with more women in the workforce, boys may increasingly regard their mothers as objects of identification. As a result, male potency may have greater psychological valence than ever for adolescent boys because, as I noted in Chapter 5, it appears to serve as a critical stabilizing force in the development of male gender identity.

7   Technical Approaches to Malignant Transference Hate

> It does not matter much what a man hates provided he hates something.
>
> —Samuel Butler

Freud (1915a) once noted that the only truly significant obstacles likely to be encountered by the analyst are those involving the management of transference. Among the panoply of transference feelings directed at the analyst, intense hatred is one of the most difficult to endure. Analysts may be drawn to the field, at least in part, because the practice of analysis itself serves as a reaction formation against hatred, aggression, and sadism (McLaughlin 1961, Menninger 1957, Schafer 1954). The experience of being hated day in and day out tends to erode one's carefully constructed defenses against hating one's patient. Moreover, the analyst's conscious altruistic wishes to help others are also thwarted by the hateful patient, occasionally leading the analyst to question whether the whole analytic endeavor in this particular instance is a waste of time and energy.

In Chapter 2, I distinguished benign and malignant forms of transference hate. As a general rule the benign form of transference hate, like its erotic counterpart, is more characteristic of neurotically organized patients, while the malignant variant, much like erotized transference, is more likely to be found in borderline patients. This distinction is not intended to be an absolute one, but it is clinically useful to conceptualize the predominant form of transference hate as related to the level of ego organization found in the patient. In so doing, however, it is well to keep in mind Little's (1966) caveat that normal, neurotic, and psychotic transferences may be observed in the same patient within a single session. Moreover, borderline patients as a group are characterized by a broad spectrum of ego-functioning, ranging from those who are analyzable to those who require extended hospitalization (Gabbard et al. 1994; Meissner 1988).

Freud was certainly aware of this spectrum of hateful transferences from the benign to the malignant, although he did not explicitly make such a distinction. While Freud viewed hate as occupying a central position in the pathogenesis of the neuroses, his writings are remarkably sketchy on the technical handling of transference hate. He devoted an entire paper to transference love, but no comparable document exists to assist the analyst in dealing with the common situation of being hated by a patient. In his most extensive, though still limited, discussion of transference hate, Freud (1940) observed that the therapeutic successes derived from periods of positive transference may be drowned by the torrents of negative transference: "The danger of these states of transference evidently lies in the patient's misunderstanding their nature and taking them for fresh real experiences instead of reflections of the past" (p. 176). He goes on to say that in these states the patient "hates the analyst as his enemy and is ready to abandon the analysis" (p. 176). His recommendations for dealing with such intense states of hatred in the patient are relatively pedestrian:

It is the analyst's task constantly to tear the patient out of his menacing illusion and to show him again and again that what he takes to be new real life is the reflection of the past. And lest he should fall into a state in which he is inaccessible to all evidence, the analyst takes care that neither the love nor the hostility reach an extreme height. This is effected by preparing him in good time for the possibilities and by not overlooking the first signs of hate. [p. 177]

Freud's straightforward recommendations may be more difficult to implement with the malignant forms of transference hate. I draw this conclusion based in part on the tenacity of the hatred encountered in such patients and in part on the formidable types of countertransference generated by malignant hatred. In this chapter I will focus on the challenges posed by malignant transference hate, and I will suggest strategies that allow the analyst to persevere long enough to engage the patient in a psychoanalytic treatment.

PATHOGENESIS OF MALIGNANT HATE

Some patients may transiently dip into malignantly hateful transferences, but otherwise maintain the "as if" aspects of the transference throughout the bulk of the analytic work. My focus here is the patient whose predominant transference is one of malignant hate, where moments of reflectiveness and relief from the intensity of the negative affect are the exception rather than the rule. One of the true paradoxes characterizing these patients is that they repeatedly seek out treatment despite their thorough dissatisfaction with each therapist. They often jump from analyst to analyst and quit each time with feelings of disappointment and resentment. They seem to seek out treatment because the very core of their being depends on having a relationship in which they attack someone who is trying to help them (Rosenfeld 1987). Kernberg (1984) noted that patients such as these, who are part of a larger group prone to negative therapeutic reactions, are often identified with a cruel, sadistic internal object that can only give some semblance of love if it is accompanied by hatred and suffering. In other words, their attachment always must come at the expense of hatred. The alternative is a state of nonexistence.

This formulation, of course, suggests a repetition of a childhood situation in which abusive figures have been in the role of caregivers. Indeed, there is some empirical evidence that relates childhood abuse and this pattern of internal object relations. Nigg et al. (1991) compared a group of borderline patients with childhood sexual abuse to a group who did not have such histories. On projective testing, the presence of an extremely malevolent introject differentiated those who had been sexually abused from those who had not.

Research at the Anna Freud Centre in London (Fonagy et al. 1994) has drawn a link between childhood trauma and the lack of the "as if" quality of transferential reactions. While not specifically addressed to the hateful patient, this type of transference, in which the analyst is not viewed as a current-day repetition of a past figure based on the patient's projections but rather is regarded as the *original* object of hate, is certainly characteristic of the malignant hate that is the focus of this chapter. Fonagy and his collaborators (1994) have concluded that childhood trauma may impair the development of what they call *reflective self function* in these patients, which they define as the "capacity to think of their own and others' actions in terms of mental states . . . [that is, the] ability to invoke mental state constructs: feelings, beliefs, intentions, conflicts, and other psychological states" (p. 241).

This inability to "mentalize" appears to relate to intergenerational patterns of abuse in that the mother and father seem unable to develop working internal models of relationships and thus fail to pass on that reflective capacity to their children.

While childhood abuse appears to be one pathogenetic pathway for the development of malignant hate, in other cases no clear abuse history can be discerned. Obviously, the possibility of an inborn temperament that is hyperirritable and easily provoked to anger may play some role in alternative forms of pathogenesis. In addition, however, certain patients seem to be suffering from smoldering resentment based on their experience or perception of chronic narcissistic injury. These patients to a large extent resemble the kinds of patients Kohut (1972) described in his explication of chronic narcissistic rage. They feel that their parents never validated or affirmed their feelings or perceptions, so they go through their lives forever misunderstood and always anticipating further misunderstandings. Often this rage is fueled by a desire for revenge.

Regardless of the specific pathway of pathogenesis, the end result is that the expectable moderating effect of love over hate as one develops mature whole-object relatedness does not take place. There appears to be a dominant object relationship between a hated object-representation and a hating self-representation (Gabbard 1989b). These patients often seem to be consumed with venomous contempt in part because the good, loving aspects of the self and the corresponding object-representations are buried deep within to prevent their destruction by the all-consuming hate. Alternatively, they may be projected into figures in the environment who are regarded as entirely good or totally loving (Boyer 1983, Giovacchini 1975, Hamilton 1986, Klein 1946, Searles 1958).

In this manner the islands of love and concern for others are further protected by safely storing them in others. This strategy may well backfire, however, because the perception that others are so saintly may produce profound envy. This development may lead the patient to project devalued and hated self- and object-representations as a way of "smearing" the saintly figure with undesirable aspects of the patient's internal world (Poggi and Ganzarain 1983).

Patients with malignant hate, then, appear to be dominated by the paranoid-schizoid mode of experiencing. They lack the moderation of the depressive mode that can help them become more reflective and think about the way they are construing relationships. The result is a conviction of certainty about their perceptions of the analyst. Once the constellation is firmly entrenched within the patient, the analyst will encounter enormous resistance to shifting the patient's perceptions. Fortunately, some make forays into a more depressive mode of mental functioning that allows for analytic work to take place. A case example will illustrate some of the challenges posed by the malignantly hateful patient.

CASE EXAMPLE

Mr. H, a 28-year-old divorced man, came to analysis after an abortive two-year attempt with another analyst. That treatment experience ended with the analyst's move to another city. (I often wondered if that was the analyst's way of extricating himself from the unpleasant experience of spending an hour a day with Mr. H.) The most startling aspect of the opening phase of the analysis was the rapidity with which the transference hate developed and the conviction expressed by the patient that his perceptions were absolutely accurate. My overriding impression was one of being falsely accused. I was, of course, accustomed to being the target of negative transference, but rarely of this intensity so early in the process. I took flight from the daily barrages by retreating into diagnostic speculation: "Obviously a borderline feature," I would think to myself.

His contempt was thoroughly justified, in his view, because of the structure of the analytic situation, which he perceived as unreasonable and inflexible. Mr. H resented my fee, and he unabashedly expressed his feeling that he deserved to be treated for nothing. One comment he made in the first few weeks of the analysis, in response to my observation that he was verbally assaultive, nicely captured his point of view: "I know you think I'm assaultive, but it's because of the way you treat me. You charge me, you even bill me when I choose to take vacations, you don't give me answers to any of my questions, and you rigidly enforce the end of the hour even if I'm in the middle of a thought. I see *you* as assaultive, so I react with hostility."

All his feelings were the direct result of how I treated him, as though he had no role in re-creating an object relationship from his past. His partially developed self had no sense of active agency connected with it—no sense of "I-ness" (Ogden 1986). He was simply buffeted by malevolent forces in his environment. One of the most striking features during the early weeks of the analytic process was the absence of anger (or any other feelings, for that matter) directed toward his previous analyst. Working from the assumption that much of the venom directed toward me was a displacement and actually belonged with the memory of his last analyst, I occasionally would interpret this connection to him. He always reacted with scorn, suggesting that I was trying to "pass the buck" to someone else for my own failings. In his own way, Mr. H may have been tuning in to an attempt on my part to sidestep the heat of the transference by deflecting it elsewhere. When I was confronted with the absence of analytic space, with no gateway to forging a viable working relationship with the patient, I was tempted to develop an alliance by encouraging him to direct his wrath elsewhere. If I had succeeded, I could then have empathized with his hatred toward someone else and, in so doing, attempt to form an alliance around the shared anger toward an "outside enemy."

When, on occasion, I was not regarded as the hated internal object, I would become idealized. This turn of events, however, led him to hate me all the more because of the emergence of his envy. "I see all your books on those shelves, and I feel a sense of loathing towards you. I could never read that many books. I can't ever hope to have the amount of knowledge that you have. I feel like getting up and tearing down all your bookshelves."

As the patient railed against me, he would often lightly pound his fist on the wall adjacent to the couch. He would exert some control over the pounding so that it would stop just short of being a disturbance to the occupant of the office next to mine. I could never be certain, however, and his behavior placed me in a disturbing dilemma. If I did nothing about the pounding, was I colluding with his "acting in" by allowing him to disturb my neighbor? If, on the other hand, I told him to stop the pounding, was I allowing myself to be manipulated by him into a nonanalytic position where he then could rightly see me as attempting to control him? He would also set up other situations that created the feeling that I was damned if I did and damned if I didn't. He would begin a session by asking if I would let him know when the session was half over because he had to leave early. When I pointed out to him that he was wearing a watch and would know when the time was up himself, he would become furious at me for refusing to help him.

Most of all, he would repeatedly try to maneuver me into a corner where I would wittingly or unwittingly imply that I did indeed hate him. The barrage of contempt day in and day out took its toll on me, and I was not always able to contain adequately the patient's projected contents. I would occasionally make sarcastic, contemptuous, or counterattacking comments as I sought to survive in the lion's den that he had created in my office. On one particular day he was accusing me of not empathizing with his point of view. I responded by saying, "You treat me with contempt and then expect me to empathize with you. I wonder if this is part of a larger pattern of expecting others to love and take your side without earning their regard." The patient responded with glee: "So you *do* hate me. I knew I could get you to admit it." On another occasion the following exchange occurred:

Patient: I don't understand why you give me no credit whatsoever for being able to hate you. Don't I get two points for expressing my anger?

Analyst: What do you see as positive about that?

Patient: Because all my life I've suppressed my anger. Now I'm finally getting it off my chest.

Analyst: You're speaking to a side of you that I have not seen. All I've seen is unrelenting hostility.

Patient: Then you must hate me! You can't handle me! I'm too tough! I get a thrill out of triumphing over you and being the only patient of yours that will not get better, that won't change in the way that you want me to.

Mr. H, of course, had made a couple of good points. At times I felt I could not handle him, and at times I certainly did hate him. One of the most distressing aspects of the analysis was that Mr. H appeared completely uninterested in receiving help from me. He confirmed the accuracy of this observation when I pointed out to him that he repeatedly defeated any effort on my part to help him understand himself. His response was explosive. "I don't fucking want your help! I want you as a target! I attempt to provoke you. I have a fantasy of throwing up on your floor or shitting on your couch. I want to rid myself of all this. I hate it when I can't provoke you into taking my anger. Then *I* have to take it. I need a place to dump. I've been using you like a pay toilet."

This outburst helped me to understand how Mr. H conceptualized the analytic process. It was indeed a toilet. It was a place where he could evacuate the bad aspects of himself and his tormenting and hated internal objects. From his point of view, projection of these mental contents was a far superior option to any other alternative. His behavior in the hours made me feel coerced into accepting the role of the hated object that hated him back. I resorted to numerous defensive maneuvers to avoid the role. At times I would withdraw and become more aloof, attempting to retreat into defensive isolation where I would be impervious to his attacks. At other times I would attempt to empathize with his need to hate as his way to survive emotionally. In still other instances I would shore up my occupational reaction formation by attempting to feel loving concern for the poor wretch. When I would shift into this mode, Mr. H would invariably experience me as being less than genuine, not to mention patronizing.

My countertransference loathing of Mr. H reached a

peak when I had a thorny scheduling problem and I asked him if he could change the hour he saw me on Wednesdays. He replied that while he could switch the hour to accommodate my wish, he was choosing not to do so. He said that it was important for him to assert his own rights rather than to allow others to "walk over me." He went on to say that it gave him tremendous pleasure to know that he could control me rather than having me always be the one in charge. His refusal to cooperate left me seething with resentment. I dreaded having to see him day after day, and I found myself wishing that he would quit. I even caught myself daydreaming about what I might do to make him quit.

As fate would have it, I was fortunate to begin a much needed two-week vacation at this point in the analysis. As the vacation neared its completion, I found myself dreading my return to work because I would have to face the unpleasant experience of a fifty-minute hour with Mr. H each day. On the night before I returned, I had the following dream:

> *Mr. H and I were in an analytic session. I was growing increasingly anxious as Mr. H continued to pound the wall next to the couch with ever-increasing intensity. Quite unexpectedly, he turned around, looked at me, then stood up and stared down at me with a defiant grin. I felt frantic that I was unable to control him, and I unleashed my pent-up fury in the form of a lecture shouted at the top of my lungs: "Analysis is for people who can control their impulses and channel them into words. If you can't do that here, if you can't cooperate with what I am trying to do, you should not be in analysis."*

In my associations to the dream, I thought of the many times during the sessions when Mr. H pounded on the wall. I had often wanted to say just those words to him. The dream helped me to understand why I had not. For me to assert the customary expectations of the analytic setting carried with it a risk. Clearly, my unconscious concern was that my intense hatred of Mr. H and my sadistic wishes to control him, so evident in the dream, would show through my efforts to clarify the nature of our task. I realized that my guilt related to these feelings was leading me to feel disempowered as an analyst. In this context I suddenly understood the meaning of my proposal of the hour change on Wednesdays as an *option* rather than as a *decision* that had already been made and with which he was expected to comply. At an unconscious level, I was equating the ordinary power and control inherent in the analytic role with omnipotent control driven by enormous aggression. Hence, my presentation of the change as a choice could be understood as a reaction formation against these powerful wishes within me.

Another insight I gleaned from the dream was that the patient had been serving as a receptacle for that part of me that desperately needed to control him. I could disavow that part of me by thinking that it was *Mr. H* who was driven by the wish to control—not me. My self-analytic work with the dream brought me in touch with the fact that my analytic "work ego" (Fleming 1961) was being eroded by the intensity of the patient's projections. I was starting to share his propensity to view action—not understanding—as the solution.

When we resumed the analysis after the vacation, it was clear that the break had done us both some good. The patient began by commenting that he had been worried ever since the ending of our last session: "I was afraid I'd pushed you into a breakdown where you would destroy furniture and attack me. I try to bait you to take on my characteristics. I hate it when you're calm—then I have to take it back in me. I feel like I want to explode. I want to rip up your office. If I can't be your best patient, maybe I can be your worst. But I'm afraid that I'll drive you crazy."

I had seen occasional glimpses of movement into an analytic space where the capacity for self-observation was present, but always in the context of extratransference relationships where he feared that he would hurt someone on whom he depended. I took advantage of this opening of analytic space and made an interpretation: "The feelings you have inside are unbearable, but if you dump them into me, you fear that you will get well at the expense of my going crazy. This worries you, because after all, feelings of hate are not the only feelings you have toward me."

The patient responded to my interpretation by making the following observation: "If I don't hate you, I feel like a primordial soup that is waiting to be pulled together. I have no identity. I want you to take care of me. I have a pretense of being independent and self-sufficient, but underneath I'm incredibly dependent and needy. I don't feel comfortable having anyone take care of me. I feel diffuse, amorphous, like an amoeba. I feel like being sarcastic with others when I start to feel uncomfortably close."

Changes had occurred on both sides of the analyst–patient dyad. I had recognized my own countertransference need to take action to control an analytic situation that was getting out of hand. In part, I was responding to a projective identification of the patient, but I was also reacting to my own anxiety in the face of a situation where I had very little control and where I felt de-skilled as an analyst because of my guilt related to my feelings of hate. On the patient's side of the dyad, a sequestered object relationship involving a concerned self-representation (with the capacity to love) and a loved object-representation (with the capacity to be hurt) had surfaced. It is possible that the patient's perception of my anger and hatred at his refusal to change the appointment time prompted the emergence of the other side of him, accompanied by depressive anxieties as the hating and loving sides of him were juxtaposed. He was also able to acknowledge the organizing effect of hate on his own sense of identity. In its absence, he felt amorphous. My interpretive effort to connect split-off aspects of himself further enhanced his capacity to look at what lay beneath the hate.

As the analysis proceeded, the patient continued to operate predominantly in a paranoid-schizoid mode. However, with each foray into depressive concerns, there was usually an associated opening of analytic space. At these moments, I would make interpretive connections for the patient that he could use to further his developing reflectiveness. When the time was right, for example, I was able to interpret that his reluctance to change the hour was connected with his fear that I would replace him with someone else. I suggested to him that he had therefore been hurt by my proposal of a schedule change. He responded with a tearful observation that he'd never heard me acknowledge his proneness to feel hurt. He went on to say that no one had recognized his pain in the past. Building on my observation that he feared being replaced, he told me that his worst fear was that after termination I would not remember him. He imagined that he would call me on the phone many years after the analysis and I would not know who he was. This confession provided an opening for me to interpret the role of hate in maintaining connectedness and avoiding abandonment. As long as he continued to hate me, he knew that I would not see him as ready for termination and could not possibly forget him.

The opening of analytic space in the process also allowed the patient to bring in genetic material that he had scrupulously avoided throughout the analysis. He spoke of his rage at his father for leaving him and his mother when the patient was only 2. He spoke of a wish to take revenge against his father but also the fear that he had driven him off with his hatred. He was soon able to link his attempts to coerce me into controlling him with an earlier wish that his father had been present to control his powerful oedipal longings toward his mother. He also had a firm conviction that his mother was indifferent to him. He recalled numerous instances when he would act up as a way of trying to evoke a response from his mother. As an adolescent he would come home drunk at night and wake her up to be sure she was aware of his drinking. He felt that even such drastic efforts were often unsuccessful, and he went through life behaving in such a way that others could not avoid being affected by him.

At the time of his successful termination, the patient experienced a resurgence of hate toward me because I would not stop him from terminating. The only way he could experience caring from others, he realized, was through their efforts to control him. If I did not stop him from terminating, I obviously did not care about him. He came to see that his hatred served to mask feelings of grief at the prospect of losing me. He made numerous reparative efforts during the last months of analysis, letting me know that he was embarrassed about the things he had said to me and about the way he had treated me. He was also able to let me know that the analysis had allowed him to grow up and experience gratitude in addition to hatred.

DISCUSSION

In my work with Mr. H, I often thought of a piece of advice I had once heard regarding what to do when one encounters an angry grizzly bear in the wilderness. According to wilderness lore, one should neither charge the bear in a counterattacking posture that is designed to drive him off nor run away from the bear out of fear. If one simply stands one's ground, the bear will usually drop his threat of attack and go elsewhere. While I have so far had the good fortune to avoid having to test the soundness of that advice, it seems to me that one can think about the technical problems of handling transference hate in an analogous way. One must walk a fine line between the temptation to counterattack and the urge to retreat into aloof disengagement. Rather, one must be a durable object who holds one's ground and attempts to contain and understand that which is being projected.

This strategy is difficult to sustain because powerful feelings of hatred, by their nature, impel one to action rather than reflection (Heimann 1950). The action chosen may include the use of interpretation as a weapon of counterattack—an attempt to put the patient in his place or suppress his hostility. These interpretations are also frequently an attempt to unload the hateful self- or object-representation projected into the analyst. However, it is usually an error of technique to return the projected parts of the patient prematurely via interpretation (Carpy 1989, Epstein 1977, 1979, Grotstein 1982, Ogden 1982, 1986, Rosenfeld 1987, Searles 1986, Sherby 1989). As in the case of Mr. H, the patient needs to keep the hateful object- or self-representation in the analyst because he is unable to integrate it within himself. Moreover, if the analyst cannot tolerate the transference role to which he has been assigned because of the unpleasant nature of the projected introject, how can he reasonably expect the patient to tolerate it? Searles (1986) warned that when the analyst tries to force the introject back into the patient through premature interpretation, there is an implied denial of any basis in reality for the patient's transference perception of the analyst. It is as though the analyst is saying to the patient: "Hate resides only in you, not in me."

In the Menninger Treatment Interventions Project (Gabbard et al. 1994, Horwitz et al. 1996), we studied the transcripts of the audiotaped psychotherapy of three borderline patients in long-term psychoanalytic psychotherapy. Two teams of researchers tracked the linkages between the therapist interventions and the resulting shifts in the patient's ability to collaborate with the therapist. Premature transference interpretation of the patient's hate and aggression resulted in deterioration of the alliance (as measured by the ability to collaborate with the therapist) in those borderline patients who had experienced childhood trauma. These patients felt misunderstood because the therapist was not appreciating the fact that real external trauma had occurred and that they were expecting further mistreatment at the hands of a therapist.

There are other compelling reasons to avoid premature interpretation of projected aspects of the patient. Unless the analyst has sat with the projected material and subjected it to the metabolizing, detoxifying process of containment (Bion 1962b), he will be returning it in the same form in which it was delivered. In its most extreme form, this variant of countertransference acting out may be as dramatic as the case of the young therapist described by Altschul (1979), who grew so exasperated at his borderline patient that he screamed "I hate you" over the telephone. While such eruptions of "countertransference psychosis" by a psychotherapist may seem unusual, I have observed them with some regularity among hospital staff engaged in the inpatient treatment of borderline patients. In these cases, the treater has been taken over by the patient's projection, and the patient's inability to integrate good and bad elements of self and object are re-created in the clinician (Altschul 1979). In the moment of countertransference acting out, the analyst, like the patient, sees action—extrusion or destruction of the "bad object"—as the only solution to the intolerable feelings of hatred within.

My hatred of Mr. H and my wish that he would quit the analysis prior to the two-week break was a re-creation of the patient's object world within my own mind. Getting rid of the patient seemed to be the only solution to my tormented internal state. My interventions were not particularly effective at that point in the analysis, and there was more than a kernel of reality in the patient's perception that I hated him and was having difficulty handling him. As Gorney (1979) has noted, when the patient's entire effort is to transform the analyst into a bad object, there may be a real erosion of the analyst's technical competence as he reacts in a role-responsive manner by becoming "bad" in his choice of interventions and their timing. Both the analytic work ego (Fleming 1961) and the necessary split between the observing and experiencing aspects of the analyst's ego (Kris 1956) are compromised by the powerful projective identification process that accompanies the malignant form of transference hate. Fortunately, my self-analytic work and the actual break in the analysis gave me the necessary distance to get back on track with Mr. H.

These considerations lead us to two crucial points in this discussion. The first is that analysts themselves may lose their own sense of analytic space and find it collapsing into a paranoid-schizoid mode of experience in which ill-advised action seems to be the only way of surviving. In the process of projective identification, the patient's lack of self-reflective function may be deposited in the analyst so that the analyst temporarily experiences the same incapacity as the patient. The second point is that interpretive work tends to be most effective when both patient and analyst are coexisting in an analytic space (i.e., both are functioning in a mode in which reflective observation is possible). From these two critical points it follows that long periods of containment that gradually allow for interpretation may be necessary to facilitate the convergence of patient and analyst in an analytic space.

Numerous authors (Boyer 1986, 1989, Buie and Adler 1982, Carpy 1989, Chessick 1977, Epstein 1979, Gabbard 1989a, Giovacchini 1975, Grotstein 1982, Little 1966, Searles 1986, Sherby 1989) have focused on the centrality of containment in the treatment of severely disturbed patients. There is a broad consensus among these authors that (1) verbal interpretations may fall on deaf ears when the patient is harboring intense negative feelings toward the analyst, (2) a new set of experiences with a new object is necessary before the patient can accept interpretive interventions, and (3) the traditional role of the analyst as a neutral observer who delivers occasional interpretations from a position of evenly suspended attention is not an adequate characterization of the requirements for the analytic treatment of more disturbed patients.

In the transcript of the psychotherapy processes studied in the Menninger Treatment Interventions Project (Gabbard et al. 1994), we consistently found a characteristic pattern of effective interpretation. A number of supportive interventions often paved the way for a transference interpretation that the patient could then hear and upon which he or she could reflect. By asking questions, clarifying the content of what one is hearing, and facilitating further expansion, the analyst creates a climate in which interpretation will be accepted.

It would be erroneous to view containment as inferior to interpretation in terms of its therapeutic potential. It is a critically important ingredient in projective identification, which is the main mode of communication in the paranoid-schizoid mode and the principal method by which self- and object-representations are modified (Gabbard 1989b, Grotstein 1981, Ogden 1986). Through the processes of metabolizing and detoxifying (Bion 1962b, Boyer 1986), the patient's projections are modified and transformed in such a way that the patient can more readily reintroject them. As a modified internal object is reintrojected by the patient, the corresponding self-representation is similarly modified in keeping with the changes in the internal object.

Containment should not be equated with a kind of passive inaction (Rosenfeld 1987). Nor should it be understood as a masochistic enduring of the patient's contemptuous attacks (Ogden 1982). It involves silent processing, but it also entails verbal clarifications of what is going on inside the patient and what is transpiring in the patient–analyst dyad. In addition, containment implies a number of other processes (Gabbard 1989a), including the identification of feeling states within the analyst, the diagnosis of the patient's internal object relations based on how they are played out in the analytic dyad through projective identification, an ongoing self-analytic process that seeks to delineate the analyst's own contributions to the struggles with the patient, the associative search for linkages between the disparate projected aspects of the patient, and the silent interpretation of what is going on inside the patient in preparation for later verbal interpretation.

As described in the treatment of Mr. H, part of the analyst's task is to trace his own defensive maneuvers as he seeks to avoid hating the patient. Hate in the patient evokes hate in the analyst (Epstein 1977), but it also tends to produce denial of hate. As Winnicott (1949) stressed, the analyst must not deny that hate actually exists within himself and that he actually hates the patient. The patient will only be able to tolerate his own hate if the analyst can hate him. In this regard my sarcasm-tinged confrontations of Mr. H, which I viewed as countertransference-related "mistakes," may have been useful in some way to the patient. In clinical discussions, it is often asked if an analyst can treat a patient he does not like. A more relevant question in the case of patients with malignant hate is whether the analyst can treat a patient he does not hate. Epstein (1977) noted that the analyst's most frequent error is to react to projections of hatred by attempting to be "all good." This deprives the patient of his primary defensive mode of projectively disavowing hatred and seeing it in the analyst instead of in himself.

Another defensive tendency that should come under scrutiny during the containment process is the temptation to collude with the patient's splitting by focusing only on the good or loving aspects of the patient (Kernberg 1984). As described in the treatment of Mr. H, one variant in this defensive posture is to encourage the displacement of hate onto an extratransference figure so the analyst can develop a therapeutic alliance based on the extrusion of hate and badness from the analyst–patient relationship.

A crucial turning point in the analysis of Mr. H was my discovery that his perception of me as a punitive figure invested in asserting omnipotent control over him was not entirely his own distortion. On the contrary, it resonated with actual wishes to control him that I was harboring within. Another defensive operation requiring monitoring during the containment process is the analyst's tendency to act as if the patient's perception is entirely a distortion, leading to a disavowal of all responsibility and a projection into the patient of qualities that actually reside in the analyst as well. In this context, Searles (1986) made the following observation:

> It is essential that the analyst acknowledge to himself that even the patient's most severe psychopathology has some counterpart, perhaps relatively small by comparison but by no means insignificant, in his own *real* personality functioning. We cannot help the borderline patient, for example, to become well if we are trying unwittingly to use him as the receptacle for our own most deeply unwanted personality components, and trying essentially to require him to bear the burden of all the severe psychopathology, in the whole relationship. [p. 22]

The analyst must walk a fine line between blasting the patient with his own hatred and denying its very existence. After hatred and anger are processed and metabolized through the containment process, they can be more constructively expressed in a way that is useful to the patient (Epstein 1977, Searles 1986, Sherby 1989). Moreover, the tolerating of intense feelings in and of itself may produce change in the patient (Carpy 1989).

During the months prior to the two-week break in the analysis of Mr. H, the patient bore witness to my numerous struggles to maintain an analytic posture in the context of his using me as a "toilet" for his unacceptable parts. My struggles were manifested in my countertrans ference enactments, in which I made sarcastic comments, withdrew into aloof silences, demonstrated by my guilt-ridden reluctance to enforce the schedule change I proposed for fear that it would betray my aggressive feelings, and attempted to transcend my hatred by assuming a saintly position vis-à-vis the patient. As Carpy (1989) noted, the patient's observation of his analyst's attempts to deal with feelings regarded as intolerable by the patient makes these feelings somewhat more tolerable and accessible for reintrojection. Projective identification begins as an attempt to destroy links between the patient and his feelings because the feelings are unbearable. Observing the analyst's capacity to bear those same feelings restores the linkages. Mr. H, for example, began to "re-own" some of the feelings he observed in me with the comment, "I try to bait you to take on my characteristics. I hate it when you're calm—then I have to take it back in me."

One other aspect of containment is the message conveyed to the patient that the analyst is a durable, persistent object that is not destroyed by the patient's attacks. Winnicott (1968) felt that the analyst's survival of the borderline patient's destructive attacks is a crucial element in helping the patient to make use of the analyst as a truly external figure outside the patient's omnipotent control. He drew a developmental analogy in this regard by noting that the mother must survive the primitive attacks of the infant for the child to proceed with development and maturation. Winnicott stressed that in both situations survival means avoiding retaliation, and he specifically cautioned against using interpretation in the midst of attacks by the patient. He viewed interpretive interventions as dangerous under such circumstances and suggested that the analyst would do better to wait until the destructive phase is over, at which point the analyst can discuss with the patient what transpired during the attacks.

To get to the most primitive transference issues, one often has to go to the brink of despair with the patient, where one questions whether or not he can continue and whether or not he is being effective as an analyst. As the case of Mr. H illustrates, the pivotal breakthrough occurred only after I reached the point of wishing that the patient would quit. In commenting on destructive transferences, Bird (1972) noted: "This dark and ominous time, when both patient and analyst are about ready to call it quits, is, according to my thesis, perhaps the only kind of transference in which the patient's most deeply destructive impulses may be analyzable" (p. 296).

Finally, as the analyst contains the many feelings arising within the patient and within himself, he will begin to become aware of the multiple functions of hate in the transference. Brenner (1982) has pointed out that while one can speak about positive or negative manifestations of transference feelings, transference as a whole is always ambivalent. Just as erotized transference may conceal enormous aggression toward the analyst, hateful transferences may conceal longings for love and acceptance. Mr. H was finally able to reveal that he had established an intense dependency on me and wished to preserve some form of connectedness to me through his hating.

In Chapter 2, I noted Bollas's (1987) term *loving hate* as an example of how some individuals bind others to them with intensely hateful feelings. Mr. H, for example, lived with a dread of indifference, the kind of nonresponsiveness that he had experienced with his mother. Only through hate could he coerce objects in his environment into passionate involvement with him. Only then did he feel alive and connected.

In a subsequent communication, Bollas (1994) noted that some patients have no confidence that they can use the analytic object to develop their own erotic self-narrative and thus attack the object in hopes of dislodging the analyst from a neutral stance. They may feel that if the analyst actually responds to such attacks, they have finally gained access to the real person of the analyst and thus feel they have broken through the analytic barrier with hate. This breakthrough may then enable them to feel connected in an erotic way.

Other functions of hate became apparent as well in the analysis of Mr. H, including its organizing effect on his amorphous sense of identity, its role in defending against grief, and its defensive function in the service of dealing with envy. Many of these functions that are mentally noted while containing may subsequently be interpreted.

The postponement of interpretation in the analysis of the malignantly hateful patient is required for several reasons. First and foremost, the patient is unlikely to be capable of making use of interpretation early in the analysis. Interpretations will be experienced as confirmation that the analyst is like everyone else—a persecutor attempting to attack or victimize the patient.

The analyst needs to wait before he interprets for his own reasons as well. It is imperative that he has a preliminary understanding of his own countertransference and has processed the patient's projections sufficiently so that he has restored his own analytic space. Only then can he be therapeutic with his interventions. Bollas (1990) has aptly noted: "And as some psychotic patients sponsor the regressions in the analyst, rather than within themselves, analysts will endure regressive episodes from which they recover through time, patience, and reflective work. When this is so, analytic insight and

interpretation are in the first place curative for the analyst, who gets better first" (p. 352).

When the analyst has accomplished this self-curative
task, he needs to wait patiently for a signal from the
patient that he is accessible to interpretation. This readiness will be indicated by evidence of the development of
a sense of "I-ness," where a mediating subject is present,
an observer who views feelings and thoughts as intrapsychic creations rather than incontrovertible factual perceptions (Ogden 1986).

When Mr. H made comments such as, "I hate it when I
can't provoke you into taking my anger," or "I try to bait
you to take on my characteristics," he was indicating
some opening of analytic space. He was thinking symbolically about what was happening in the analyst—
patient relationship (i.e., he was distinguishing between
symbol and symbolized). When he expressed open concern that he might drive me crazy, he had clearly arrived
at the depressive position and its associated anxiety that
he might harm someone he had grown to care about. He
had begun to think about what he was doing to me as
analogous to the climactic scene in William Friedkin's
1974 classic horror film, *The Exorcist*, where the demon
possessing the little girl leaves her and enters the
psychiatrist-priest, leading him to plummet to his death.
Mr. H felt he could only get over his "madness" at the cost
of driving me mad. Carpy (1989), who also has advocated
the postponement of interpretation, pointed out that the
patient is capable of using the interpretation only when
he can recognize aspects of himself in the analyst.

When the split-off and sequestered aspect of the patient's self-containing feelings of love and concern finally
surfaces, the analyst's task is to reconnect the split parts
through interpretation (Gabbard 1989b, Kernberg 1984). I
pointed out to Mr. H, for example, that his hatred coex-

isted with feelings of concern for me. The integration of the loving and hating aspects of the self will be threatening at first, and the patient will continue to revert to hate. Resistance to integration or, for that matter, change of any kind can be related to a host of factors (Gabbard 1989a):

1. The denigration of others prevents the patient from being aware of painful feelings of envy.
2. The refusal to link up more positive representations with the negative, hateful representations prevents the loving aspects of self and object from being contaminated and destroyed by the influences of hate. There is a pervasive attack on linkages to good objects in the environment as well as internal linkages between good and bad self-representations and between good and bad object-representations (Bion 1959, Grinberg et al. 1977, Grotstein 1981).
3. The fantasy of revenge may be the greatest pleasure of all to the patient, and to give up the hate may carry with it the loss of the revenge fantasy.
4. As implied before, the patient's identity may be organized around hatred, and the modification of the hating self-representation or of the hated object-representation is often experienced as a form of annihilation.
5. The patient may preserve a sense of meaning by hating, and change may cause the patient to confront a sense of living in a meaningless state.
6. A hateful relationship is better than none at all, and a modification of the patient's internal object relations may be experienced as the loss of any sense of connectedness to both external and internal objects. Hence, resistance to change may also be understood as an avoidance of separation anxiety.

Some or all of these resistance factors may have been noted during periods of containment. Those observations made while containing the hate may then be brought forth through interpretation because the patient can acknowledge the existence of unconscious determinants. In the case of Mr. H, I was able to help him see the role of hate in avoiding feelings of abandonment and loss. The function of hate in reducing envy may also be interpreted, but only with caution. Too often such interpretations are experienced as "put-downs." The analyst is likely to get further by focusing on how the shame and pain of envy prevent the patient from expressing his full capacity to love (Rosenfeld 1987). The feeling of being accepted by the analyst for what one is may in and of itself do more to reduce envy than excessive interpretive activity.

With each interpretation that connects the islands of love with the hateful core of the patient, the patient gains a greater sense of subjective agency. A different mode of analytic work is now within the patient's grasp as a result of his entering and sustaining an analytic space. As Ogden (1989) has observed, one result of analysis is that the patient will begin to feel understood and will begin to regard the analyst as someone who is capable of concern as well as hate.

The goal of termination with these patients is not to eradicate their hate, only to temper it with love. At the end of the analysis of Mr. H, he still hated me and told me so. He hated me for letting him grow up and leave. But he also told me that I was the first person who'd ever really listened to him and that he would miss me. I also harbored feelings of hate toward him and was relieved by his departure. Yet I had many other feelings as well. I would miss him, too.

Altman (1977) has conjectured that analysts tend to place an excessive emphasis on love because of their need to disown hate. He cautioned that love is not a cure-all and that the experience of love would give us greater pleasure if we did not use it primarily to mask underlying hate. He even suggested that the more openly we allow ourselves to hate, the more completely we might be able to love. In Chapter 2, I identified eight different reasons that analysts might hate their patients from the word "go." This preexisting subjectivity will then be acted on as analysts immerse themselves in the malignant transference hatred of the patient described in this chapter, and all the preexisting reasons for hating the patient will be exacerbated and intensified because of the patient's overt contempt. In the eye of this tempest, it is useful for the analyst to remember Altman's words of wisdom and know that the patient, too, may be finding a way to love through open expressions of hate. Perhaps there is even a sense of hope in malignant transference hate in that the patient is hoping the analyst can tolerate being a "bad enough object" until the patient can risk the realm of love and tenderness.

8   PASSIVE HATE IN THE TRANSFERENCE

> There is room for the idea that significant relating
> and communicating is silent.
>
> —D. W. Winnicott

It is the psychoanalyst's lot in life to endure prolonged silences in the course of his practice. Much has been written about the optimal technical approach to periods of silence in the resistant neurotic patient. As these patients are generally amenable to verbal interventions, a variety of interpretations, confrontations, and inquiries have been advocated and used with varying degrees of success. Since the neurotic patient is ordinarily capable of forming a therapeutic alliance with the analyst in pursuit of a common goal (i.e., analyzing the resistance), such silences are often relatively short lived.

Much less has been written about the more seriously disturbed patient who torments those who attempt to help him. Through noncooperation, these patients express their hate passively and silently. In long-term psychoanalytic hospital work, one not uncommonly encounters personality-disordered patients who systematically defeat all treatment efforts. While some employ noisy splitting maneuvers for this purpose (Gabbard 1986), others use passive, silent resistance. These latter patients do not sign themselves out of the hospital, yet they seem incapable of developing an alliance with those who seek to help them. In the most refractory cases, the analyst may feel like he is "doing nothing" for protracted periods of time while the patient refuses to collaborate in the analytic task. Verbal interventions may simply intensify the patient's commitment to thwart the analyst and result in more intense passivity.

The analyst who is confronted with these circumstances must devise strategies to persevere in the face of the slings and arrows of outrageous resistance. How does one endure the monotony? The assault on one's therapeutic effectiveness? The helplessness? The frustration? The hatred of one's tormentor? The wish to give up?

The analyst's systematic understanding of the here-and-now transference-countertransference situation may enable him to survive such adverse developments. In the most optimistic scenario, it may even lead to a breakthrough of the stalemate. In actual fact, of course, the analyst is not "doing nothing," as it might appear to the naive observer. On the contrary, with the help of his own associative train of thought and his knowledge of theory, he actively seeks to understand the patient's silence and the vicissitudes of the internal object relations that lie behind it.

THEORETICAL AND TECHNICAL CONSIDERATIONS

All considerations of theory and technique with the silently resistant, hateful patient must follow from one basic assumption: a relationship is always present, even in the absence of verbalization. Moreover, the presence of a relationship between patient and analyst implies that there are transference and countertransference elements to be understood and analyzed. As Rangell (1982) has observed, Freud's assertion that patients suffering from "narcissistic neuroses" do not form transferences is one of his few clinical observations that has not been validated by subsequent analytic experience. The apparent absence of transference *is* the transference (Brenner 1982). One component of "doing nothing," then, is the analyst's systematic examination of the vicissitudes of transference and countertransference, even if conducted in total silence. As the analyst sits in the stillness of the consulting room, he ponders the question, "What object relationship paradigms from the past are being repeated in the present?"

With the primitively organized hateful patient, transference and countertransference are best understood as externalizations of internal object relations (Ogden 1983). Via projective identification, the analyst is the recipient of both the patient's internal object-representations and his internal self-representations. A number of authors (Bion 1967, Grotstein 1981, Heimann 1950, Malin and Grotstein 1966, Ogden 1982) have written about the therapeutic processing of these projective identifications. One of the principal functions of the analyst is to serve as a container for the self- and object-representations, as well as the affects connected with them, that are projected into the analyst by the patient. Bion (1967) linked his model of the "container-contained" to his understanding of the developmental process of the infant, who projects the unwanted aspects of his internal world (the contained) into the breast-mother, who serves as a container. The mother holds and processes the projected elements and returns them in modified and detoxified form to the infant. In a similar manner the analyst contains and modifies the patient's projections before the patient reintrojects them. In both the original developmental situation and the later therapeutic one, the result is growth and integration of one's internal self- and object-representations.

As I stressed in both Chapters 3 and 4, however, the analyst is not simply a blank screen or a container without contents of its own. The projective identification process works both ways, especially in cases of refractory silent patients, where the patient becomes a container for the analyst's projections. This aspect of treatment is stunningly portrayed in Bergman's *Persona*, where a nurse is given responsibility for a patient who has become completely mute. The absence of verbal information from the patient makes her an ideal repository for the projections of the nurse-therapist, who becomes increasingly out of control as she treats her patient as if she were an embodiment of her own (the nurse's) internal objects. Searles (1975) similarly noted that the patient attempts to treat the analyst by becoming what the analyst wants him to be, and he links these efforts to the infant's need to "cure" the mother.

The form of silent mental processing that is being advocated here requires an openness or receptivity to the patient's projections. The analyst must retain enough reflectiveness to observe what is happening to him while he is experiencing the powerful affects associated with the projected contents. In a similar vein, one must monitor what one projects into the patient. The analyst may not be able to process and understand the projective identifications until after he has been "coerced" by the patient into playing a role in the patient's internal drama. The analyst's task is to keep this role-playing in the realm of a feeling state or a partial enactment. The feeling of wanting to strike the patient, for example, may lead to a recognition of projective identification, which in turn leads to a processing of the interaction that heads off an actual striking out by the patient.

After the analyst has recognized his collusion in the object world of the patient, he may wish to return the projection to the patient via interpretation. More often, however, with the recalcitrant, hostile patient, who has sworn an oath of silence, the interpretation will only heighten the resistance. Hence, the analyst must silently note his observation, formulate the interaction in his own mind, and allow the understanding to inform his subsequent interaction with the patient. The analyst's task is succinctly summed up by Ogden (1982):

> The perspective of projective identification neither requires nor excludes the use of verbal interpretations; the therapist attempts to find a way of talking with and being with the patient that will constitute a medium through which the therapist may accept unintegratable aspects of the patient's internal object world and return them to the patient in a form that the patient can accept and learn from. [p. 42]

Quite apart from any interpretive efforts, then, the analyst's response to the projections provides a new object and affect for internalization by the patient. In this regard he breaks the repetitive cycle of pathological object relations that has characterized the patient's life. These patterns originated in early relationships with parental figures—what Epstein (1979) has referred to as primary maturational failure. The patient evokes similar reactions in his adult life, and these can be labelled *secondary* maturational failures. The reactions of others to the patient so consistently fit this pattern that he rarely experiences a maturationally corrective response. Epstein has suggested that the analyst's strategy is to figure out a way to be with the patient that *is* maturationally corrective. In other words, the analyst attempts to provide a relationship in which he or she does *not* respond to the patient's projections like everyone else and therefore avoids another *secondary* maturational failure. Obviously, this strategy is a goal that follows numerous instances of responding *like* objects from the patient's past.

One final theoretical point comes from Winnicott's (1963) observations regarding the need not to communicate: "There is an intermediate stage in healthy development in which the patient's most important experience in relation to the good or potentially satisfying object is the refusal of it" (p. 182). He asserted that at the core of the true self in all of us is a segment that must remain incommunicado. This isolation preserves an authenticity that is sacred to the evolving self. Winnicott insisted that our technique must accommodate the patient who is communicating to us that he is not communicating. Being "alone," yet in the presence of the analyst, may fulfill an important developmental need that the analyst should not violate by bombarding the patient with interpretations. Winnicott noted that a lengthy period of silence may be the most therapeutic experience for certain patients, and the analyst who patiently waits may be more helpful than one who insists on verbal communication.

Winnicott's technical recommendations grow out of his theoretical understanding of an important transition in the infant's internal object world. The maternal object is originally perceived by the infant as a *subjective* phenomenon, an extension of the infant. As a result of development, the subjective object is transformed into an *objective* object, one that is partly created by the infant and partly the by-product of the infant's increasing attunement with external reality. Explicit communication is a requirement for the objective object but is entirely unnecessary when relating to the subjective object. In Winnicott's view, overt communication always runs the risk of creating a false self that merely complies with the demands of the object. When this lack of authenticity begins to disturb the developing child, he retreats into silent communication with the subjective object as a way of restoring a sense of a true and real self. Hence, Winnicott postulated that there is a fundamental split in the self: One part communicates explicitly with objective objects, while another communicates silently with subjective objects. The latter aspect of the self must be respected and validated for healthy development to proceed.

THE CASE OF JOHN

A fragment of an actual analysis may be helpful in illustrating these theoretical and technical points as they apply to prolonged periods when the analyst is apparently doing nothing. John was an 18-year-old young man who came to the Menninger Hospital after defeating all previous treatment experiences. He had failed to graduate from high school despite above average intelligence and numerous tutorial sessions, and he had been fired from several jobs. His academic and vocational endeavors were torpedoed largely because of his refusal to get out of bed. On the numerous mornings when John stayed in bed, his father would typically return home from work and scream at him to get up and get dressed. These coercive efforts culminated in his father's attempts to physically lift John out of bed and dress him. As John tipped the scales at around 240 pounds, all such heroic efforts were doomed to failure.

On a typical day, John would rise late in the afternoon and go to the tennis courts, where he apparently distinguished himself and won several tournaments. Other areas of poor impulse control, however, caused the family a good deal of distress. On two occasions, John had disappeared for days with the family station wagon; on another, he had impulsively stolen a car. Outpatient psychotherapy had been unsuccessful because John had refused to attend the sessions. After a girlfriend jilted him, he made an impulsive suicide attempt and ended up in a hospital near his home. There he stayed in bed until 5 P.M. every day and refused to participate in any of the treatment activities. His psychiatrist finally referred him to the Menninger Hospital, and he indicated in his referral that all his efforts to force John to talk during therapy sessions had been for naught.

When he arrived at the Menninger Hospital, John voluntarily signed himself into the institution and seemed motivated to overcome his inability to "follow through on commitments." A thorough diagnostic evaluation revealed no signs of psychosis or major depression. The social worker assigned to the case described John's mother as intrusive and overinvolved. His father came across as demanding and authoritarian. Psychological testing revealed borderline ego functioning and paranoid-schizoid tendencies. He seemed incapable of conceptualizing his internal experience, so he resorted to communication through action. Specifically, the testing suggested that when he felt forced to submit to what he perceived as unrealistic expectations, he became resentful and enraged. He responded to these unacceptable feelings by retreating into a passive, withdrawn state of silence.

During the first few preparatory sessions of his analytic work with me, he talked openly about his history and his wish to turn his life around. He failed to show up for his fourth session, and the unit staff called to inform me that he would not get out of bed. When he did not attend the next session, I went to his hospital room as was the common practice at that time. John was lying in bed, clearly awake, but with his eyes closed, feigning sleep. In a rather calm tone of voice, I asked him to get out of bed and come to my office. I informed him that I could not help him accomplish his goal of turning his life around if he would not come to my office and talk with me. My statements were met, of course, with stony silence. I advised him that he was repeating his pattern here and asked him if that was really what he wanted to do. More silence. I felt myself becoming increasingly irritated, and as I stood at his bedside, I had a conscious fantasy of pulling him out of bed and forcing him to sit up and talk to me. I sat down in his desk chair and joined him in silence. I reflected on how surprised I was by the intensity of my anger. Since patients typically repeat their family situations in the hospital, I should have taken this repetition as a matter of course.

I continued to sit in John's room for a few more sessions. As my anger subsided, I realized how utterly powerless and helpless I felt in my attempts to get through to John and find a way to communicate with him. Although it was premature to offer interpretations, I nevertheless asked periodic questions regarding the function of his silence, all of which were met with unwavering quiet. When I heard from a nurse that he arose in the evening and played cards with his peers, I was again irritated. I asked him why he could get up to play cards but could not get up for our sessions. No response. As I left his room at the end of one session, a nurse informed me that he had hung up on his parents the night before when they asked him why he would not get out of bed.

As I sat with John the following day, I reflected further on the internal object relations that were being played out in the stark silence of his room. I had responded to John's passive resistance much as his father had. I unconsciously identified with the projected internal object characterized by an angry demanding expectation that he should do what I wanted him to do. My reaction occurred in muted form as compared with his father's, but I could certainly empathize with that more extreme reaction. My anger regarding his selective interest in getting up to play cards undoubtedly paralleled his father's anger about his ability to get up for tennis but not for school. The information from the nurse about the phone call helped me understand that the more I expected him to conform to my expectations, the more he would withdraw.

I spent several more sessions silently associating and interpreting to myself the various meanings of the interaction between John and me. I continued to experience alternating feelings of anger and helplessness. It was extraordinarily useful for me to contain and process these feelings for a number of sessions without attempting to force the projections back into John. Such interventions would have been experienced as an intrusion or violation of John's privacy and his right not to communicate in a verbal mode. Moreover, containing the feelings allowed me to make further connections to John's own internal object relations. For example, when I felt strongly that I wanted to "unload" some of the feelings back onto the patient with a verbal barrage, I sensed also that I was very likely identifying with the same projected internal object derived from the intrusive and overinvolved mother. On the other hand, in those moments when I felt most helpless and powerless, it became clear that I was identifying with an aspect of John's self-experience. John *was* communicating to me. He was letting me know how it felt to be powerless and helpless, as he so often did.

As my attention ebbed and flowed during those many hours of silence, I noted how strongly invested I was, at least at times, in making John talk. Although at some level I was undoubtedly identifying with the demanding father, I associated to my own need to change John as a representation of an object in my own intrapsychic world. This object-representation of mine, which was undoubtedly influenced by parental figures in my childhood, had been externalized in this analytic process because it paralleled in many ways the interaction between John and his father. My own tendency to expect John to conform to my wishes provided a kernel of reality (Ogden 1982) onto which John could conveniently project his demanding internal object associated with his father.

I realized that as long as I conformed to the demanding father, I would not be providing a potentially therapeutic or corrective experience for John and we would be at a stalemate. Even as I sat silently, I was nevertheless expecting something from him; I was clearly not content for him to be silent. To disengage from the expectation that he should talk would also be to disengage from a pathological and repetitive projective identification process involving a demanding object-representation and a recalcitrant and oppositional self-representation. Following Searles's (1965) recommendation regarding periods of silence in treatment of schizophrenic patients, I began bringing reading material to the sessions. At the beginning of each hour, I explained to John that I was going to read during our time together but told him that I would be happy to put down my reading at any time if he wished to discuss anything with me; however, I would be equally content to pass the time with him in silence.

I began this practice after approximately one month of silence. I continued to read and pass the sessions in silence for nearly three more months. As I became absorbed in my reading over a period of time, I realized that I had successfully disengaged from my wish to make John talk. I was content to allow him his private, quiet space while I occupied myself with my own interests. In the third month of this arrangement, an evening nurse informed me that John was getting quite angry at me because he felt I was "treating him like a baby" by sitting with him in his room every day. The astute nurse replied that if he truly disliked what was going on, all he had to do was get up and come to my office each morning for our sessions.

Shortly thereafter, I was shocked to leave my office one morning on the way to the hospital unit only to find John sitting in the waiting room outside my office. I shall never forget the gleeful, triumphant look on his face when he saw my surprise. I invited him into my office, where we continued the analysis from that point on. Although he was not sure why he had decided to get up and come to my office, it was clear to me that my disengagement from the projective identification process and the restoration of an analytic space where I could think my own thoughts had allowed John to take back his anger and hate and begin to own them as aspects of himself. He was then able to use them constructively to motivate himself for treatment. Throughout the rest of hospital stay, he continued to get up at 8 A.M. every morning and participate in all the treatment activities and in his analysis.

DISCUSSION

Psychoanalysis may be characterized as much by what the analyst does not do as by what he does. The decision not to make any verbal interventions may be the most therapeutically effective strategy with which to approach the refractory silent patient. The case of John illustrates Ogden's (1982) point that psychoanalytic work does not need to be interpretive to be considered psychoanalytic. A systematic examination of the months of silence already described allows us to enumerate a number of significant intrapsychic and interpersonal phenomena that transpired during a period where the analyst to all outward appearances seemed to be doing nothing:

1. *Diagnosis of the patient's internal object relations.* By serving as a container for the patient's projective identification, I was able to formulate a tentative diagnostic understanding of the patient's internal world. At various times, I identified with: a demanding, coercive object-representation (most often associated with father); a violating, intrusive object-representation (most often associated with mother); and a helpless and powerless self-representation. Obviously, an intimate knowledge of the patient's internal object relations helps the analyst gain a greater understanding of the patient's pathological interpersonal relations as well.

2. *Self-analysis.* As I contained various projections from the patient, I also made associative linkages to my own internal object- and self-representations. This form of self-analysis enabled me to clarify certain aspects of the analytic interaction in which I was using the patient as a container for my own projections and thus enacting repetitive interactions from my own life. The restoration of analytic space and the capacity to think one's own thoughts is just as crucial to the self-analytic task as it is to the analysis of the patient.

3. *Disengagement from the projective identification process.* My processing of the patient's projected contents enabled me to avoid behaving like a projected aspect of the patient's internal world. Instead of responding in a manner that Grinberg (1979b) referred to as projective counteridentification (i.e., as a demanding internal object to the patient's passive resistant self), I was able to

provide a maturationally corrective experience. In Epstein's (1979) terms, I was able to figure out a way to be with the patient that *corrected* rather than *perpetuated* the secondary maturational failures to which the patient had become accustomed.

4. *Disengagement from expectations.* Bion (1970) repeatedly advised the analyst to approach the patient without expectations, desire, or memory. As I became aware that even my silent and patient waiting for John to talk was perceived by him as a pathological repetition of the demands and expectations of his parents, I was gradually able to divorce myself from my own need to engage in a verbal and mutual understanding of the analytic interaction. I am convinced that my own contentment with my role of quietly reading in John's presence was crucial to his eventual emergence from his withdrawal. At some point he undoubtedly sensed that his passivity was no longer thwarting my efforts to make him talk, thus losing its psychological importance.

Another way of understanding the change in the patient's ego functioning as a result of the period of silence is that I had passed an unconscious "test" constructed by the patient. Through extensive study of actual transcripts of analyses with neurotics, Weiss and colleagues (1986) have evolved a hypothesis that suggests such tests may be of paramount importance in a successful analysis. According to this hypothesis, a patient develops pathological beliefs based on early interactions with parental figures and seeks unconsciously to disconfirm these beliefs in analysis so that development can proceed. The analyst is treated the same way as the patient treated his parents to see if the analyst will respond similarly to them. In other words, when I failed to respond with demands and expectations to the patient's silence and passivity, I disconfirmed his belief that all parental figures would violate his privacy and force him to conform to their expectations. Relief and an increase in generalized ego functioning often result from such disconfirmations. Although the work of Weiss and his colleagues was based on neurotic patients in classical analyses, one can assume that a similar mechanism may operate in more disturbed patients such as John.

5. *Modification of projections for reintrojection.* The processing of the self- and object-representations deposited in me by John allowed him to take them back in a modified and more tolerable form. John's conversation with the evening nurse suggests that the intense rage of the demanding and overbearing internal object associated with father was modified to a more constructive form of anger. He was able to verbalize his feelings of anger at me for what he experienced as an infantilization of him, and he was able to use it to mobilize his ego resources to break the cycle of self-destructive passivity. Similarly, the persecutory and coercive quality of the internal object was "detoxified" into a more reasonable internal demand to change.

6. *Legitimization of the private, noncommunicative core of the self.* In disengaging myself from pressuring John to speak, I also communicated that I respected his need for silence. In speaking of the adolescent's need to isolate himself, Winnicott (1963) noted: "This preservation of personal isolation is part of the search for identity, and for the establishment of a personal technique for communicating which does not lead to violation of the central self" (p. 190). Winnicott observed that many adolescents experience psychoanalysis as a kind of spiritual rape because their evolving identity is repeatedly intruded upon by the curious analyst. The formation of a therapeutic alliance is generally considered to be critically important in the treatment of the borderline patient

(Gabbard et al. 1988, 1994). In patients such as John, silent respect for the patient's central self may be the only viable technical approach to fostering the therapeutic alliance.

As the analyst legitimizes the patient's choice not to communicate through words, he also allows for the transition from being perceived as a subjective object to one that is predominantly perceived as an objective object. Winnicott warned of the danger inherent in verbally intruding on the patient before this important transition has been completed. A premature violation of this "subjective object" period may overwhelm the patient and lead to psychotic disorganization. Searles (1986) seemed to grasp Winnicott's point in his observation that

> Winnicott's concept of the good enough holding environment implies that the analyst be not merely relatively stably there, for the patient, but also relatively destructible (psychologically) by the patient, time and again, as the patient's persistent needs for autistic (omnipotent) functioning still require. Hence the analyst needs intuitively to provide his own absence, perhaps as often as his own presence, to the patient at timely moments. [p. 351]

By way of concluding my discussion, I would like to offer some reflections on the role played by my decision to bring reading material to the session. It was only when I began to read that I fully appreciated the patient's sadism and hostility toward me. I felt a sense of freedom that led me to recognize how masochistically enslaved to my tormentor I had been in the four weeks of silence that preceded the decision to read. The act of reading had liberated me from those shackles.

About a year after I originally published this case report in the *International Journal of Psycho-Analysis*, I received a letter from a colleague in the United Kingdom who informed me that his study group had recently discussed my paper. He noted that one discussant had suggested that I should not have read because a mother would never read while tending to an infant. Three members of the study group, all of whom had been mothers of infants, immediately disagreed. One revealed she always read in the wee hours of the night while rocking her infant back to sleep. The reason was simple—it was to keep from going mad. I think I know what she meant.

EPILOGUE:
MYTHS, MOVIES, AND MAGIC

In the twilight of his life, Freud (1937) turned his attention to Empedocles of Acragas, the multifaceted physician and philosopher. Born in 495 B.C., Empedocles had concluded that two fundamental principles, roughly translated as love (φιλία) and strife (νείκος), were always at war with each other in their efforts to gain the upper hand. While love sought to unify, strife sought to divide and fragment. In this Greek philosopher's cosmology, these two forces alternated in dominance, each enjoying periods of triumph over its antagonist.

As one might suspect, Freud seized on these ancient words from the Golden Age of Western civilization and commented on the striking similarities between the fundamental principles of Empedocles and the primal instincts of eros and destructiveness that he had identified. Freud, of course, linked the principle of strife with the death instinct. Even though we have now relegated the death instinct to the status of a way station on the journey to our modern understanding of human motivation, there can be little doubt that the intrapsychic struggle between love and destructive hate has always been at the heart of human mythopoiesis.

The fall of Satan and his expulsion from Paradise is one product of that myth-making capacity that reflects the human desire to cleanse ourselves of all negativity and exist in a pure, unadulterated state of love and bliss. Acknowledging and owning our own hatred and destructiveness is resisted with every fiber of our being. Racial and ethnic prejudices and the never-ending geopolitical conflicts are intimately linked with the projective disavowal of unacceptable aspects of ourselves and the perception of them in others.

Yet, the irony is that when Satan fell from grace, we all fell with him. We are firmly ensconced in varying degrees of envy, aggression, sadism, hatred, and destructiveness. At some level, our yearning to love and attach carries with it the promise of fusing with another and transcending this host of negative experiences that fills us with self-loathing.

The longing to fuse with the beloved also has an extensive history in Greek and Roman mythology. From Ovid's *Metamorphoses*, for example, comes the myth of Baucis and Philemon. Although Ovid was Roman, the myth probably has Greek origins. Baucis and Philemon were an aging couple who welcomed Jupiter in the guise of a mortal into their home after many other denizens of their village had refused him entry. In return, they were granted any wish they requested. They chose to die at the same moment so neither would have to experience the anguish of separation from the other. Their wish was granted, and in death they were transformed into two trees standing close together, growing from one double trunk. The desperate wish to avoid separateness and to become one person that underlies many loving relationships is unmistakable in this myth.

The myth of Baucis and Philemon is a mythic illustration of the Liebestod fantasy—the wish to die with a loved one. It is a powerful wish for merger often traced to the Celtic legend of *Tristan and Iseult.* Wagnerian operas, such as *The Ring Cycle* and *Tristan und Isolde,* use this theme to dramatic effect. Gediman (1995) has stressed that the Liebestod fantasy is linked to a duel wish in the lovers: to fend off anxieties of irrevocable loss or "bad death" and to express the longing for a "good death" via symbiotic union.

Plato also spoke of a wish to fuse in his *Symposium.* He referenced Aristophanes as the source of the legend that humans had derived from a third sex. These overarching beings had originally been a fusion of both male and female characteristics, with four feet, four hands, two faces, and both male and female genitals. After Zeus decided to sever them in half, all nature became divided in the same way. Ever since, according to this legend, each human creature has been striving to reunite with his or her other half and once again fuse.

The psychoanalytically informed reader cannot fail to see the connection between this myth and Freud's (1905b) observation that the finding of an object is a refinding of it. Indeed, to return to a Miltonian view, the search for an ideal romantic partner is a quest that is reminiscent of regaining the paradise lost of one's infancy. The unconscious fantasy is often that the beloved will help one recapture the symbiotic bliss of the early months of life and that this omnipotent other can banish all experiences of unpleasure, rage, and anxiety.

A similar expectation is often raised when a patient enters into a relationship with an analyst. "Maybe this time," the patient's unconscious muses, "I will finally receive the healing love that I have been denied all my life (or at least since I was forced to face the world on my own)." Many patients carry a powerful unconscious fantasy that psychoanalytic cure rests on some version of unconditional loving acceptance by the analyst. Some analysts may harbor similar unconscious fantasies about their role vis-à-vis the patient (Gabbard 1995c).

This perspective on psychoanalysis as essentially a love cure is ubiquitous in our modern spinner of myths, the Hollywood cinema. In our systematic study (Gabbard and Gabbard 1987) of over 250 Hollywood films that featured some type of psychotherapy or psychoanalytic work, film after film seemed to suggest that some form of loving interaction with one's therapist is far more important than any understanding or insight gained in the treatment process. Even in films that have reasonably positive depictions of psychotherapy, such as Robert Redford's 1980 *Ordinary People*, the psychotherapist's affirmation that he is a friend and his moving embrace of the patient are depicted as the primary healing force at work.

In films where the analyst is female and the patient is male, the love cure is accompanied by sexual healing as well (Gabbard and Gabbard 1989). Moreover, the healing in these cases goes both ways. There have been at least twenty-seven films in which an unhappy female therapist with no personal life is swept off her feet by a handsome male patient. The female analyst is shown to be at least as disturbed as the patient (if not more so), and as her romantic and sexual involvement heals her patient, she, too, is transformed into a vibrant, sexually alive woman by the love of her male patient. To mention only a few illustrative examples of this genre, Ingrid Bergman is transformed by Gregory Peck in *Spellbound* (1945); Mai Zetterling is loved to health by Danny Kaye in *Knock on Wood* (1954); Tony Curtis romances Natalie Wood in *Sex and the Single Girl* (1964); George C. Scott awakens

Joanne Woodward in *They Might Be Giants* (1971); Barbra Streisand is healed by Nick Nolte in *Prince of Tides* (1991); and Lena Olin finds meaning in her life through romantic and sexual involvement with her bipolar patient, Richard Gere, in *Mr. Jones* (1993).

At one level of discourse, these films are restoring women to their traditional roles in the patriarchal Hollywood cinema as erotic objects of display for the visual pleasure of the male audience (Mulvey 1977). The contempt for the professional role of women is hardly concealed in such depictions. Nevertheless, at another level these films depict psychoanalytic or psychotherapeutic cure as a recapturing of the paradise of early mother–infant bliss that was lost long ago, the paradise that never really existed quite as it is remembered. In almost all of these films, the destructiveness of such sexual liaisons between analyst and patient are completely ignored by the lovers themselves and all others in their professional sphere.

In the entire annals of the Hollywood cinema, we could only identify two films that featured a female therapist helping a male patient without falling in love with him and becoming sexually involved. In each of these films, *Last Embrace* (1979) and *Private Worlds* (1935), the treatment occupies no more than a few seconds of screen time and is entirely peripheral to the film's major plot lines.

Over the years of sitting behind my analytic couch, listening to the ebb and flow of patients' lives, and getting to know the cast of characters that parade before me in each unique psychological drama, I have come to recognize the powerful role of a particular unconscious fantasy of many patients. It is largely a fantasy of magic. Analysis represents to them an opportunity to shed the qualities they find the most repugnant. This fantasy generally includes a conceptualization of analysis as a purifying process that will help them exile the Satan within and thus achieve a transcendent perfection where only love exists, uncontaminated by hate. The achievement of this fantasy is, of course, thwarted at every turn, as much by human nature as by the analytic process itself, which is dedicated to an unflinching search for truth about oneself (however subjective or constructed that truth may be).

The account in the prologue of this book of my disconcerting session with Ms. S long ago is emblematic of how hatred and aggression come to the surface when the patient's unconscious goals are frustrated, and in the course of the analysis the analyst thus has numerous opportunities to help the patient integrate his or her darker side. Indeed, one of the key themes in many analyses is the emergence of hatred and anguish in the analysand when faced with apparently unrequited love toward the analyst. In another of Ovid's tales, Phoebus is madly in love with Daphne after being pierced by Cupid's arrow. Ovid makes it clear, however, that Cupid's decision to inflict this love on Phoebus was based in the malicious wrath he harbored toward Phoebus. He ingeniously chose another arrow from his quiver and released it directly into Daphne. *This* arrow, though, had the impact of making Daphne take flight from love. Hence, Phoebus pursued her in vain and experienced all the anguish of an impossible love that was beyond his grasp.

It is an irony of the analytic situation that while the patient's agenda may be to transcend negative affects and undesirable self-representations, the analyst's agenda is to help the patient reown these aspects of the self that are disavowed and/or projected elsewhere. I share Rycroft's (1985) view that "psychoanalytic treatment is not so much a matter of making the unconscious conscious, or of widening and strengthening the ego, as of providing a setting in which healing can occur and connections with previously repressed, split-off and lost aspects of the self can be re-established" (p. 123). As analysts, we help patients learn to live within their own skin, squarely within the dialectic created by love and hate and by life and destructiveness. In this regard, the psychoanalytic process is inevitably a bittersweet tale involving a singular mixture of discovery and loss. Just as our patients have the opportunity to examine their own internal cast of characters, so do we as analysts go through a series of projections, introjections, and reintrojections as we reassess our inner worlds and come to situate ourselves more firmly within *our* own skins. Both analyst and analysand are ultimately sadder, but wiser—impoverished, but enriched.

The passions of love and hate will always be with us, however we try to maneuver around them. Rather than to expel hate, we must learn to integrate it and temper it with love so that our inherent aggression is harnessed in more constructive directions. We would all do well to heed the words of Havelock Ellis (1937), whose advice is as wise today as ever:

> It is passion, more passion and fuller, that we need. The moralist who bans passion is not of our times; his place these many years is with the dead. For we know what happens in a world when those who ban passion have triumphed. When Love is suppressed, Hate takes its place. . . . It is more passion and ever more that we need if we are to undo the work of Hate, if we are to add to the gaiety and splendor of life, to the sum of human achievement, to the aspiration of human ecstasy. [p. 61]

References

Abend, S. M. (1989). Countertransference and psychoanalytic technique. *Psychoanalytic Quarterly* 48:374–395.

Akhtar, S. (1995). Some reflections on the nature of hatred and its emergence in the treatment process: discussion of Kernberg's chapter "Hatred as a core of aggression." In *The Birth of Hatred: Developmental, Clinical and Technical Aspects of Intense Aggression*, ed. S. Akhtar, S. Kramer, and H. Parens, pp. 85–101. Northvale, NJ: Jason Aronson.

Altschul, V. A. (1979). The hateful therapist and the countertransference psychosis. *NAPPH Journal* 11:15–23.

Altman, L. L. (1977). Some vicissitudes of love. *Journal of the American Psychoanalytic Association* 25:35–52.

Aron, L. (1990). One-person and two-person psychologies and the method of psychoanalysis. *Psychoanalytical Psychology* 7:475–485.

——— (1991). The patient's experience of the analyst's subjectivity. *Psychoanalytic Dialogues* 1:29–51.

Bak, R. C. (1968). The phallic woman: the ubiquitous fantasy in perversions. *Psychoanalytic Study of the Child* 23:15–36. New York: International Universities Press.

Balint, M. (1948). On genital love. *International Journal of Psycho-Analysis* 28:34–40.

Benedek, E. P. (1973). Training the woman resident to be a psychiatrist. *American Journal of Psychiatry* 130:1131–1135.

Benjamin, J. (1988). *The Bonds of Love: Psychoanalysis, Feminism, and the Problem of Domination*. New York: Pantheon.

―――― (1991). Father and daughter: identification with difference—a contribution to gender heterodoxy. *Psychoanalytic Dialogues* 1:277–299.

―――― (1995). *Like Subjects, Love Objects: Essays on Recognition and Sexual Difference*. New Haven, CT: Yale University Press.

Bergmann, M. S. (1980). On the intrapsychic function of falling in love. *Psychoanalytic Quarterly* 44:56–77.

―――― (1985-1986). Transference love and love in real life. *International Journal of Psychoanalytic Psychotherapy* 11:27–45.

―――― (1987). *The Anatomy of Loving: The Story of Man's Quest to Know What Love Is*. New York: Columbia University Press.

―――― (1994). The challenge of erotized transference to psychoanalytic technique. *Psychoanalytic Inquiry* 14:499–518.

Bibring-Lehner, G. (1936). A contribution to the subject of transference-resistance. *International Journal of Psycho-Analysis* 17:181–189.

Bion, W. R. (1955). Language and the schizophrenic. In *New Directions in Psychoanalysis*, ed. M. Klein, P. Heimann, and R. E. Money-Kyrle, pp. 220–239. London: Tavistock.

―――― (1957). Differentiation of the psychotic from the nonpsychotic personalities. *International Journal of Psycho-Analysis* 38:266–275; also in *Second Thoughts: Selected Papers on Psycho-Analysis*, pp. 43–64. New York: Jason Aronson, 1984.

―――― (1958). On arrogance. *International Journal of Psycho-Analysis* 39:144–146; also in *Second Thoughts: Selected Papers on Psycho-Analysis*, pp. 86–92. New York: Jason Aronson, 1984.

―――― (1959). Attacks on linking. *International Journal of Psycho-Analysis* 40:308–315; also in *Second Thoughts: Selected Papers on Psycho-Analysis*, pp. 93–109. New York: Jason Aronson, 1984.

―――― (1962a). The psycho-analytic study of thinking, II. a

theory of thinking. *International Journal of Psycho-Analysis* 43:306–310; also in *Second Thoughts: Selected Papers on Psycho-Analysis,* pp. 110–119. London: Heinemann, 1967.

—— (1962b). *Learning From Experience.* New York: Basic Books. [new printing, New York: Jason Aronson, 1983]

—— (1963). *Elements of Psycho-analysis.* London: Heinemann. [new printing, New York: Jason Aronson, 1983]

—— (1967). *Second Thoughts: Selected Papers on Psycho-Analysis.* New York: Jason Aronson.

—— (1970). *Attention and Interpretation: A Scientific Approach to Insight in Psycho-Analysis and Groups.* New York: Basic Books. [new printing, New York: Jason Aronson, 1983]

Bird, B. (1972). Notes on transference: universal phenomenon and hardest part of analysis. *Journal of the American Psychoanalytic Association* 20:267–301.

Blos, P. (1962). *On Adolescence: A Psychoanalytic Interpretation.* New York: Free Press.

—— (1991). The role of the early father in male adolescent development. In *The Course of Life, vol. IV. Adolescence,* ed. S. I. Greenspan and G. H. Pollack, pp. 1–16. Madison, CT: International Universities Press.

Blum, H. P. (1973). The concept of erotized transference. *Journal of the American Psychoanalytic Association* 21:61–76.

—— (1976). Masochism, the ego ideal, and the psychology of women. *Journal of the American Psychoanalytic Association* 24(suppl):157–191.

—— (1995). Sanctified aggression, hate, and the alteration of standards and values. In *The Birth of Hatred: Developmental, Clinical and Technical Aspects of Intense Aggression,* ed. S. Akhtar, S. Kramer, and H. Parens, pp. 17–37. Northvale, NJ: Jason Aronson.

Blum, H. P., and Blum, E. J. (1986). Reflections on transference and the countertransference in the treatment of women. In *Between Analyst and Patient,* ed. H. C. Meyers, pp. 177–192. Hillsdale, NJ: Analytic Press.

Boesky, D. (1990). The psychoanalytic process and its components. *Psychoanalytic Quarterly* 59:550–584.

Bollas, C. (1987). *The Shadow of the Object: Psychoanalysis of the Unthought Known.* New York: Columbia University Press.

—— (1990). Regression in the countertransference. In *Master Clinicians on Treating the Regressed Patient*, ed. L. B. Boyer and P. L. Giovacchini, pp. 339–352. Northvale, NJ: Jason Aronson.

—— (1994). Aspects of the erotic transference. *Psychoanalytic Inquiry* 14:572–590.

Bolognini, S. (1994). Transference: erotised, erotic, loving, affectionate. *International Journal of Psycho-Analysis* 75:73–86.

Boyer, B. (1983). *The Regressed Patient.* New York: Jason Aronson.

—— (1986). Technical aspects of treating the regressed patient. *Contemporary Psychoanalysis* 22:25–44.

—— (1989). Countertransference and technique in working with the regressed patient. *International Journal of Psycho-Analysis* 70:701–714.

Brenner, C. (1982). *The Mind in Conflict.* New York: International Universities Press.

Breuer, J., and Freud, S. (1895). Studies on hysteria. *Standard Edition* 2:vii-xxxi, 1–311.

Buie, D., and Adler, G. (1982). The definitive treatment of the borderline patient. *International Journal of Psycho-Analysis* 9:51–87.

Carpy, D. V. (1989). Tolerating the countertransference: a mutative process. *International Journal of Psycho-Analysis* 70:287–294.

Chessick, R. D. (1977). *Intensive Psychotherapy of the Borderline Patient.* New York: Jason Aronson.

Chused, J. F. (1991). The evocative power of enactments. *Journal of the American Psychoanalytical Association* 39:615–639.

Coen, S. J. (1992). *The Misuse of Persons: Analyzing Pathological Dependency.* Hillsdale, NJ: Analytic Press.

———— (1994). Barriers to love between patient and analyst. *Journal of the American Psychoanalytic Association* 42:1107–1135.

Compton, A. (1981). On the psychoanalytic theory of instinctual drives. II: the sexual drives and the ego drives. *Psychoanalytical Quarterly* 50:219–237.

Cooper, A. M. (1992). Psychic change: development of the theory of psychoanalytic techniques. *International Journal of Psycho-Analysis* 73:245–250.

Davies, J. M. (1994a). Love in the afternoon: a relational reconsideration of desire and dread in the countertransference. *Psychoanalytical Dialogue* 4:153–170.

———— (1994b). Desire and dread in the analyst: Reply to Glen Gabbard's commentary on "Love in the Afternoon." *Psychoanalytic Dialogues,* 4:503–508.

Dicks, H. V. (1963). Object relations theory and marital studies. *British Journal of Psychology* 36:125–129.

Dimen, M. (1991). Deconstructing difference: gender, splitting, and transitional space. *Psychoanalytical Dialogue* 1:335–352.

Dupont, J., ed. (1988). *The Clinical Diary of Sándor Ferenczi,* trans. by M. Balint and N. Z. Jackson. Cambridge, MA: Harvard University Press.

———— (1995). The story of a transgression. *Journal of the American Psychoanalytic Association* 43:823–834.

Eagle, M. (1993). Enactments, transference, and symptomatic cure: a case history. *Psychoanalytic Dialogues,* 3:93–110.

Ehrenberg, D. B. (1994). Reply to reviews by Barrett, Blechner, and Schwartz of *The Intimate Edge: Extending the Reach of Psychoanalytic Interaction. Psychoanalytic Dialogues* 4:303–316.

Eigen, M. (1985). Toward Bion's starting point: between catastrophe and faith. *International Journal of Psycho-Analysis* 66:321–330.

Ellis, H. (1937). *On Life and Sex: Essays of Love and Virtue, I.* Garden City, NY: Garden City.

Epstein, L. (1977). The therapeutic function of hate in the countertransference. *Contemporary Psychoanalysis* 13:442–468.

—— (1979). Countertransference with borderline patients. In *Countertransference: The Therapist's Contribution to a Therapeutic Situation*, ed. L. Epstein and A. H. Feiner, pp. 375–405. New York: Jason Aronson.

Erikson, E. H. (1980). *Identity and the Life Cycle.* New York: Norton.

Fairbairn, W. R. D. (1954). *An Object-Relations Theory of Personality.* New York: Basic Books.

Fast, I. (1984). *Gender Identity: A Differentiation Model (Advances in Psychoanalysis: Theory, Research, and Practice, Volume 2).* Hillsdale, NJ: Analytic Press.

Field, N. (1989). Listening with the body: an exploration in the countertransference. *British Journal of Psychotherapy* 5:512–522.

Fleming, J. (1961). What analytic work requires of an analyst: a job analysis. *Journal of the American Psychoanalytic Association* 9:719–729.

Fonagy, P., Steele, M., Steele, H., et al. (1994). The Emanuel Miller Memorial Lecture 1992: the theory and practice of resilience. *Journal of Child Psychology and Psychiatry* 35:231–257.

Freud, A. (1958). Adolescence. *Psychoanalytic Study of the Child* 13:255–278. New York: International Universities Press.

Freud, S. (1900). The interpretation of dreams. *Standard Edition* 4 and 5:ix–xxxii, 1–627.

—— (1905a). Fragment of an analysis of a case of hysteria. *Standard Edition* 7:1–122.

—— (1905b). Three essays on the theory of sexuality. *Standard Edition* 7:123–245.

—— (1907). Delusions and dreams in Jensen's *Gradiva*. *Standard Edition* 9:1–95.

—— (1909a). Analysis of a phobia in a five–year-old boy. *Standard Edition* 10:1–149.

—— (1909b). Notes upon a case of obsessional neurosis. *Standard Edition* 10:151–320.

—— (1912). The dynamics of transference. *Standard Edition* 12:97–108.

—— (1914). On narcissism: an introduction. *Standard Edition* 14:67–102.

—— (1915a). Instincts and their vicissitudes. *Standard Edition* 14:109–140.

—— (1915b). Observations on transference-love. *Standard Edition* 12:157–173.

—— (1918). The taboo of virginity (Contributions to the psychology of love III.) *Standard Edition* 11:191–208.

—— (1921). Group psychology and the analysis of the ego. *Standard Edition* 18:65–143.

—— (1923). The ego and the id. *Standard Edition* 19:1–66.

—— (1925). An autobiographical study. *Standard Edition* 20:1–74.

—— (1930). Civilization and its discontents. *Standard Edition* 21:157–145.

—— (1937). Analysis terminable and interminable. *Standard Edition* 23:209–253.

—— (1940). An outline of psychoanalysis. *Standard Edition* 23:139–207.

Friedman, L. (1991). A reading of Freud's papers on technique. *Psychoanalytic Quarterly* 60:564–595.

—— (1994). Ferrum, Ignis, and Medicina: return to the crucible. Plenary presentation at the annual meeting of the American Psychoanalytic Association, May.

Fromm-Reichmann, F. (1989). Reminiscences of Europe. In *Psychoanalysis and Psychosis,* ed. A. S. Silver, pp. 469–481. Madison, CT: International Universities Press.

Gabbard, G. O. (1986). The treatment of the "special" patient in a psychoanalytic hospital. *International Review of Psycho-Analysis* 13:333–347.

—— (1989a). On "doing nothing" in the psychoanalytic

treatment of the refractory borderline patient. *International Journal of Psycho-Analysis* 70:527–534.

—— (1989b). Patients who hate. *Psychiatry* 52:96–106.

—— (1989c). *Sexual Exploitation in Professional Relationships*. Washington, DC: American Psychiatric Press.

—— (1991a). Commentary: Do we need theory? *Bulletin of the Menninger Clinic* 55(1):22–29.

—— (1991b). Technical approaches to transference hate in the analysis of borderline patients. *International Journal of Psycho–Analysis* 72:625–637.

—— (1991c). Psychodynamics of sexual boundary violations. *Psychiatric Annals* 21:651–655.

—— (1992). Commentary on "Dissociative processes and transference–countertransference paradigms . . ." by Jody Messler Davies and Mary Gale Frawley. *Psychoanalytic Dialogues* 2:37–47.

—— (1993a). Introduction to classic article, "Observations on transference love." *Journal of Psychotherapy Practice and Research* 2:171–172.

—— (1993b). On hate in love relationships: the narcissism of minor differences revisited. *Psychoanalytic Quarterly* 62:229–238.

—— (1994a). Commentary on papers by Tansey, Hirsch, and Davies. *Psychoanalytic Dialogues* 4:203–213.

—— (1994b). On love and lust in erotic transference. *Journal of the American Psychoanalytic Association* 42:385–403.

—— (1994c). *Psychodynamic Psychiatry in Clinical Practice: The DSM-IV Edition*. Washington, DC: American Psychiatric Press.

—— (1994d). Psychotherapists who transgress sexual boundaries with patients. *Bulletin of the Menninger Clinic* 58:124–135.

—— (1994e). Sexual excitement and countertransference love in the analyst. *Journal of the American Psychoanalytic Association* 42:1083–1106.

—— (1995a). The early history of boundary violations in

psychoanalysis. *Journal of the American Psychoanalytic Association* 43(4):1115–1136.

——— (1995b). Countertransference: the emerging common ground. *International Journal of Psycho-Analysis* 76:475–485.

——— (1995c). When the patient is a therapist: special challenges in the analysis of mental health professionals. *Psychoanalytic Review* 82:709–725.

——— (in press). Discussion of Boston Psychoanalytic Society and Institute Conference on "Psychoanalysis and sexual abuse." *Psychoanalytic Inquiry*.

Gabbard, G. O., and Gabbard, K. (1987). *Psychiatry and the Cinema*. Chicago: University of Chicago Press.

——— (1989). The female psychoanalyst in the movies. *Journal of the American Psychoanalytic Association* 37:1031–1049.

Gabbard, G. O., Horwitz, L., Allen, J. G., et al. (1994). Transference interpretation in the psychotherapy of borderline patients: a high-risk, high-gain phenomenon. *Harvard Review of Psychiatry* 2:59–69.

Gabbard, G. O., Horwitz, L., Frieswyk, S., et al. (1988). The effect of therapist interventions on the therapeutic alliance with borderline patients. *Journal of the American Psychoanalytic Association* 36:697–777.

Gabbard, G. O., and Lester, E. P. (1995). *Boundaries and Boundary Violations in Psychoanalysis*. New York: Basic Books.

Gabbard, G. O., and Wilkinson, S. M. (1994). *Management of Countertransference with Borderline Patients*. Washington, DC: American Psychiatric Press.

Galdston, R. (1987). The longest pleasure: a psychoanalytic study of hatred. *International Journal of Psycho-Analysis* 68:371–378.

Galenson, E., and Roiphe, H. (1976). Some suggested revisions concerning early female development. *Journal of the American Psychoanalytical Association* 24(suppl):29–57.

Gediman, H. K. (1995). *Fantasies of Love and Death in Life and*

Art: A Psychoanalytic Study of the Normal and the Pathological. New York: New York University Press.

Gill, M. M. (1982). *Analysis of transference, Vol. 1: Theory and technique.* New York: International Universities Press.

—— (1993). One-person and two-person perspectives: Freud's "Observations on Transference-Love." In *On Freud's "Observations on Transference Love,"* ed. E. S. Person, A. Hagelin, and P. Fonagy, pp. 114–129. New Haven, CT: Yale University Press.

—— (1994). *Psychoanalysis in Transition: A Personal View.* Hillsdale, NJ: Analytic Press.

Giovacchini, P. L. (1975). Various aspects of the psychoanalytic process. In *Tactics and Techniques of Psychoanalytic Psychotherapy, Volume II: Countertransference,* ed. L. B. Boyer and P. L. Giovacchini, pp. 5–94. New York: Jason Aronson.

Goldberger, M., and Evans, D. (1985). On transference manifestations in male patients with female analysts. *International Journal of Psycho-Analysis* 66:295–309.

Gorkin, M. (1985). Varieties of sexualized countertransference. *Psychoanalytic Review* 72:421–440.

—— (1987). *The Uses of Countertransference.* Northvale, NJ: Jason Aronson.

Gorney, J. E. (1979). The negative therapeutic interaction. *Contemporary Psychoanalysis* 15:288–337.

Gornick, L. K. (1986). Developing a new narrative: the woman therapist and the male patient. *Psychoanalytic Psychology* 3(4):299–325.

Green, A. (1973). On negative capability: a critical review of W. R. Bion's attention and interpretation. *International Journal of Psycho-Analysis* 54:115–119.

Greenacre, P. (1970). The transitional object and the fetish: with special reference to the role of illusion. In *Emotional Growth Vol. 1,* pp. 335–352. New York: International Universities Press, 1971.

Greenberg, J. R. (1991a). *Oedipus and Beyond: A Clinical Theory.* Cambridge, MA: Harvard University Press.

———— (1991b). Countertransference and reality. *Psychoanalytic Dialogues,* 1:52–73.

———— (1995). Self-disclosure: Is it psychoanalytic? *Contemporary Psychoanalysis* 31:193–205.

Greenson, R. R. (1967). *The Technique and Practice of Psychoanalysis, Volume I.* New York: International Universities Press.

———— (1968). Dis-identifying from mother: its special importance for the boy. *International Journal of Psycho-Analysis* 49:370–374.

Grinberg, L. (1979a). Countertransference and projective counteridentification. In *Countertransference,* ed. L. Epstein and A. H. Feiner, pp. 169–191. New York: Jason Aronson.

———— (1979b). Countertransference with borderline patients. In *Countertransference,* ed. L. Epstein and A. H. Feiner, pp. 375–405. New York: Jason Aronson.

Grinberg, L., Sor, D., and De Bianchedi, E. T. (1977). *Introduction to the Work of Bion.* New York: Jason Aronson.

Grotstein, J. S. (1981). *Splitting and Projective Identification.* New York: Jason Aronson.

———— (1982). The analysis of a borderline patient. In *Technical Factors in the Treatment of the Severely Disturbed Patient,* ed. P. L. Giovacchini and L. B. Boyer, pp. 261–288. New York: Jason Aronson.

Grubrich-Simitis, I. (1986). Six letters of Sigmund Freud and Sándor Ferenczi on the interrelationship of psychoanalytic theory and technique. *International Review of Psycho-Analysis* 13:259–277.

Guidi, N. (1993). Unobjectionable negative transference. *Annual of Psychoanalysis* 21:107–121.

Hamilton, N. G. (1986). Positive projective identification. *International Journal of Psycho-Analysis* 67:489–496.

Heimann, P. (1950). On counter-transference. *International Journal of Psycho-Analysis* 31:81–84.

Hill, D. (1994). The special place of the erotic transference in psychoanalysis. *Psychoanalytic Inquiry* 14:483–498.

Hirsch, I. (1993a). Countertransference enactments and some

issues related to external factors in the analyst's life. *Psychoanalytic Dialogues* 3:343–366.

—— (1993b). Reply to commentaries by Kindler and Shapiro. *Psychoanalytic Dialogues* 3:395–399.

—— (1994). Countertransference love and theoretical model. *Psychoanalytic Dialogues* 4:171–192.

Hoffer, A. (1993). Is love in the analytic relationship "real"? *Psychoanalytic Inquiry* 13:343–356.

Hoffman, I. Z. (1983). The patient as interpreter of the analyst's experience. *Contemporary Psychoanalysis* 19:389–422.

—— (1991). Discussion: Toward a social constructivist view of the psychoanalytic situation. *Psychoanalytic Dialogues* 1:74–105.

—— (1992). Some practical considerations of a social-constructivist view of the psychoanalytic situation. *Psychoanalytic Dialogues* 2:287–304.

—— (1994). Dialectical thinking and therapeutic action in the psychoanalytic process. *Psychoanalytic Quarterly* 63:187–218.

Horwitz, L., Gabbard, G. O., Allen, J. G., et al. (1996). *Borderline Personality Disorder: Tailoring the Psychotherapy to the Patient*. Washington, DC: American Psychiatric Press.

Jacobs, T. J. (1986). On countertransference enactments. *Journal of the American Psychoanalytical Association* 34:289–307.

—— (1993a). The inner experiences of the analyst: their contribution to the analytic process. *International Journal of Psycho-Analysis* 74:7–14.

—— (1993b). Insight and experience: commentary on M. Eagle's "Enactments, transference, and symptomatic cure." *Psychoanalytic Dialogues* 3:123–127.

Jacobson, E. (1951). Development of the wish for a child in boys. *Psychoanalytic Study of the Child* 5:139–152. New York: International Universities Press.

Jacobson, J. G. (1994). Signal affects and our psychoanalytic confusion of tongues. *Journal of the American Psychoanalytic Association* 42:15–42.

Joseph, B. (1993). On transference love: some current observations. In *On Freud's "Observations on Transference Love,"* ed. E. S. Person, A. Hagelin, and P. Fonagy, pp. 102-113. New Haven, CT: Yale University Press.

Joseph, B. (1989). *Psychic Equilibrium and Psychic Change: Selected Papers of Betty Joseph,* ed. M. Feldman and E. B. Spillius. London and New York: Tavistock/Routledge.

Karme, L. (1979). The analysis of the male patient by a female analyst: the problem of the negative oedipal transference. *International Journal of Psycho-Analysis* 60:253–261.

Kernberg, O. F. (1974). Mature love: prerequisites and characteristics. *Journal of the American Psychoanalytic Association* 22:743–768.

——— (1977). Boundaries and structure in love relations. *Journal of the American Psychoanalytic Association* 25:81–114.

——— (1984). *Severe Personality Disorders: Psychotherapeutic Strategies.* New Haven, CT: Yale University Press.

——— (1987). Projection and projective identification: developmental and clinical aspects, in *Projection, Identification, Projective Identification,* ed. J. Sandler, pp. 93–115. Madison, CT: International Universities Press.

——— (1991). Aggression and love in the relationship of the couple. *Journal of the American Psychoanalytic Association* 39:45–70.

——— (1994a). Aggression, trauma, and hatred in the treatment of borderline patients. *Psychiatric Clinics of North America* 17:701–714.

——— (1994b). Love in the analytic setting. *Journal of the American Psychoanalytic Association* 42:1137–1157.

——— (1995a). Hatred as a core affect of aggression. In *The Birth of Hatred: Developmental, Clinical, and Technical Aspects of Intense Aggression,* ed. S. Akhtar, S. Kramer, and H. Parens, pp. 55–82. Northvale, NJ: Jason Aronson.

——— (1995b). *Love Relations: Normality and Pathology.* New Haven: Yale University Press.

Klein, M. (1946). Notes on some schizoid mechanisms. In *Envy and Gratitude and Other Works, 1946–1963*, pp. 1–24. New York: Delacorte Press/Seymour Laurence, 1975.

—— (1955). On identification. In *Envy and Gratitude and Other Works, 1946–1963*, pp. 141–175. New York: Delacorte Press/Seymour Laurence, 1975.

Knoblauch, S. H. (1995). To speak or not to speak? How and when is that the question? Commentary on papers by Davies and Gabbard, *Psychoanalytic Dialogues* 5:151–155.

Kohut, H. (1972). Thoughts on narcissism and a narcissistic rage. *Psychoanalytic Study of the Child* 27:360–400. New Haven, CT: Yale University Press.

—— (1984). *How Does Analysis Cure?* ed. A. Goldberg. Chicago: University of Chicago Press.

Kris, E. (1956). On some vicissitudes of insight in psychoanalysis. *International Journal of Psycho-Analysis* 37:445–455.

Kumin, I. (1985). Erotic horror: desire and resistance in the psychoanalytic situation. *International Journal of Psychoanalytic Psychotherapy* 11:3–20.

Kundera, M. (1980). *The Book of Laughter and Forgetting*, trans. M. H. Heim. New York: Knopf.

Lear, J. (1990). *Love and Its Place in Nature: A Philosophical Interpretation of Freudian Psychoanalysis*. New York: The Noonday Press (Farrar, Straus, and Giroux).

Lester, E. P. (1985). The female analyst and the erotized transference, trans. M. H. Heim. *International Journal of Psycho-Analysis* 66:283–293.

Levine, H. B. (1994). The analyst's participation in the analytic process. *International Journal of Psycho-Analysis* 75:665–676.

Little, M. (1966). Transference in borderline states. *International Journal of Psycho-Analysis* 47:476–485.

Loewald, H. W. (1970). Psychoanalytic theory and psychoanalytic process. In *Papers on Psychoanalysis*, pp. 277–301. New Haven: Yale University Press, 1980.

Maguire, M. (1995). *Men, Women, Passion, and Power: Gender Issues in Psychotherapy*. London: Routledge.

Mahler, M. S., Pine, F., and Bergman, A. (1975). *The Psychological Birth of the Human Infant: Symbiosis and Individuation.* New York: Basic Books.

Malin, A., and Grotstein, J. S. (1966). Projective identification in the therapeutic process. *International Journal of Psycho-Analysis* 47:26–31.

Maroda, K. (1991). *The Power of Countertransference.* New York: Wiley.

Mayer, E. L. (1994). A case of "severe boundary violations" between analyst and patient. Paper presented at the December American Psychoanalytic Association Panel.

McCullers, C. (1951). *The Ballad of the Sad Cafe.* Cambridge, MA: Riverside Press.

McDougall, J. (1995). *The Many Faces of Eros: A Psychoanalytic Exploration of Human Sexuality.* New York: Norton.

McGuire, W., ed. (1974). *The Freud/Jung Letters: The Correspondence between Sigmund Freud and C. G. Jung,* trans. R. Manheim and R. F. C. Hull. Princeton, NJ: Princeton University Press.

McLaughlin, J. T. (1961). The analyst and the Hippocratic Oath. *Journal of the American Psychoanalytic Association* 9:106–123.

——— (1991). Clinical and theoretical aspects of enactment. *Journal of the American Psychoanalytic Association* 39:595–614.

Meissner, W. W. (1988). *Treatment of Patients in the Borderline Spectrum.* Northvale, NJ: Jason Aronson.

Menninger, K. (1942). *Love Against Hate.* New York: Harcourt, Brace & Company.

——— (1957). Psychological factors in the choice of medicine as a profession. *Bulletin of the Menninger Clinic* 21:51–58.

Meyers, H. C. (1991). Perversion in fantasy and furtive enactments. In *Perversions and Near-Perversions in Clinical Practice: New Psychoanalytic Perspectives,* ed. E. I. Fogel and W. A. Myers, pp. 93–108. New Haven, CT: Yale University Press.

Mitchell, S. A. (1988). *Relational Concepts in Psychoanalysis: An Integration.* Cambridge, MA: Harvard University Press.

——— (1993a). Aggression and the endangered self. *Psychoanalytic Quarterly* 62:351–382.

——— (1993b). *Hope and Dread in Psychoanalysis.* New York: Basic Books.

Modell, A. H. (1991). The therapeutic relationship as a paradoxical experience. *Psychoanalytic Dialogues* 1:13–28.

Money-Kyrle, R. E. (1956). Normal counter-transference and some of its deviations. *International Journal of Psycho-Analysis* 37:360–366.

Mulvey, L. (1977). Visual pleasure and narrative cinema. In *Women and the Cinema: A Critical Anthology*, ed. K. Kay and G. Peary, pp. 412–428. New York: Dutton.

Myers, H. (1987). How do women treat men? In *The Psychology of Men*, ed. G. I. Fogel, F. M. Lane, and R. S. Liebert, pp. 262–275. New York: Basic Books.

Natterson, J. (1991). *Beyond Countertransference: The Therapist's Subjectivity in the Therapeutic Process.* Northvale, NJ: Jason Aronson.

Nigg, J. T., Silk, K. R., Westen, D., et al. (1991). Object representations in the early memories of sexually abused borderline patients. *American Journal of Psychiatry* 148:864–869.

Ogden, T. H. (1979). On projective identification. *International Journal of Psycho-Analysis* 60:357–373.

——— (1982). *Projective Identification and Psychotherapeutic Technique.* New York: Jason Aronson.

——— (1983). The concept of internal object relations. *International Journal of Psycho-Analysis* 64:227–241.

——— (1986). *The Matrix of the Mind: Object Relations and the Psychoanalytic Dialogue.* Northvale, NJ: Jason Aronson.

——— (1989). *The Primitive Edge of Experience.* Northvale, NJ: Jason Aronson.

——— (1992a). The dialectically constituted/decentred subject of psychoanalysis, I: the Freudian subject. *International Journal of Psycho-Analysis* 73:517–526.

—————— (1992b). The dialectically constituted/decentred subject of psychoanalysis, II: the contributions of Klein and Winnicott. *International Journal of Psycho-Analysis* 73:613–626.

—————— (1994). *Subjects of Analysis.* Northvale, NJ: Jason Aronson.

—————— (1995). Analyzing forms of aliveness and deadness of the transference-countertransference. *International Journal of Psycho-Analysis,* 76:695–710.

Ovid (Publius Ovidius Naso). *Metamorphoses,* Vol. I, II. Ed. T. E. Page, E. Capps, and W. H. D. Rouse. Trans. F. J. Miller. London: William Heinemann Ltd. and Cambridge, MA: Harvard University Press, 1936. (first printed in 1916).

Panel (1992). Enactments in psychoanalysis. M. Johan, reporter. *Journal of the American Psychoanalytic Association* 40:827–841.

Pao, P. N. (1965). The role of hatred in the ego. *Psychoanalytic Quarterly* 34:257–264.

Parens, H. (1979). *The Development of Aggression in Early Childhood.* New York: Jason Aronson.

—————— (1995). Notes on perversions of the superego by hate: discussion of Blum's chapter "Sanctified aggression, hatred, and the alteration of standards and values." In *The Birth of Hatred: Developmental Clinical and Technical Aspects of Intense Aggression,* ed. by S. Akhtar, S. Kramer, and H. Parens, pp. 41–52. Northvale, NJ: Jason Aronson.

Paris, J., ed. (1993). *Borderline Personality Disorder: Etiology and Treatment.* Washington, DC: American Psychiatric Press.

Person, E. S. (1983). The influence of values in psychoanalysis: the case of female psychology. *Psychoanalytic Inquiry* 3:623-646.

—————— (1985). The erotic transference in women and in men: differences and consequences. *Journal of the American Psychoanalytic Association* 13:159–180.

—————— (1986). The omni-available woman and lesbian sex: two fantasy themes and their relationship to the male developmental experience. In *The Psychology of Men,* ed. G. I.

Fogel, F. M. Lane, and R. S. Liebert, pp. 71–94. New York: Basic Books.

——— (1988). *Dreams of Love and Fateful Encounters: Romance in Our Time.* New York: Norton.

Phillips, A. (1994). *On Flirtation.* Cambridge, MA: Harvard University Press.

Pine, F. (1990). *Drive, Ego, Object and Self.* New York: Basic Books.

Poggi, R. G., and Ganzarain, R. (1983). Countertransference hate. *Bulletin of the Menninger Clinic* 47:15–35.

Pope, K. S., Keith-Spiegel, P., and Tabachnick, B. G. (1986). Sexual attraction to clients: the human therapist and the (sometimes) inhuman training system. *American Psychology* 42:993–1006.

Porder, M. S. (1987). Projective identification: an alternative hypothesis. *Psychoanalytic Quarterly* 56:431–451.

Pulver, S. E. (1992). Psychic change: insight or relationship? *International Journal of Psycho-Analysis* 73:199–208.

——— (1993). The eclectic analyst, or the many roads to insight and change. *Journal of the American Psychoanalytic Association* 41:339–357.

Racker, H. (1968). *Transference and Counter-transference.* New York: International Universities Press.

Rangell, L. (1982). The self in psychoanalytic theory. *Journal of the American Psychoanalytic Association* 30:863–891.

Raphling, D. L. (1991). Love and Morality. Paper presented at the meeting of the American Psychoanalytic Association Seminar for Clinicians, New York, October.

Renik, O. (1990). Analysis of a woman's homosexual strivings by a male analyst. *Psychoanalytic Quarterly* 59:41–53.

——— (1991). Men and women love in the same way—only differently. Paper presented at the meeting of the American Psychoanalytic Association Seminar for Clinicians, New York, October.

——— (1993). Analytic interaction: conceptualizing technique in light of the analyst's irreducible subjectivity. *Psychoanalytic Quarterly* 62:553–571.

—— (1995a). The role of an analyst's expectations in clinical technique: reflections on the concept of resistance. *Journal of the American Psychoanalytic Association* 43:83–94.

—— (1995b). The ideal of the anonymous analyst and the problem of self-disclosure. *Psychoanalytic Quarterly* 64:466–495.

Richards, A., and Richards, A. K. (1995). Notes on psychoanalytic theory and its consequences for technique. *Journal of Clinical Psychoanalysis* 4:429–456.

Ritvo, S. (1971). Late adolescence: developmental and clinical considerations. *Psychoanalytic Study of the Child* 26:241–263. New Haven: Yale University Press.

Roiphe, H., and Galenson, E. (1981). *Infantile Origins of Sexual Identity.* New York: International Universities Press.

Rosenfeld, H. A. (1952). Notes on the psycho-analysis of the super-ego conflict of an acute schizophrenic patient. *International Journal of Psycho-Analysis* 31:111–131; also in *New Directions in Psycho-Analysis*, pp. 180-219. London: Tavistock, 1955.

—— (1987). *Impasse and Interpretation: Therapeutic and Anti-therapeutic Factors in the Psychoanalytic Treatment of Psychotic, Borderline, and Neurotic Patients.* London and New York: Tavistock.

Ross, J. M. (1977). Towards fatherhood: the epigenesis of paternal identity during a boy's first decade. *International Review of Psycho-Analysis* 4:327–347.

Roughton, R. E. (1993). Useful aspects of acting out: repetition, enactment, and actualization. *Journal of the American Psychoanalytic Association* 41:443–472.

Russ, H. (1993). Erotic transference through countertransference: the female therapist and the male patient. *Psychoanalytic Psychology* 10:393–406.

Rycroft, C. (1985). *Psychoanalysis and Beyond*, ed. P. Fuller. Chicago: University of Chicago Press.

Samuels, A. (1985). Symbolic dimensions of eros in transference/

countertransference. *International Review of Psycho-Analysis* 12:199–207.

Sandler, J. (1976). Countertransference and role responsiveness. *International Review of Psycho-Analysis* 3:43–47.

—— (1983). Reflections on some relations between psychoanalytic concepts and psychoanalytic practice. *International Journal of Psycho-Analysis* 64:35–45.

—— (1987). The concept of projective identification. In *Projection, Identification, Projective Identification*, ed. J. Sandler, pp. 13–26. Madison, CT: International Universities Press.

—— (1993). On communication from patient to analyst: not everything is projective identification. *International Journal of Psycho-Analysis* 74:1097–1107.

Schafer, R. (1954). *Psychoanalytic Interpretation in Rorschach Testing: Theory and Application.* New York: Grune & Stratton.

—— (1977). The interpretation of transference and the conditions for loving. *Journal of the American Psychoanalytic Association* 25:335–362.

—— (1992). *Retelling a Life: Narration and Dialogue in Psychoanalysis.* New York: Basic Books.

—— (1993). Five readings of Freud's "Observations on Transference-love." In *On Freud's "Observations on Transference-Love,"* ed. E. S. Person, A. Hagelin, and P. Fonagy, pp. 75–95. New Haven, CT: Yale University Press.

Scharff, J. S. (1992). *Projective and Introjective Identification and the Use of the Therapist's Self.* Northvale, NJ: Jason Aronson.

Searles, H. F. (1958). Positive feelings in the relationship between the schizophrenic and his mother. In *Collected Papers on Schizophrenia and Related Subjects*, pp. 216–253. New York: International Universities Press.

—— (1959). Oedipal love in the countertransference. *International Journal of Psycho-Analysis* 40:180–190.

—— (1965). *Collected Papers on Schizophrenia and Related Subjects.* New York: International Universities Press.

———— (1975). The patient as therapist to his analyst. In *Tactics and Techniques in Psychoanalytic Psychotherapy, Volume II: Countertransference*, ed. P. L. Giovacchini, pp. 95–151. New York: International Universities Press.

———— (1979). *Countertransference and Related Subjects: Selected Papers*. New York: International Universities Press.

———— (1986). *My Work with Borderline Patients*. Northvale, NJ: Jason Aronson.

Segal, H. (1964). *An Introduction to the Work of Melanie Klein (2nd ed.)*. New York: Basic Books.

Shapiro, S. A. (1993). Gender-role stereotypes and the clinical process: commentary on papers by Gruenthal and Hirsch. *Psychoanalytic Dialogue* 3:371–387.

Sherby, L. B. (1989). Love and hate in the treatment of borderline patients. *Contemporary Psychoanalysis* 25:574–591.

Spillius, E. B. (1992). Clinical experiences of projective identification. In *Clinical Lectures on Klein and Bion*, ed. R. Anderson, pp. 59–73. London and New York: Tavistock/Routledge.

Stoller, R. J. (1968). *Sex and Gender: On the Development of Masculinity and Femininity*. New York: Science House.

———— (1973). Facts and fancies: an examination of Freud's concept of bisexuality. In *Women and Analysis: Dialogues on Psychoanalytic Views of Femininity*, ed J. Strouse, pp. 343–364. Boston: Hall, 1985.

———— (1975). *Perversion: The Erotic Form of Hatred*. New York: Pantheon.

———— (1979). *Sexual Excitement: Dynamics of Erotic Life*. New York: Pantheon.

———— (1985). *Observing the Erotic Imagination*. New Haven, CT: Yale University Press.

Stolorow, R. D., and Atwood, G. E. (1992). *Contexts of Being: The Intersubjective Foundations of Psychological Life*. Hillsdale, NJ: Analytic Press.

Symington, N. (1990). The possibility of human freedom and its transmission (with particular reference to the thought of Bion). *International Journal of Psycho-Analysis* 71:95–106.

Tansey, M. J. (1994). Sexual attraction and phobic dread in the countertransference. *Psychoanalytic Dialogue* 4:139–152.

Tansey, M. J., and Burke, W. (1989). *Understanding Countertransference: From Projective Identification to Empathy.* Hillsdale, NJ: Analytic Press.

Ticho, E. A. (1975). The effects of the analyst's personality on psychoanalytic treatment. *Psychoanalytic Forum,* 4:135-163.

Torras de Beà, E. (1987). A contribution to the papers on transference by Eva Lester, Marianne Goldberger and Dorothy Evans. *International Journal of Psycho-Analysis* 68:63–67.

Trop, J. L. (1988). Erotic and eroticized transference: a self psychological perspective. *Psychoanalytic Psychology* 5:269–284.

Twemlow, S. W., and Gabbard, G. O. (1989). The lovesick therapist. In *Sexual Exploitation in Professional Relationships,* ed. G. O. Gabbard, pp. 71–88. Washington, DC: American Psychiatric Press.

Tyson, P. (1982). A developmental line of gender identity, gender role, and choice of love object. *Journal of the American Psychoanalytic Association* 30:61–86.

——— (1986). The female analyst and the male analysand. Paper presented to the San Francisco Psychoanalytic Institute.

Viederman, M. (1988). The nature of passionate love. In *Passionate Attachments: Thinking About Love,* ed. W. Gaylin and E. Person, pp. 1–14. New York: Free Press.

Wäelder, R. (1936). The principle of multiple function: observations on over-determination. *Psychoanalytic Quarterly* 5:45–62.

Waksman, J. D. (1986). The countertransference of the child analyst. *International Review of Psycho-Analysis* 13:405–415

Weiss, J., Sampson, H., and the Mount Zion Psychotherapy

Research Group (1986). *The Psychoanalytic Process: Theory, Clinical Observation and Empirical Research.* New York: Guilford.

Welles, J. K., and Wrye, H. K. (1991). The maternal erotic countertransference. *International Journal of Psycho-Analysis* 72:93–106.

Wilkinson, S. M., and Gabbard, G. O. (1995). On romantic space. *Psychoanalytic Psychology* 12:201–219.

Winnicott, D. W. (1949). Hate in the counter-transference. *International Journal of Psycho-Analysis* 30:69–74.

——— (1954). Metapsychological and clinical aspects of regression within the psycho-analytic set-up. In *Collected Papers: Through Paediatrics to Psycho-Analysis*, pp. 278–294. New York: Basic Books, 1958.

——— (1960). The theory of the parent–infant relationship. In *The Maturational Processes and the Facilitating Environment: Studies in the Theory of Emotional Development*, pp. 37–55. New York: International Universities Press, 1965.

——— (1963). Communicating and not communicating leading to a study of certain opposites. In *The Maturational Processes and the Facilitating Environment: Studies in the Theory of Emotional Development*, pp. 179–192. New York: International Universities Press, 1965.

——— (1968). The use of an object and relating through identification. In *Psycho-analytic Explorations*, ed. C. Winnicott, R. Shepherd, and M. Davis, pp. 218–227. Cambridge, MA: Harvard University Press, 1989.

Wrye, H. K. (1993). Erotic terror: male patients' horror of the early maternal erotic transference. *Psychoanalytic Inquiry* 13:240–257.

CREDITS

The author gratefully acknowledges permission to reprint portions of the following material:

INDEX